THE DRAGON
MILLENNIUM

THE DRAGON MILLENNIUM

Chinese Business in the Coming World Economy

EDITED BY

Frank-Jürgen Richter

QUORUM BOOKS
Westport, Connecticut • London

Library of Congress Cataloging-in-Publication Data

The dragon millennium : Chinese business in the coming world economy /
   edited by Frank-Jürgen Richter.
      p.   cm.
   Includes bibliographical references and index.
   ISBN 1–56720–353–1 (alk. paper)
      1. Industries—China.   2. China—Economic policy—1976–
   I. Richter, Frank-Jürgen.
   HC427.92.D73   2000
   338.951—dc21   99–36601

British Library Cataloguing in Publication Data is available.

Library of Congress Catalog Card Number: 99–36601
ISBN: 1–56720–353–1

First published in 2000

Quorum Books, 88 Post Road West, Westport, CT 06881
An imprint of Greenwood Publishing Group, Inc.
www.quorumbooks.com

Printed in the United States of America

The paper used in this book complies with the
Permanent Paper Standard issued by the National
Information Standards Organization (Z39.48–1984).

10 9 8 7 6 5 4 3 2 1

Contents

Tables and Figures

TABLES

FIGURES

Preface

China has already become the world's third-largest economic power, and it currently presents enormous business opportunities. Despite the current Asian economic crisis, the year 2000 will mark the beginning of the Dragon Millennium.

This edited collection explores the future organization of Chinese business. Looking at the complex questions associated with the concept of ownership and control in China, the book first discusses economic policy and the development of the firm in China. The development path of some selected industries is then examined. The book also pinpoints the challenges that multinational companies face in China and portrays the endeavor of Chinese firms to grow globally. A discussion of a hypothetical Chinese way of management closes the book.

The contributors offer a genuine Chinese approach to theory and practice of management and organization in China, concentrating more thoroughly on the complexity of Chinese organizations than former mainstream work. All contributors are members of the worldwide Chinese business and academic community. The research presented inspires further academic discourse and managerial policy in the face of evolving Chinese reality. The book supplies expert knowledge and support for business practitioners, policy analysts, scholars, and students in China and abroad.

Frank-Jürgen Richter
Beijing, China

Introduction:
Chinese Visionaries Predict
China's Future Organization of Business

Frank-Jürgen Richter

In the nearly two decades since Deng Xiaoping introduced market reforms to China, the country has posted some of the most eye-popping economic numbers of the century. China's gross domestic product grew an average of 9.4 percent a year between 1978 and 1995, lifting an astonishing 200 million people above the poverty line. If China continues to grow at a similar pace, the kind of economic transformation that took developed countries roughly 80 years to complete would be condensed into a quarter century.

In China the dragon is the symbol of the emperor, the son of Heaven, and represents male vigor. It is considered to be a good-natured creature and is believed to be blessed with magic powers. These powers include being able to shrink to the size of a silkworm, to fill the space between Heaven and Earth, and to choose to be invisible or visible. One of the most charismatic animal signs in Chinese astrology, the dragon is full of energy, power, and very good fortune. It has a vibrant, intelligent nature, and its actions are decisive and confident.

According to Chinese astrology, the passage of time is measured by a cycle of 60 years. The twelve astrological animals appear five times during the 60-year cycle, and they appear in a slightly different form every year. The year 2000, which marks the beginning of the Dragon Millennium, is an ''Angry Dragon.'' As its name suggests, this is a volatile, unleashed dragon. Because of its powerful swings of mood, it is not an easy creature to be or to live with. It has a real chance at greatness, wealth, and fame, but the costs might be very high. As a matter of fact, the Chinese economy is at a crossroads. The recent fall of Japan and the Asian Tigers (South Korea, Singapore, Malaysia, Thailand, and Indonesia) may impact China as well. If the Dragon suffers as the Tigers already have, one may only hope that the Dragon will not get too angry in experiencing stormy and dramatic relationships with its partners on the economic and political stage.

My intention is not to publish another mainstream reader derived from the Western point of view, but to present a genuine Chinese approach. Hence, I have elicited contributions from members of the worldwide Chinese business and academic community. Although my approach to the dragon is rather scientific, I believe the contributions I have gathered in one volume will be a good way to inform the reader about China's rise to global eminence and the transformation of its corporations. In twelve chapters, Chinese visionaries predict their economic future and the future of the global world of business. In my assessment, the future of the world economy is heavily dependent on the future growth of China. I do not follow the mainstream opinion that China needs the West more than the West needs China. On the contrary, Western firms must participate in the growth of the Chinese market to remain globally competitive. China now presents one of the most attractive opportunities for business in the Far East and is fast becoming something of a new frontier for Western business pioneers eager to stake their claims. However, I believe that how the West interacts with China will be one of the defining issues of the next millennium.

China has the chance to become the largest national economy sometime in the next millennium, probably still in the first half of the twenty-first century. To predict China's future, however, is a difficult or even impossible endeavor. China is a complex society due to its deeply embedded and multilayered cultural heritage, its rapid rate of recent modernization, and its vast scale, which encompasses strong local identities and traditions. Who would have predicted in the old days of the Cultural Revolution, for instance, that Deng Xiaoping would introduce rational economics and modernize China? Most probably only some naive scholars who mystify the China of their dreams. Napoleon's 200-year-old warning that when the Chinese dragon awoke from its slumber it would shake the world has at last been proven true. Futurists, however—if they are serious— do not predict the future; they project different outcomes for it. By this I do not intend to predict the future of the Chinese political landscape or talk about the superiority of "values," no matter if they are of Asian or Western origin. Rather, I think that the globalized world is shifting its emphasis from politics to economics. The current Asian crisis shows how intertwined the world's economies are and how contagious the Asian crisis may be. The probability that any projection will occur is a matter of personal conviction.

In 1997, when the Asian financial crisis started taking its toll, Chinese Premier Zhu Rongji announced a bold plan to keep the economy on track. He promised to make the collapsing state sector profitable in three years and to pump large amounts into infrastructure. A confident Zhu predicted he could keep China growing at 8 percent a year. But the government didn't foresee just how bad the Asian economies would get. At the same time, Hong Kong's losing battle to fight off speculators is heightening fears that Hong Kong and China may be next in line to devalue their currencies.

Zhu Rongji's efforts to clean up China's shaky financial sector could further dampen growth and force the authorities to resort to devaluation. The bankruptcy of Guangdong International Trust & Investment Corp. (GITIC) has spooked foreign lenders, who may not get their money back. So international bankers are calling in their China loans early, refusing to roll over others, and fearing in lending new money. Despite its mounting economic woes, however, the country still has a huge current account surplus, not to mention its foreign currency reserves.

In 1998 the government announced that it would issue additional bonds to fund power, telecommunications, transportation, housing, and irrigation projects and to raise its banking lending quota. Yet there are doubts that such fiscal stimuli will be enough. China is dealing with serious overcapacity in most industrial sectors. Inventories have swelled to half of the total economy, and fears of skyrocketing unemployment have put a damper on consumer spending. Deflation pressure is high. While most economists may agree that Keynesian-style fiscal stimulus has moved Beijing closer to its growth target, there are dangers. The rush to spend may waste scarce resources while the real improvement of China's fundamentals is delayed. Therefore, the government is postponing some reforms to avoid further swelling of the ranks of the unemployed, which are already growing due to the ongoing privatization of state-owned enterprises (SOEs).

This book brings together twelve forecasts made by Chinese economists and practitioners from institutions in both China and overseas. I purposely added scenarios written by Overseas Chinese, as the economies of China and Overseas Chinese businesses grow together.

The contributions center around several major issues. What kind of corporation is most appropriate for China's present stage of economic development? What will be the corporate characteristics most suited to China's current transitional economy? What will be the best organizational form for the next millennium? Can this kind of corporation provide the needed agility for Chinese companies in the global economy? Furthermore, how do these firms establish their development strategies? How do they conduct their competitive performance? What are their competition achievements? What are their main formation elements?

In Part I, "Economic Policy and the Development of the Firm," the complex questions associated with the concept of ownership and control in China are qualified. About half of China's more than 300,000 SOEs now lose money. The efforts to reform them have been stepped up since the 15th Party Congress in 1997, when Chinese leaders laid down the government's policy to "grasp the large, release the small." The reform allows the SOEs to be merged, bankrupted, or sold to private investors. The state would maintain control over only 1,000 large and strategically important firms and would actively groom several to compete as multinational conglomerates.

The contributors point to the challenges facing China as the country seeks to

structure and to coordinate its distinctive forms of organization. Although ownership of most Chinese assets will still be by collective units, individual entrepreneurs will be able to build sizable firms. The economic balance between
state-owned and private firms is one of the most important issues of China's
future.

In Chapter 1, David Li examines the behavior of the Chinese SOEs in the
reform era. He illustrates that despite facing strong profit incentives, Chinese
SOEs are still greatly influenced by the government and dependent on the government. Their profits consist of those earned in the market and rents bargained
from the government, which tends to impose its objectives on the enterprise.
After negotiations with the government, state enterprises maximize market profit
by making short-term production decisions. However, when the final realized
profit is negative, state enterprises are not accountable for the losses. The implication is that the Chinese enterprise reform provides high incentives for the
SOEs to pursue short-term efficiency but poor incentives for them to pursue
long-term dynamic efficiency. Therefore, disentangling the government–enterprise relation is a key step to complete the reform of the Chinese SOEs.

In Chapter 2, Qi Hantang gives a detailed account of the genesis and development of Chinese township and village enterprises up until the present day.
The peasants in these enterprises have developed different industries, forms of
ownership, investment channels, and operational modes. Although dividing this
developmental process into distinct stages is problematic, he believes that it
makes sense to do so because it helps us capture the important events in the
history of Chinese township and village enterprises. He concludes that township
and village enterprises have been a true alternative to the conventional wisdom
of SOEs.

In Chapter 3, Wang Xueli and Zhang Lijun address the future of private
enterprises in China. The word "private" had been a sensitive term in the
economic system of China for a long time, while in fact the private enterprises
become more and more outstanding during the reform process. The surprise that
the private enterprises bring into the national economy is their rapid growth
compared with state enterprises. It looks as if the bottleneck of their further
development has occurred. The chapter gives an inside picture of Chinese private
enterprises, then analyzes the main problems and their causes associated with
the private enterprises at present. Finally, suggestions for the future development
of Chinese private enterprises are proposed. It is believed that their influence
on the economic development of China is potentially profound.

In Part II, "Outlook on Selected Industries," the development path of some
industries is illustrated, highlighting the finance, automobile, and petroleum industries. The contributors mainly concentrate on the different performance pattern and development speed of firms in these industries. The needs and
characteristics of various industries and market segments differ greatly. China
will continue to evolve rapidly, and the markets and competitive landscape will
continue to change.

The authors study the pitfalls and underlying trends of the mentioned industries facing the country in the next several decades. In anticipation of Chinese macroeconomic goal and approach, Chinese high economic growth will be coupled with various challenges and vulnerabilities, mainly in the areas of population, environmental, and market responsiveness.

In Chapter 4, Chen Baizhu and Feng Yi aim to contribute to the understanding of the changing political and economic framework within which banking institutions developed in China. In contrast to its high economic growth, China's financial sector, though evolving slowly, has not yet been reformed into an efficient, modern financial system consistent with a privatized economy. The authors argue that the conflict between China's current financial system and its underlying economic structure will be intensified, which will significantly impede future economic growth unless further reform is undertaken in the financial market. Recommendations about the future development of China's banking industry are provided.

In Chapter 5, Chen Jin focuses on the automobile industry, which is becoming an important element for the development of the Chinese economy. The realistic comparison is conducted on Chinese carmakers' various adaptation behaviors as a result of environmental change and management resources, the way of changing former organizational behavior, and the formation of their development strategies. The Chinese automakers have introduced technology in quite different ways (along with environmental changes) since the 1980s. Notably, the former small and medium-sized enterprises developed much faster than the former large-sized enterprises. The author predicts a further concentration process in the automobile industry as new entrants spur competition.

In Chapter 6, Deng Shengliang and Xu Xiaojie describe the ambitious economic restructuring program approved by the Chinese National People's Congress to break the government meddling of the oil and gas industry. The program calls for a great overhaul of oil industry regulation and reorganization of state-owned oil companies in line with an integrated operation- and competition-oriented development approach. The chapter starts from the overhaul at the end of century and its far-reaching repercussions on macroeconomic development. Emphasis is given not only to organizational changes but also to reorientation of the central government energy policy and a shift of oil corporate strategies. China's role and preferences in these regards and its impacts on the world petro-economies are addressed. The authors end the chapter with a summary of some underpinnings of the dragon's move in the next decades.

The objective of Part III, "Competition, Cooperation, and Capitalism," is to identify the challenges that multinational companies face in China and to describe how Chinese firms try to enter foreign markets. Because of the country's vast size and huge development potential, many multinationals believe they must compete there. The myth of the great China market, a vast population ready to absorb unlimited quantities of Western goods, may have attracted many investors to establish ventures in China. For those who came in the mid-1980s, the market, as a matter of fact, was wide open. The situation changed dramatically in the mid-1990s. The Chinese market is now considered to be rather volatile and sluggish and falls behind former bullish prospects.

The contributors believe that the engagement of multinationals in China has to be perceived as a win-win situation that encompasses Chinese partner firms, suppliers, and customers, as well as the socioeconomic environment in general. For multinationals, the challenge is finding a way to coexist with the eager dragon. Certainly it would be unwise for any Western businessperson to stray into the lair without learning the dragon's ways. Chinese firms, on the other hand, have to adapt to the capitalist framework of their targeted markets if they want to become global players.

Edward Tse in Chapter 7 is concerned about how multinationals grow their businesses profitably after they complete their market entries into China. Given the complexity of operating in China, it is not surprising that some companies have made fundamental mistakes in managing their businesses. Initially, many firms held a simplistic view of the Chinese market and lacked a real understanding of its dynamics. He recommends that Western managers try to better understand China's regulatory context, focus on future, rather than existing, consumer demand, and build a strong local organization. Multinationals need to develop a rigorous, cohesive approach to competing in the Chinese market.

In Chapter 8, Luo Yadong covers two issues: project selection and location selection in China. These issues are important because they influence the effectiveness and efficiency of international investment in China. This chapter begins with an introduction of conceptual foundations on the issues, followed by governmental policies on project orientation and locational preference. Managerial guidelines on selecting appropriate locations and the right type of projects are reiterated. Economies of scale and investment commitment are considered crucial for market expansion in China.

Chapter 9 analyzes the internationalization process of Chinese enterprises. Lu Tong presents findings of survey research on a sample of Chinese financial services and trading companies with offices and subsidiaries in the United Kingdom. The literature on state-owned enterprises, general trading companies, and Third World multinationals provides a framework for interpreting the results. The evidence is of recent and limited-scale internationalization. A small number of companies may achieve their goal of becoming successful global players. The potential for technology transfer to China is considerable but has not been recognized in a formal sense.

In Part IV, "The Lure of Chinese Management," the specifics of a hypothetical Chinese way of managing firms are discussed. It seems that it is now China's turn to be perceived as exotic and fashionable, as Japan was in the mid-1980s. The important difference is that while Japan's development was revered as a model from which one could learn—the one that attracted students from the West, eager to study Japanese management practices—Chinese management is still seen as virgin territory. Inflexible SOEs that carry the burden of the planned economy are surely not the model the West can draw from.

However, there are signs that a specific Chinese way of management is slowly evolving. Chinese management is rooted in the country's Confucian heritage as well as the kinship-based leadership paradigm of Overseas Chinese businesses in Southeast Asia. It is believed that the coming strength of Chinese management may not be its perfection but its pragmatism and flexibility. How and why Chinese management will develop, what the stakes are for Western management scientists, and how the leverage of Chinese management can be channeled are subjects discussed in this section.

In Chapter 10, Siu Wai-Sum proposes a tentative theory of Chinese small business management, drawing from the experience of Hong Kong entrepreneurs. He examines how and to what extent Chinese small firms have managed to survive, grow, and succeed or, more specifically, how Chinese owner-managers manage employees, make business decisions, and formulate business plans. The results appear to suggest that Western and Chinese owner-managers are different in planning, communication, and human resource management. The reasons for such differences are unclear, but a possible explanation may be found in the influence of cultural values.

The agenda of Cheah Hock Beng in Chapter 11 is that the Chinese economy will not rely significantly on the activities of large firms engaged in the production of radically innovative goods and services. Instead, its international competitiveness will depend on adaptive entrepreneurs, engaged in small-scale enterprise, product and process imitation, subcontracting, and spatial arbitrage. This will help China catch up with previously more economically developed and technologically advanced nations. Such adaptive entrepreneurial activities may receive government support and help narrow the economic and performance gaps with the Western world. The author envisions that China will continue to rely on and benefit from gains emanating from adaptive entrepreneurship in the foreseeable future.

In Chapter 12, Ip Po-Keung proposes a concept of virtuous corporations using a notion of virtues drawn from the Confucian resources. A set of Confucian virtues is identified: *Jen, I, Li*, wisdom, trustworthiness, honesty, integrity, responsibility, and hard work, among others. Core values, including Confucian values like harmony, *Jen* as caring, and trust, together with other virtues, perform the constitutive and regulative functions in building the morality and spirituality of the corporation. The role of virtues in the development of the virtuous corporation is examined. Ways of institutionalizing virtue development as building the spirituality of the corporation are discussed. The downside of Confucian virtuous corporations and the way to deal with them is also discussed.

Of course, this book can hardly document all the varieties of business organizations in China, nor can it predict all those that will emerge in the future. The evidence from this volume, nevertheless, is that although Chinese firms are still at an early stage in evolving their management strategies, they will definitely be important players in the world economy.

However, the benefits of this Chinese way of management have been decreasing as the internal and external constraints intensify. The recent economic crisis that affected various Asian countries since 1997 and that is likely to spread to other regions in the world represents a significant transformation of the domestic and global economic contexts. Intensified competition for export markets from other Asian countries whose currencies have depreciated significantly will compound surplus productive capacity in a range of industries and intensify deflationary pressures.

In these circumstances, it is necessary to look ahead at the Dragon Millennium, after the crisis has altered the financial and industrial structures, within China as well as in the world at large. Then it would be necessary to rebuild new forms of organizations that are more efficient and more appropriate for the next millennium. It is principally in that context, not just the present one, that the role of a typical Chinese way of management must be considered and that the rise of the Chinese dragon may be contemplated.

China will continue to evolve rapidly, and the market and competitive landscape will continue to change. In the next millennium, the Chinese dragon may be a fierce competitor. But it also could be a formidable customer or partner. China is not going to change, however, just to suit the wishes of the West. It is vital that all those involved in the dragon's move, in China and abroad, keep their mind as open as possible about the many opportunities and risks that naturally accompany such historical development. It is this book's aim to contribute to this task. Welcome to the expedition of the millennium!

Part I

Economic Policy and the Development of the Firm

Chapter 1

Chinese State-Owned Enterprises under the Dual Influence of the Government and the Market

David Li

INTRODUCTION

This chapter studies the behavior of China's state-owned enterprises (SOEs) under reform. The focus is on the crucial issue of government–enterprise relations. The central argument is that although the reform has provided the Chinese SOEs with strong profit incentives, the SOEs are still both influenced by the government and dependent on the government for various kinds of favors. Therefore, in order to complete China's SOE reform, the key is to further restructure the government–enterprise relation.

This chapter illustrates the Chinese SOEs' dual dependence on the government and the market by analyzing the dual-track pricing system, an early and representative measure of reform. Although the dual-track pricing system was formally phased out in the early 1990s and different forms of SOE reforms have been experimented with and implemented since then, many problems continue to plague the Chinese SOEs, such as profit losing, excessive employment, and a heavy debt burden. A fundamental cause for these problems continues to be the dual influence of the government and the market on the Chinese SOEs. Instead of low-priced materials, today's SOEs are dependent on the government for many other forms of subsidies (or favorable policies) such as cheap credit, land, export permits, tax exemptions, permits to issue initial public offerings (IPOs), and so on. Meanwhile, in its negotiations with SOEs, the government imposes its own objectives on the enterprise, economic or non-economic, such as larger employment and higher output growth. In a word, the dual influence of the government and the market on the SOEs is a persistent feature of the SOEs that gives rise to many of the observed inefficiencies of the SOEs.

In order to characterize SOE behavior, this chapter models an operation cycle of a Chinese SOE and then utilizes a firm-level data set to provide relevant evidence. In the context of the dual-track pricing system, at the beginning of the operation cycle, the manager and the government negotiate a contract on the input/output quotas as well as profit-sharing rules. Afterward, the SOE starts production by making its input/output decision. At the end of the operation cycle, when profit is realized, the manager and government bargain again on subsidies. The focus of the analysis is on the quota negotiation at the first stage of the operation cycle, when the SOE manager behaves like a rent-seeker, since a large amount of profit is at stake. Through the bargaining process, the government partially imposes its objective onto the enterprise. After the negotiation of the contract, the enterprise faces the market and tries to maximize its market profit by choosing the best input/output combination. Finally, when the realized profit is negative, the enterprise relies upon the government to cover the loss.

This chapter is related to two groups of works in formal economics literature on China's SOE reform. The first group consists of a large body of works that are centered on the debate on whether there is major progress or efficiency improvement of the Chinese SOEs. They include, for example, Chen et al. (1989), Jefferson, Rawski, and Zheng (1992), Fan and Woo (1992), and Woo et al. (1994). We are not directly concerned with the debate, but our analysis indicates that there is enormous room for further progress of the SOE reform in the direction of reducing the influence of the government on SOEs. The second group of works studies the behavior of SOEs. Groves et al. (1994) provide evidence to show that managers of the Chinese SOEs have taken advantage of various reform measures to improve SOE performance. They do not directly discuss the costs of government control of SOEs. Qian (1996) summarizes that there are two sources of inefficiencies in SOEs: those due to agency costs and those due to government control. Li (1998) illustrates that there is a trade-off between these two kinds of cost and that in the Chinese context there are net benefits of reducing government control. In this chapter, we are interested in analyzing the detailed interactions between the government and SOEs and attempt to pin down the costs of government control of SOEs.

In the following section we develop a theoretical framework to study the interactions between the Chinese government and SOEs. Then we provide relevant empirical evidence. The chapter ends with a consideration of policy implications.

THEORETICAL ANALYSIS

In order to articulate the main argument of this chapter, we focus on a stylized scenario of the operation of a Chinese state enterprise. That is, we build a simple model that can help us think through the incentives and behavior of government officials and enterprise managers. We briefly describe the essence of the model while skipping the technical discussions. Interested readers are referred to Li (1998). The model focuses on a hypothesized operation cycle of a Chinese SOE in the context of the dual-track pricing system. The insights of the analysis are more general than those associated with the dual-track system. The operation cycle contains three time periods. Period 1 is planning and bargaining between the SOE and the government. Period 2 is production, and period 3 is distribution of profit. In periods 1 and 2, the government and the SOE have extensive interactions.

In period 1, the SOE and the government bargain about the quota. Given that the planned prices are typically different from the market prices, an output quota that stipulates that the SOE must deliver a fixed amount of output to the government at the planned price (which is typically lower than the market price) represents a tax on the government. Conversely, an input quota represents a subsidy. Thus, in period 1, the SOE and the government are bargaining about taxes or subsidies to the enterprise, which are often termed rents by economists.

In period 2, the SOE produces by choosing its input-output combination. At the end of period 2, the profit is determined. It consists of a deterministic component that is fully anticipated by both the SOE and the government at the beginning of period 1 and a random noise from the production and marketing process.

Period 3 is distribution. If the realized profit is positive, then the SOE and the government divide the total profit according to a profit tax rate. However, if the profit is negative, then another round of negotiation will arise. Since in reality bankruptcy is nonexistent, the SOE and the government negotiate on how many subsidies the SOE will get or how much loss should be sustained by the SOE. This is a phenomenon called the soft budget constraint.

The objective function of the SOE is to maximize the retained profit, which is closely linked to bonuses and welfare spending of the SOE. Findings of many studies (Jefferson, Rawski, and Zheng, 1992; Groves et al., 1994) lend support to such an objective function of the enterprise. In the following, we identify the SOE with the manager, since in a model of short horizon, job security of managers is not an issue.

The government's objective consists of two goals. On the one hand, the government treasures the revenue obtained from the SOE's profit, since the economic and political power of the government is dependent on this. On the other hand, the government, which is controlled by professional career bureaucrats, likes to see a large output and employment from the enterprise. A high output benefits the bureaucrat in at least two ways. A large output represents a large domain of control of the bureaucracy. Also, a large output is associated with high employment, which reduces various social problems. The desire for output, as argued by Shleifer and Vishny (1994), is a coherent feature of the politics of the old socialist system. As a matter of fact, the output index is one of the most important figures in the Chinese industrial statistics, and the performance of the bureaucrats is judged by it.

The first prediction of the model is that in period 2, when the quota negotiation has settled, the SOE chooses an input/output combination that maximizes the firm's profit, which is calculated at market prices. In other words, from the point of view of the SOE's input and output choices, the quota and the planned prices are not relevant. That is, only the market prices are driving the production decisions of the SOE, despite the presence of planned prices. This is the main rationale of the dual-track reform. One implication of this result is that after the reform the Chinese SOEs short-term productivity should be improved due to more efficient production decisions. Indeed, this is a common conclusion of many studies, such as Chen et al. (1989).

However, one has to be cautious in interpreting the preceding conclusion, which gives an impression that the soft budget constraint does not have bad consequences. The current framework is concerned only with static input/output decisions and leaves out the issue of investment decision, which is distorted in the presence of the soft budget constraint. Moreover, the process of bargaining for quotas can be very efficiency-reducing for SOEs. As argued later, the quota system is in the way of enhancing long-term efficiency.

The second prediction of the model is concerned with the quota allocation. It shows that the quota allocation depends on the government's intensity of preference for profit and how high the market price is over the planned price. The stronger the government's concern with profit (i.e., less with output) or the higher the market price over the planned price, the lower the quota. Therefore, if we believe that local governments are more concerned with profits, as is often the case, than those SOEs under the control of local government have lower quotas. Also, during the early 1990s, when the gap between the market and planned prices was narrowing, quotas indeed were diminishing.

One special case of the second prediction deserves special attention. Suppose that the government is very concerned with output, and then, the prediction shows that the quota is very high so that it is likely that the SOE generates a negative profit. Shleifer and Vishny (1994) use this to explain the soft budget constraint. Here we define this as ex ante soft budget constraint, since there is another kind of soft budget constraint, when the SOE has a loss unexpectedly, and we define that as the ex post soft budget constraint.

The third and fourth conclusions are reached by extending the basic model described earlier. The third one is about investment decisions or demand for investment of SOEs. If we expand the model to include investment considerations, we can predict that there is excessive demand for investment by SOEs (similar to Kornai, 1992; Li, 1994). In other words, SOEs' investment decisions, which are unlike static input/output decisions and have long-term consequences, are socially inefficient. Facing such a high demand for investment, the government is unlikely to allocate investment funds efficiently. This gives rise to one kind of dynamic inefficiencies across SOEs, since truly efficient SOEs may not get the needed capital.

The last conclusion of the theoretical analysis is that rent-seeking, which in our context is the process bargaining for the most favorable quotas by the SOEs, is a severe impediment to efficiency improvement in the SOE. As Murphy,

Shleifer, and Vishny (1993) have argued, rent-seeking has a scale economy yielding higher and higher returns to the rent-seekers, while improving productive efficiency does not. Thus, it can be shown in the generalized model that in equilibrium, managers will spend a lot of time dealing with the bureaucrats instead of within the SOE or in the marketplace. The end result is that the equilibrium productivity is low. Clearly, this is a rather socially undesirable situation.

To summarize, investment hunger with misallocation of capital and excessive rent-seeking are implied by the model as two undesirable aspects of the Chinese enterprise reform. These are problems that can prevent Chinese state enterprises from making effective long-run decisions, despite the fact that their short-run production decisions can be efficient, as shown before. Therefore, the implication is that in the long run, there may be limits to the positive effects of the Chinese enterprise reform, although the measured productivity of the SOEs can be higher after the reform due to better static production decisions.

EMPIRICAL EVIDENCE

Three groups of evidence are provided in this section. They are on the profit-maximizing behavior of Chinese SOEs during reform, the rent-seeking behavior of SOEs, and the extent of the soft budget constraint in Chinese SOEs (refer to Li, 1994 for the econometric analysis behind this section).

The data used are from a so-called Enterprise Panel Survey (EPS) project, which aimed to evaluate the performance of China's enterprises, and hence that of the reform. The EPS was initiated in 1985. About 800 industrial enterprises were chosen, and quarterly data were collected from each of the enterprises starting from the first quarter of 1986. The data available for the present research are limited to the first ten quarters, namely, the first quarter of 1986 to the second quarter of 1988. About 600 SOEs had their data recorded for all ten quarters. For a more detailed description of the data set, see Fan, Li, and Peng (1989).

The Profit Incentive of SOEs

The preceding analysis implies that the input/output decisions of an SOE after reform should be consistent with profit maximization. Statistical tests can be run on this prediction (for details, see Li, 1994). The test results are very close to those of similar tests conducted on U.S. firms. Thus, one concludes that, like U.S. firms, the Chinese SOEs' input-output choice is rather close to profit maximization. In addition to the formal statistical tests, an overwhelming amount of anecdotal evidence shows that during reform, managers of Chinese SOEs have been rather concerned with profits when making short-term production decisions, although the efficiency of their long-term production decisions is a different issue.

Rent-Seeking in Negotiating for Quotas

We now provide evidence on rent-seeking by SOEs when negotiating quotas with the government. Simple summary statistics show that across the years, output quotas decreased. SOEs controlled by higher branches of government tend to get higher quotas. Larger SOEs get higher quotas. Finally, mining and the raw material industry get the highest quota, while heavy manufacturing gets the lowest.

We can further analyze the pattern of quota allocation. A few patterns are worth mentioning. First, surprisingly, the ratio of market price to planned price does not really explain the size of quota of a firm. Perhaps budgetary transfers are used extensively in negotiating the quota. Second, SOEs controlled by higher-level governments (e.g., the central government) have higher output quotas. This is consistent with the hypothesis that higher-level governments have more political considerations and care more about controlling cheap output, while lower-level SOEs care more about fiscal revenue. There is plenty of anecdotal evidence on this. Third, similar to the second finding, larger SOEs tend to have higher quotas. Part of the reason seems to be that larger SOEs are usually controlled by higher-level governments. Fourth, when the SOE is leased or contracted out to managers, its quota is low. We interpret this as the bargaining power effect. The fact that a manager is able to take over an SOE indicates the manager is already in a good position to bargain with the bureaucrat.

Besides the determination of the quota, another very important issue is to estimate the magnitude of the rent at stake in the government–enterprise negotiation. The size of the rent directly determines how much effort the manager should devote to dealing with the government bureaucrat instead of enhancing efficiency internally. A natural measure of the impact of rent is obtained by comparing the rent with the SOE's total gross (before tax) profit. Note that the rent can be either positive or negative. We find that the absolute value of rent to that of gross profit for SOEs with non-zero rents is 1.665. That is, the government's manipulation of quota-generated rents, which on average are much bigger than the final profit of the SOE. Also, these rents are in general of the opposite sign of the market profit. In addition, note the large standard deviation of 4.335, which indicates that there were large variations in the rent-to-profit ratio.

Another finding regarding the rent is that the government's manipulation of the quota actually amounts to equalizing the final profits. Specifically, rent-losing SOEs are almost all market profit makers (only 3 out 241 cases—less than 1.5%—are not). On the other hand, most of the market profit losers enjoy positive rent provided by the government (3 out of [97 + 3] cases—less than 3%—did not). A second observation is that the sheer magnitude of rent enjoyed by the profit losers is much higher than that by profit makers, implying how important the rent is for the rent-earners and thus how much effort the managers must have put in.

Overall, the findings on the quota negotiations can be summarized as follows. First, the allocation of the quota is generally consistent with bargaining theory. This gives us more confidence in the assumption that government desires both profit and output. Second, the large size of the rent suggests that it is highly necessary for the manager to devote great effort to dealing with bureaucrats. Finally, the rent is found to be independent of the enterprise type, and this suggests that the rent is open to managers of all enterprises.

Evidence on Profit Losing and the Soft Budget Constraint

The theoretical analysis of the previous section indicates that ex post (after profit is realized) bargaining between the SOE and the government is a major source of inefficiency. A very damaging outcome of the ex post bargaining is the so-called soft budget constraint, which refers to situations where profit-losing SOEs bargain for subsidies and survive.

Given the importance of the soft budget constraint, we focus on cases of profit-losing SOEs in the sample. A tricky issue is the profit figure, which has to be carefully calculated, since the accounting profit many times already includes government subsidies. The gross profit figure which we will use is recalculated by taking all production costs from the sales revenue. Not counted as a cost item are contributions to the SOE's welfare funds, which is for extra bonus and perks and therefore should be regarded as part of the retained profit.

According to the reconstructed gross profit, we find that profit losing is much more prevalent than what the accounting profit shows. A major reason is that a lot of subsidies are already provided before the SOE ever reports losing profit. Another observation is that even the recalculated profit-losing rate is consistently lower than 20 percent, while the widely accepted profit-losing rate in China is 30 percent. Sample selection bias is the major reason for this. It is much easier to collect data from profit-making SOEs than profit-losing SOEs, and therefore the sample definitely consists of disproportionately more profit-making, "good" SOEs.

Who are the profit losers? One useful classification is dividing them into chronic losers and random losers. Chronic profit losers may be caused by distorting governmental policies and are not necessarily due to mismanagement. They correspond to the ex ante soft budget constraint discussed earlier. Random profit losers are due to either mismanagement of the manager or just bad luck. The analysis reveals that the distribution of years of losing profit is rather skewed toward one year. That means that most of the SOEs in the sample appear to be random profit losers. Of course, sample bias may have caused this pattern.

Who are the most likely profit losers? In other words, what are the characteristics of the profit-losing SOEs? In order to answer these questions, a sequence of econometric analysis is conducted. We find that surprisingly, other things being equal, large SOEs are less likely to be in the red. One possible explanation is that for these SOEs, many favorable treatments are already incorporated before the accounting profit is calculated, such as low-interest loans. Also, we find that industry type matters. SOEs in mining and raw material industry are most likely to be in the red, while SOEs in light industry or the chemical industry are least likely to be in the red.

The next question is about the severity of the so-called soft budget constraint. One possible index of the softness of the budget constraint is the correlation between the SOE's retained profit and the SOE's total gross profit. We use this index and find that the budget constraint is softer for the random profit losers than for the chronic ones. For the random losers, the average correlation between the retained profit and the gross profit is actually −10.9 percent. That means the big one-time losers can expect to get more positive retained profit than the small one-time losers. A likely explanation is that with these random profit losers, the government has less accurate information about the reason for the profit loss. Therefore, the SOE can always argue that it has really tried very hard and that the profit loss is due to bad luck. The big losers can even make a bigger case out of this than the small ones. This explanation is backed by the size effect in the regression: medium-sized and, to some extent, large-sized SOEs faced softer budget constraint. Also, very interestingly, SOEs under more reform measures are found to have more subsidies. This is perhaps due to the fact that SOEs under special reform programs enjoy higher bargaining powers than others.

As for the chronic losers, we find that the retained profit is in general independent of the negative profit—the correlation coefficient is statistically indistinguishable from 0. This result for the chronic losers is not surprising, since their losing profit is often due to exogenous reasons and in many times fully expected by all. Moreover, we find that no particular type of SOE enjoyed better treatment, except for SOEs undergoing special reform measures. Similar intuitions discussed in random profit losing are applicable here.

Overall, the findings on the soft budget constraint can be summarized by stating that the soft budget constraint is still very prevalent after the reform. Profit losing is, to a large extent, an outcome of government intervention, such as imposing a high quota. Random profit losers enjoy better treatment from the government than the chronic ones, partly due to their informational advantage (as illustrated by Dewatripont and Maskin, 1990).

CONCLUDING REMARKS

This chapter examines the behavior of the Chinese SOEs under reform. The central argument is that the Chinese SOEs in the reform era are under the dual influence of the government and the market, and this explains major inefficiency and poor performance of China's SOEs. More specifically, there are three aspects of the behavior of the Chinese SOEs. First, SOE managers tend to engage in very active rent-seeking, looking for underpriced inputs, low-interest credit, land, export permits, and so on. In the process, the government takes the opportunity to impose its own objectives onto the SOEs. During the years of the dual-track pricing reform, our evidence shows that the rent can be higher than 50 percent of an SOE's profit earned from the market. Second, once the relevant rents are earned, Chinese SOEs seem to be efficient in choosing their input-output combination to maximize profit. This is a desirable effect of the reform and perhaps accounted for the documented productivity improvement during early years of reform. Third, the problem of the soft budget constraint, taking the form of subsidizing both chronic and random (occasional) profit losers, is prevalent in the reform era. This implies that the investment decision of the SOE is severely distorted.

The implication of the analysis is straightforward. The remaining problems with the Chinese SOEs are results of excessive influence of the government, giving rise to heavy rent-seeking and the soft budget constraint. Thus, the reform has been incomplete in redefining the government–enterprise relation. Intensive reforms in the direction of disentangling government–enterprise relations are critically needed in order to complete the task of transforming the ailing Chinese SOEs.

A natural question at the end of any lengthy analysis of China's SOE is: What is the future of Chinese SOEs and China's enterprise reform? Overall, one can be guardedly optimistic. The Chinese leadership seems to have long recognized that the complicated government–enterprise relationship is the key issue of enterprise reform. Accordingly, various reform efforts have been made to push for a proper resolution of this issue. The most recent wave of reforms aimed at the SOEs came after the Chinese Communist Party's 17th Congress in 1997. Small SOEs are being privatized. Very soon, the remaining issue will be only with medium-sized and large SOEs. Rapid privatization of these SOEs is unlikely to happen and unlikely to be desirable, since a large number of supporting institutions such as corporate governance and financial discipline need to emerge in order for privatized medium-sized and large-sized enterprises to perform well. Thus, most likely, another decade is needed for China to fully resolve the SOE problem. Until then, China's economic reform cannot be proclaimed complete and successful.

ACKNOWLEDGMENT

The chapter is a revision of an earlier paper entitled ''The Behavior of Chinese State Owned Enterprises after the Reform.'' I would like to thank Fan Qimiao, Roger Gordon, Dale Jorgenson, Lee Lung-fei, and Xu Chenggang for valuable discussions and suggestions.

REFERENCES

Appelbaum, E. (1978) Testing Neoclassical Production Theory. *Journal of Econometrics* 7, pp. 87–102.

Chen, K., Wang, H., Zheng, Y., Jefferson, G., and Rawski, T. (1989). Productivity Changes in Chinese Industry: 1953–1985. *Journal of Comparative Economics* 12, pp. 73–83.

Dewatripont, M., and Maskin, E. (1995). Credit and Efficiency in Centralized and Decentralized Economies. *Review of Economic Studies* 62, pp. 541–556.

Fan, G., and Woo, W. (1992). Decentralized Socialism and Macroeconomic Stability: Lessons from China. Mimeo, University of California, Davis.

Fan, Q., Li, L., and Peng, Z. (1989). The CESRRI Enterprises Panel Survey System: An Introduction. London: S.T. International Centre for Economics and Related Disciplines (STICERD), London School of Economics.

Groves, T., Hong, Y., McMillian, J., and Naughton, B. (1994). Automony and Incentives in Chinese State Enterprises. *Quarterly Journal of Economics* 109(1), pp. 38–51.

Jefferson, G., Rawski, T., and Zheng, X. (1992). Growth, Efficiency, and the Convergence in China's State and Collective Industry. *Journal of Economic Development and Cultural Change* 40(2), pp. 12–20.

Kornai, J. (1992). *The Socialist System*. Princeton, NJ: Princeton University Press.

Li, D. (1994). Chinese State Enterprises under the Dual-Influence of the Government and the Market. Working paper, Department of Economics, University of Michigan.

Li, D. (1998). The Costs and Benefits of Government Control of Enterprises in Transition: Theory and Evidence from China. Working paper, Department of Economics, University of Michigan.

Murphy, K., Shleifer, A., and Vishny, R. (1993). Why Is Rent-Seeking So Costly to Growth? *American Economic Review* 83(2), pp. 43–57.

Qian, Y. (October 1996). Enterprise Reform in China: Agency Problems and Political Control. *Economics of Transition* 4(2), pp. 427–448.

Shleifer, A., and Vishny, R. (1994). Politicians and SOEs. *Quarterly Journal of Economics*. 94(439), pp. 995–1026.

Woo, W., Hai, W., Jin, Y., and Fan, G. (June 1994). How Successful Has China's State Enterprise Reform Been? *Journal of Comparative Economics* 18, pp. 410–437.

Chapter 2

The Evolution of Chinese
Township and Village Enterprises

Qi Hantang

THE SEEDS OF CBEs (1949–1957)

The seeds of Chinese commune and brigade enterprises (CBEs)—the predeces-
sor of township and village enterprises (TVEs)—consisted of rural sideline production (*nongcun fuye*)[1] and agricultural cooperatives (*nongye hezuoshe*), with
the former serving as the foundation and the latter as the support.

In 1949, when the People's Republic of China (PRC) was founded, the output
value of the rural commercial products made by artisans and craftsmen (*nongcun
shangpinxing shougongye chanzhi*) was about ¥1,500 million, while that of the
rural self-sufficient products plus that from the initial processing of agricultural
produce were about ¥5,200 million. These two figures amounted to ¥6,700 million, making up 14.7 percent of the total output value of the whole country's
industry and agriculture: 20.5 percent of the gross output value of agriculture,
and 35.4 percent of the gross output value of industry (including the output
value of the rural non-commercial handicraft industry). At that time, 70 percent
of the industrial products needed by the peasants came from the handicraft
industry, which presented itself as an important component of the rural economy
(Zhang,[2] 1990: 7; *China TVE Yearbook [1978–1987]*: 24).

On 15 December 1951, the Central Committee of the CPC issued a document
in draft form to the Party Committees at all levels, who were then required to
try the ideas suggested. The document, entitled *Resolution on Mutual Aid and
Cooperation in Agricultural Production (China TVE Yearbook [1978–1987]*:
24–25), stated that in some areas it was possible to integrate agriculture and
sideline production:

In the conditions favorable to the local situation to develop mutual aid and cooperation
in which agriculture and sideline production (handicraft industry, processing production,

transportation, and so on) are combined, a reasonable division of labor and work should be carried out according to requirements of agriculture and sideline production and to the special skills of individual people.

The document also pointed out that the Party and government should help peasants set up "producers' cooperatives of all kinds in sideline production and handicraft industry." By 1952 the output value of the rural commercial handicraft industry, together with that of self-sufficient handicraft industry and that of the initial processing of agricultural produce, added up to ¥11.1 billion. It had increased by 65.7 percent as compared with 1949, with a yearly increase of 18.3 percent, making up 13.4 percent of the gross output value of industry and agriculture, 21.6 percent of the output value of agriculture (including that of commercial products made by rural artisans and craftsmen). There were 4,670,000 artisans and craftsmen in the rural areas, making up 63.5 percent of the total people involved in the handicraft industry in China (Zhang, 1990: 8; *China TVE Yearbook [1978–1987]*: 24).

After the nationwide agrarian reform, the Party Central Committee put forward the general line (*zong luxian*) for the transition period[3] and the socialist transformation of agriculture and handicraft industry was launched throughout the country, known in China as the movement to organize cooperatives (*hezuo-hua yundong*). China's agricultural cooperative transformation took place in three stages, starting at a low level with mutual aid teams (*huzhuzu*)[4] and advancing to higher levels with elementary cooperatives (*chujishe*)[5] and advanced cooperatives (*gaojishe*).[6]

In 1953 the central authorities adopted an encouraging policy on the development of the rural sideline production. In the spirit of the Party Central Committee and the State Council, several million full-time and over 10 million part-time artisans and craftsmen joined the agricultural cooperative. According to their individual specialty, the cooperative organized the labor force into production groups or teams. Each sideline production team (group) was composed of specialists who performed specific tasks. On the basis of the characteristics of each sideline production and its relation with agricultural production, the agricultural cooperative adopted different ways of managing these teams. Some exercised unified management and unified distribution, while some others, under unified leadership and in arrangement with the agricultural cooperative, carried out independent management and assumed sole responsibility for their profits and/or losses.

The scope of operation of the agricultural cooperative included the handicraft industry, processing, transportation, service trades, and so on. Since they belonged to the agricultural cooperative, all these industries were considered sideline productions and were not separated from agriculture. However, they were creating conditions for the development of nonagricultural industries in rural areas. In 1955, in his *Notes to "The Socialist Tide in China's Rural Areas,"* Mao Zedong (1977: 254) pointed out:

It is right that sideline production must have a good market. It should not be developed blindly. For China, as a whole, rural sideline production is intended in a very large part to serve the rural area, but at the same time, it must also be of some service to the urban area and to the export trade, and the latter is likely to be extended in the years to come.

During the years between 1949 (the founding year of the PRC) and 1957, rural sideline production made unsteady progress, sometimes rising and sometimes falling. By 1957 the gross output value of sideline production reached ¥14,580 million, increasing by 23.9 percent as compared with 1952 (Zhang, 1990: 12).

THE BIRTH OF CBEs (1958–1965)

On 17 August 1958 the Political Bureau of the Central Committee of China's People's Congress (CPC) held an enlarged meeting (*kuoda huiyi*) in Bei Daihe, at which the *Resolution on the Establishment of the People's Communes in Rural Areas* was approved. It was decided (*China TVE Yearbook [1978–1987]*: 25) that

The people's communes are to be established in which farming, forestry, animal husbandry, sideline production, and fisheries will be developed in an all-round way; and in which the workers, peasants, soldiers, students, and businessmen will help each other and work together.

These were, in fact, the ideas of Mao Zedong, who envisioned the people's commune as a basic unit in China's society and as a bridge leading to communism. The whole country, especially in rural areas, immediately responded. By the end of 1958, 740,000 agricultural cooperatives all over the country were merged into 26,000 people's communes (Huang, 1998: 30). These communes had two special features: they were large in scale and publicly owned. The former cooperative had been composed of 100 or 200 households, whereas the people's commune consisted of 4,000 to 20,000 households. In general, there was one township for each commune. After scores of cooperatives with different economic conditions and wealth levels had been merged into one commune, the commune set up a highly centralized unified management and egalitarian distribution system and sometimes distributed the necessities of life in place of wages (including a communal canteen where peasants ate without paying),[7] which was called in China a supply system (*gongji zhi*).[8] All the small retailers and peddlers, open markets, and even household sideline production were regarded as the "tails of capitalism" and were banned accordingly (Huang, 1998: 30–31).

The *Resolution* also pointed out (*China TVE Yearbook [1978–1987]*: 25) that "the development of rural industry calls for a certain labor force being transferred from the agricultural production front." In December 1958 the 6th Plenary Session of the 8th Central Committee of the CPC passed the *Resolution on Some Questions Concerning the People's Communes*, which pointed out more definitely that (*China TVE Yearbook [1978–1987]*: 25) the development of the system of the people's commune in rural areas pointed the way toward the gradual industrialization of rural areas and that the people's commune must engage in industry in a big way (*daban gongye*). At that time it was thought that the industrial development of the people's commune would not only quicken China's industrialization but also help bring about common ownership in rural areas and reduce the difference between urban and rural areas.

To start enterprises, the people's communes gathered funds from various channels (*China TVE Yearbook [1978–1987]*: 25). First, they simply transferred the enterprises originally run by the agricultural cooperatives and changed them into commune-owned enterprises. Next, they raised money from commune members by campaigning for property to be shared by all (*gongchan feng*) and campaigning for equal allocation and indiscriminate transfer of resources (*ping-diao feng*). Then, they changed about 35 percent of the 100,000 handicraft co-operatives (groups) to the communes' industries. Finally, some publicly owned enterprises in rural areas were transferred to a lower administrative level, that is, the people's communes. In a word, the people's communes began to run enterprises by administrative means, which failed to differentiate between different types of ownership. With the previously-mentioned "two campaigns," they showed no consideration for the practical situation, nor did they care in the least about the economic and social effects. The CBEs came into being at a time when everyone was clamoring for industry (*daban gongye*), such as iron and steel and transportation; and the Chinese peasants brought this about at great cost to themselves. This was also observed by Chang (1993: 224); during the Great Leap Forward, agricultural collectives were instantly merged into rural people's communes to mobilize and organize labor and other resources on a massive scale for rural infrastructure and industrial projects. Millions of small shops and factories were set up by the people's communes at that time.

In view of the serious problems that emerged in both the Great Leap Forward and the movement for people's communes, the central authorities took some measures to rectify, merge, and close down the CBEs. The situation had changed after these measures. The Great Leap Forward delayed farmwork, which resulted in what is referred to as the three-year difficult period from 1959 to 1961, which brought about serious damage to the rural economy in China. In order to concentrate all the rural resources on agriculture, the central authorities made the following decisions (*China TVE Yearbook [1978–1987]*: 25). In the years that followed, the people's communes and the production brigades should not start new enterprises. Those enterprises with no conditions for normal production or not welcomed by the masses should all be closed down. As part of the readjustment and retrenchment efforts following the Great Leap Forward, a majority of rural industrial enterprises were closed down in 1961–1962 (Chang, 1993: 225). In 1961 the total output value of CBEs nosedived to ¥1.98 billion, and the figure dropped further to ¥790 million in 1962 and ¥410 million in

1963. During the following six years these enterprises saw a small rebound in their output value, but they remained basically stagnant (Byrd and Lin, 1990: 10). By 1965 the commune enterprises were reduced to 120,000. The output value of commune industries decreased from ¥1,980 million to ¥530 million.

As a result of this, the development of the fragile rural economy, which had just reemerged, began to lose its internal vitality. It also became difficult for the peasants to improve their lives. This could be seen in the following respects. First, agriculture at that time relied mainly on manual operations, and most of the agricultural means of production were produced by commune or brigade enterprises. When these enterprises were closed down, the handicraft industry of the brigade could not be restored immediately, thus causing a great shortage of small and middle-sized farm tools. Second, the extended agricultural reproduction relied on the development of sideline production to complement agriculture. However, as sideline production shrank, there were no funds that could be invested in farmwork, the development of which was therefore directly hindered. Third, the main source of the peasants' cash income was sideline occupations. The near-collapse of the sideline occupations thus immediately affected the peasants' income.

THE RESURGENCE OF CBEs (1966–1978)

The Cultural Revolution (1966–1977) caused years of upheaval for China, during which, CBEs did not continue to sag, though it was impossible for them to develop quickly and healthily. According to Chang (1993: 226), the rural industrialization drive in the Cultural Revolution period seemed to have produced the intended effects of modernizing agriculture and diversifying the rural economy. That was because before and during the Cultural Revolution there were a number of factors conducive to the development of CBEs. For example, from January 1961 to June 1963, some industrial sectors in cities were reduced in scale by sending technical personnel in different fields to rural areas; from 1968, school-leavers started to be sent down to the countryside and mountain areas (known in China as *shangshan xiaxiang*). Both groups brought with them knowledge, technology, and information about commodities. They also helped communes and brigades set up factories, utilizing their various *guanxi* (contacts) in the cities. At that time commodities on the market were in great shortage because of the halt in production for the revolution (*tingchan nao geming*) in urban factories. As a result of these, the CBEs gradually recovered. In 1970 the industrial enterprises run by the people's communes alone amounted to 44,700, increasing 2.7 times as compared with 12,200 in 1965 before the great Cultural Revolution, the net increase being 32,500. In 1965 the output value of commune industries was ¥530 million. In 1970 it reached ¥2,660 million, with a net increase of ¥2,130 million, a five-fold increase over 1965 (Zhang, 1990: 19).

In August 1970, presided over by the late Premier Zhou Enlai, a Northern

Region Agriculture Conference involving thirteen provinces was held by the State Council, which made two resolutions. One was: "In Agriculture, Learn from Dazhai (*nongye xue Dazhai*)"[9]; the other was to mechanize farming. The conference stressed that manual work alone without mechanized farming could not raise agricultural labor productivity quickly. If nothing could be done to change the situation in which 600 million peasants were busily engaged in farming, it would be impossible to create enough labor force to reconstruct industries. At that time people had very narrow views of the role of the CBEs, namely to mechanize farming (see Chen Xigen, 1989: 28–29). The output value of the whole country's commune and brigade industries rose from ¥6,760 million in 1970 to ¥19,780 million in 1975, with an average annual increase of 24.1 percent. The proportion of commune industrial output value rose from 40.8 percent to 43.9 percent within the same period. The average output value of each commune enterprise also rose from ¥58,200 to ¥112,100, which indicated that the enterprises were continuously growing larger.

On 15 October 1975, the State Council convened the National Conference, "In Agriculture, Learning from Dazhai." In the summary report of the conference, the following was put forward: "We must adhere to the socialist road when developing CBEs, which should mainly serve agricultural production, serve the people's daily life, and when possible serve big industries (*da gongye*)[10] and the export trade." The report also advocated making full use of local resources instead of fighting for raw materials with big industries. In the spirit of the conference that CBEs should be developed, on 7 November 1975 the Ministry of Agriculture and Forestry referred a report to the State Council, requesting its approval for setting up an Enterprise Administration for the People's Commune (*renmin gongshe qiye guanli ju*), whose major tasks were to (1) investigate the development of CBEs and study relevant principles and policies; (2) summarize and exchange the experience of developing the CBEs; and (3) assist concerned ministries and commissions to solve the problems in production, supply, and marketing of the CBEs. This report was ratified by the State Council on 1 February 1976.

After 1976, when the Gang of Four was overthrown, CBEs developed further. By 1978, when the 3rd Plenary Session of the 11th Central Committee of the CPC was held, the communes and brigades had 1.52 million enterprises in all, which provided jobs for a rural surplus labor force of 28.26 million. The output value came up to ¥49,100 million, an increase of 111 percent as compared with ¥23,400 million in 1975, the average increase rate being 28.2 percent a year. Of this output value, industrial value was ¥38,500 million, making up 78.4 percent of the total output value. Objectively speaking, during the great Cultural Revolution, though CBEs were criticized as something of a capitalist nature, they had several good opportunities for their resurgence.

THE FAST GROWTH OF CBEs (1979–1983)

In December 1978, the Chinese Communist Party convened its 3rd Plenary Session of the 11th Central Committee, which was of great historic significance. At the plenary session, a strategic decision was made to shift energies to a socialist modernization drive. The session emphasized that much would be done to solve the serious imbalance in the national economy. It also made a decision that the development of agriculture be quickened. In the *Decision on Several Questions concerning Speeding up the Agricultural Development*[11] the Party Central Committee (TVEB, 1987: 22) pointed out: ''CBEs should have a big development, and the proportion of the income from the CBEs against the income from the commune's three-level economy should be raised progressively.''

In the spirit of the 3rd Plenary Session of the 11th Central Committee of the CPC, on 3 July 1979 the State Council issued *Regulations on Some Questions concerning the Development of CBEs (Draft for Trial Implementation)*. The *Regulations* (TVEB, 1987: 11) pointed out that ''CBEs are economic units owned by socialist collectives. Those run by the commune belong to the commune; those run by the brigade belong to the brigade.'' The *Regulations* also formulated a series of supportive policies. For example, at least half of the investment made by the state to assist the people's communes should be used to help those poor and weak CBEs, agricultural banks should offer some low-interest loans, and the policy of low taxes or no tax on CBEs should be implemented. Furthermore, all trades and professions should actively support CBEs. The Party committees and governments at all levels made corresponding decisions and set up regulations on developing CBEs, taking the local situation into account. All these decisions and regulations created a favorable environment for the development of CBEs. This is why many cadres at the grassroots level and peasants called this period of time ''the first spring'' of the development of China's TVEs.

During 1979 and 1980, the policy of adjustment, reform, rectification, and improvement (*tiaozheng, gaige, zhengdun, tigao*) was applied to China's national economy, but the imbalance in the national economy was not fundamentally solved. In the autumn of 1980, the State Council convened a provincial governors' meeting, at which some people raised the problem of small and/or backward enterprises squeezing the big and/or advanced ones (see *Agricultural Economic Journal*, 1981). In April 1981, a national conference on industrial restructuring was held in Chengdu[12] at which CBEs became the target of fierce criticism (see Chen Xigen, 1989: 30).

According to instructions from the central authorities, from 1979 onward the departments at all levels in charge of CBEs carried out reorganization in a big way. The reorganization focused on the development of production, the improvement of management, and the setting up of a rational order of production. In 1981 more instructions were given on the reorganization of the CBEs, calling for a general checkup on enterprise assets, a clearing up of debts and credits, and the setting up and strengthening of the system of handling funds and materials. Besides, it was also demanded that all unsound practices should be opposed and abandoned, such as squandering funds, embezzling and wasting resources, giving dinners or sending gifts in order to curry favor, offering bribes, and distributing bonuses indiscriminately. After cutting 55,800 enterprises in the previous year, the CBEs closed down another 87,100 in 1981. While the number of enterprises continued to decrease between 1979 and 1981, the growth rates of the number of persons employed in the CBEs and of their gross output value underwent a fluctuation.

The Rural Policy Research Center of the Secretariat of the Central Committee of the CPC chaired the drafting of *Some Regulations of the State Council on the CBEs' Carrying out the Adjustment Policy in the National Economy.* Approved by the Secretariat of the Central Committee of the CPC and the state affairs meeting of the State Council, the *Regulations* were issued in the form of Document 77 of the State Council for enforcement on 4 May 1981.[13] The significance of the *Regulations* was that the CBEs were not to be abolished but were to be allowed to exist and continue to develop while subordinating themselves to the adjustment. Therefore, the *Regulations* in a sense saved the CBEs. It laid down the policy (TVEB, 1987: 34) for reorganizing the CBEs, which was:

[They] should be firmly subordinated to the overall situation and adjusted accordingly; at the same time, [we] should respect the autonomy of the communes and brigades, . . . all those enterprises that do not compete with the existing big factories for raw materials, that have a good market for their products, and that make a profit from their business, should not be compulsorily closed down.

In May 1982, the Ministry of Agriculture, Animal Husbandry, and Fishery transmitted the document submitted by the CBE Administration, *A Findings Report on the Contract Management Responsibility System in CBEs.* In July the ministry conducted a national forum on the contract management responsibility system (*jingying chengbao zerenzhi*) in CBEs, exchanging experiences in different places. Between 4 and 13 November 1982, the ministry conducted a forum on the reorganization of CBEs (*China TVE Yearbook [1978–1987]*: 658). On 29 November, the Ministry transmitted the summary of the forum to all Enterprise Administrations for the People's Commune at the levels of province, municipality, and autonomous region. At the forum two important reform measures of profound significance were put forward. One measure (TVEB, 1987: 77) was that "the enterprises run and owned by communes, or run and owned by brigades should then belong to all members of the whole communes or the whole brigades. The enterprises should strengthen the foundation of masses, establish and perfect the system of democratic management." The other measure (TVEB, 1987: 78) was that they should change the situation in which responsibility, power, and benefit in the management of the enterprises were poorly coordinated and in which equal distribution of income was implemented. Instead, they should adopt the system of economic responsibility in varied forms.

In order to carry out the policy of economic adjustment and use an economic lever to restrict the development of CBEs, the state made two important amendments to the tax revenue of CBEs. First, 20 products or so produced and sold by the CBEs such as tobacco, wine, sugar, cotton yarn, and silk would be taxed without exception. Second, the CBEs in the suburbs were originally required to pay 20 percent income tax out of their profit, but now this was to be changed into an eight-level, progressive taxation system (*China TVE Yearbook [1978–1987]*: 658). By the end of 1982, the number of CBEs rose to 1.36 million in all, increasing by 1.45 percent over the previous year. The output value of these enterprises was ¥85,308 million, making up an increase of 14.46 percent as compared with the previous year. In 1983, while the number of CBEs (mainly brigade enterprises) (TVEB, 1986) decreased by 15,300, other indexes such as number of employees and gross output value continued to increase.

THE CHANGE OF NAME TO TOWNSHIP AND VILLAGE ENTERPRISES (TVEs) (1984)

As urban and rural economic restructuring deepened, and the economic policy gradually became elastic and flexible, the peasants broke through some constraints and began to try various ways to develop the economy. Despite the fact that only communes and brigades were allowed to run enterprises, the peasants began to raise funds to run individual household enterprises and joint household ones. Although the peasants were not allowed to engage in trade, they began to make private transactions over a wider range of commodities. Breaking through the restriction of "three locals" (*san jiudi*), namely, drawing materials locally, producing locally, and selling products locally, they absorbed foreign and domestic capital to run joint ventures.

On 1 January 1984 an important document, *Circular of the Central Committee of the CPC on Rural Work in 1984* (colloquially called Document 1 [1984] for short), was issued, in which a special regulation concerning individual (private) enterprises hiring workers was laid down:

Presently, in enterprises with hired laborers above the set number, some of them have implemented systems that are different from those of the private enterprises. For example, they turn some surplus of the after-tax profit to the collective assets; they set a quota of dividends on shares and of the income of the owners; they return a certain proportion of profits to the workers, etc. This contains to varying degrees an element of a cooperative venture, and it is necessary to help them continue to improve. These enterprises may not be treated as capitalist businesses.

This flexibility concerning the number of workers in private enterprises was achieved by obscuring the difference in ownership. In the event, large individual enterprises were registered as collective ones.

The Ministry of Agriculture, Animal Husbandry, and Forestry held a national work conference on CBEs on 2–12 January 1984 (*China TVE Yearbook [1978–1987]*: 547). At the conference the then-minister He Kang gave a talk entitled ''Rectify and Reform, Better the Performance, Create a New Situation for CBEs.'' The conference focused on discussing the *Report on Creating a New Situation for CBEs*, to be submitted by the Ministry to the Party Central Committee and the State Council. It was pointed out in the report that CBEs had already become an important force in the national economy; China's agricultural modernization would always need to dispose of surplus labor and to raise a huge amount of capital; both of the tasks could not be fulfilled without the development of CBEs (TVEB, 1987: 114, 115). On 1 March 1984, the Party Central Committee and the State Council in the form of Document 4[14] transmitted this report, to which important comments were added. The key points of the comments were as follows.

First, the Party Central Committee pointed out that developing TVEs was the only road to the invigoration of rural economy. What they needed to do was to open up new avenues of production, to make an appropriate allocation of the surplus labor that kept on emerging, to make full use of the spare labor in rural areas, to gradually change the situation in which 800 million people were all engaged in farming, and to bring into full play rural commodity production. Only by doing all this could the rural areas become rich, and the large amount of funds needed for agricultural modernization accumulate bit by bit. Second, the Party Central Committee approved the role played by TVEs, saying that they were an important force in the national economy, a major component part of a diversified economy, a significant supplement to state-owned enterprises (SOEs), a weighty pillar of agricultural production, a very important way for the broad masses of peasants to march toward common prosperity, and a new important source of state revenue. Third, the Party Central Committee drew up a general policy to direct the development of TVEs, in other words, to vigorously support, actively guide, and administer TVEs so as to promote their development in a healthy way. Not long after, the general policy was further summed up in the following policy: *jiji fuchi, heli guihua, zhengque yindao, jiaqiang guanli* (active support, rational plan, correct guidance, strengthen management). Fourth, it was decided to rename CBEs as TVEs, the scope of which was widened. In addition to the enterprises formerly run by the township (including district and town) and village, the concept of TVEs included cooperative enterprises jointly run by some commune members, other forms of cooperative industries, and individually owned enterprises (TVEB, 1987: 111–113).

It is important to mention here that the 5th National People's Congress (NPC) adopted at its fifth session on 4 December 1982 the fourth Constitution of the PRC, which restored government at township level (Constitution of the PRC, 1985: 31), which proclaimed in the name of the Constitution the collapse of the people's commune system. On 12 October 1983 the Party Central Committee and the State Council issued *Circular on the Separation of the Government from the Commune and on the Establishment of Township Governments*, requiring the work of separation and establishment to be "completed by the end of 1984." (According to *People's Daily* overseas edition (17 July 1998: 1), Xiangyang Town of Guanghan City in Sichuang Province was the first township in China where the separation of government from commune was carried out in 1979, the commune system was abolished, and the township was reestablished in 1980.) The *Circular* (TVEB, 1987: 97) pointed out that "the scale of a township should be based on the jurisdiction of the former commune, or be appropriately reduced if the original jurisdiction of the commune is too large . . . in market towns with suitable conditions town governments may be set up."

All these carried a foreshadowing of the change of the name from CBEs to TVEs.

After the Party Central Committee issued Documents 1 and 4, the Party Committees and the governments of each province, autonomous region, and municipality directly under the central government laid down, on the basis of local reality, some regulations in succession concerning the development of TVEs. They realized that to revitalize local economy, they must first of all develop TVEs, which they thought was a strategic measure to fight poverty and bring wealth to the people. The peasants as well as the vast numbers of cadres at the grassroots level believed that the Party Central Committee's Document 4 affirmed the positive role of TVEs and laid down a supportive policy for the development of these enterprises, thus bringing "the second spring" for the TVEs. By the end of 1984 China had 6,065,200 TVEs in all, which employed 52.08 million people. The total output value reached ¥170,989 million, an increase of 68.16 percent over 1983. This achievement was particularly striking when we compare the figure of 15.61 percent, the average annual growth rate of TVE output value from 1979 to 1983 (calculated from *China Statistical Yearbook 1990*).

The following were some objective and subjective factors, that might explain why TVEs were able to develop so quickly in the year 1984.

- At the 12th National Congress of the CPC, a goal was set that the output value of industry and agriculture would be quadrupled by the end of this century, and the Chinese people would enjoy a fairly comfortable life. After that, both the leaders at all levels and the peasants had a strong desire to revitalize the local economy and to enable the people to shake off poverty and become rich as quickly as possible.

- In China's rural areas, when the first step of reform, namely, an agricultural responsibility system of contracting output to households, was, on the whole, completed, there was a need to rationalize the structure of production. It was felt that whether this reform could succeed or not depended on the development of TVEs.

- For years, the development of TVEs had been held back, but now the Party Central Committee's "red-titled" documents (*hongtou wenjian*) gave the green light.[15] A series of supporting policies was laid down with actual support from concerned departments at all levels; hence, an environment advantageous for development was taking shape.

• From 1979 onward, after the five years' adjustment, rectification, reform, and improvement, TVEs were firmly established, and their self-developing power was strengthened.

THE DEVELOPMENT OF TVEs (1985–1987)

On 1 January 1985, the Central Committee of the CPC and the State Council issued *Ten Policies for Further Invigorating the Rural Economy*. On 1 January 1986, the Party Central Committee and the State Council issued *The Arrangement of Rural Work in 1986*. Both documents continued to give support to TVEs. For example, the former required implementing the preferential credit and taxation policy toward the TVEs (*China Agriculture Yearbook 1985*: 1), and the latter addressed the issue of coordinated development between agriculture and rural industry.

After that, China's economy experienced four uncontrollable problems (*si shikong*), namely, in capital construction, the use of foreign exchange, bank credit, and funds for consumption. In addition, natural disasters affected grain production during those years. Some people attributed the four problems to the TVEs and believed that the decrease of grain production was due to the fact that too much importance was attached to the development of the TVEs while agricultural production was neglected. In some places many restrictive measures were taken, such as controlling credit funds; putting a tax on bonuses; withdrawing preferential taxation from all TVEs of the country while practicing the eight-level progressive taxation system in an all-around way; and imposing various restrictions on TVEs in the name of strengthening industrial management. Even under those unfavorable circumstances, TVEs steadily flourished. In 1986 the output value of TVEs amounted to ¥354,087 million, taking up 19 percent of the national gross social output value, with 48 percent of that in rural areas, and equal to the whole country's gross social output value in 1969.

On 20–24 December 1987 the National Rural Work Conference,[16] focusing on TVEs, convened in Beijing. The summary of this conference stated that it was important to strengthen leadership in TVEs, which actually encouraged intervention by governments at all levels to ensure that state policies were carried out in these enterprises (*China Agriculture Yearbook 1988*: 202). The fact was that even though the development of TVEs was the cause of the overheating of the economy in 1986 and 1987, this was to be solved through intervention by local governments, which were obviously not interested in limiting their local expansion mainly in economic terms.

The year 1987 was of historical significance, as TVE total output value (¥474,310 million) exceeded that of agriculture (¥467,570 million) for the first time (both figures are cited from *China Statistical Yearbook 1990*[17]), due to the rapid development of TVEs. This was also observed by Lu (1993: 232). The township and village industries are the major parts of TVEs, and the industrial output value of TVEs reached ¥324,349 million in 1987, equivalent to China's total output value of industry in 1975 (¥320,700 million). TVEs had become an important component in China's national economy, the main pillar of the rural economy, and a vital aspect of industry.

THE ADJUSTMENT OF TVEs (1988–1991)

On 21–24 December 1988, the National TVE Work Conference convened in Beijing, which held that because inflation was emerging in China's economic life, the economy was growing too fast, and the social demand was larger than the total supply, the state must adopt a series of measures such as reducing the social demand, downsizing the scale of capital construction, cutting down the capital credit, and tightening the planning and distribution of the main production materials in order to actively tide TVEs over this crisis. In a word, governmental intervention was regarded as a necessity in order to consolidate further development.

On 15 March 1989, the State Council issued *Decision on the Main Points of the Current Industrial Policies*, which pointed out that there existed some serious problems in the industrial structure, and accordingly, that it was essential to adjust the industrial structure, with priority given to the development of the agriculture, energy, transportation and raw materials sectors. That decision was mainly aimed at urban, state-owned industries. However, TVEs had become an important aspect of overall industrial policy making and were targeted as well (State Council Rural Development Research Center, 1989: 50; *China Agriculture Yearbook 1990*: 485):

TVEs should carry out the State industrial policies, actively adjust their production structure, and develop healthily and steadily. We should support those TVEs and small enterprises, which process agricultural and sideline products (*nongfu chanpin*), which procure materials and market products abroad (*liangtou zaiwai*), which produce energy and raw materials, and which are economically efficient. The TVEs that compete for raw materials with State key enterprises, cause serious environmental pollution and are economically inefficient must be compelled to change their production or close down. It is necessary to guide TVEs to produce auxiliary products for big enterprises, and under suitable conditions, encourage big enterprises to transfer some products or production processes to small enterprises, thus strengthening the specialized cooperation between urban and rural areas and avoiding duplicate construction.

Then-Premier Li Peng, in his Report on Work of Government "Firmly Carry out the Guiding Policy of Economic Reorganization and Deepening Reform," delivered on 20 March 1989 at the second meeting of the 7th Plenary Session of the NPC,[18] urged that "TVEs must accordingly reduce the speed of development during the period of economic reorganization; as for the capital needs of TVEs, they must mainly rely on their own accumulation." Li Peng's speech at the National Production Work Conference on 11 October 1989, "Correctly Appraise the Current Economic Situation and Further the Economic Reorganization,'' went further. In the first quarter of that year, the output growth rate of TVEs was still over 20 percent but had been reduced to under 10 percent. There was a main issue for TVEs of how to utilize local resources and materials in rural areas. The markets for the TVEs are partly in the city but mainly in the countryside. They should supply the necessary goods for agricultural production and life in rural areas.

In 1989, facing a severe crisis—lack of capital, energy, and materials, increasing prices for production materials, and a weakening market—a total of 3,000 TVEs were closed, stopped, merged, and changed; more than 20,000 construction projects involving TVEs were halted; and investment was reduced by ¥10,000 million. The total output of TVEs was ¥742,838 million,[19] a growth of 14.36 percent compared to the previous year and a reduction in the growth rate of 21.98 percent compared to the previous year (*China Statistical Yearbook 1990*). The policies announced in late 1988 to control and consolidate the economy provided the pretext for a partial return to state planning and an attack on TVEs, which were accused of overheating the economy and undermining state-owned urban sectors. Severe credit restrictions and a tightening of raw materials sent these enterprises into a tailspin from the second quarter in 1989 until well into 1991–1992 (Morgan, 1994: 220–221). One million TVEs reportedly were closed during the 1988–1991 austerity campaign (Zweig, 1992: 12). Although the gross output value of TVEs continued to grow, the annual growth rate of gross output value of TVEs dropped from 36.43 percent in 1988 to 14.36 percent in 1989 and further to 13.91 percent in 1990 (calculated from the data in *China Statistical Yearbook 1994*: 346).

In 1990 the economy appeared weakened and in recession, while the economic structure seemed not to have improved. In line with the support given to enterprises to overcome their difficulties, the central government pointed out that banks at all levels should give suitable support by circulating funds to TVEs. In March 1990 Li Peng reduced the role of TVEs to merely improving the countryside. In terms of policy, the leadership sought to control the too fast growth of TVEs by a combination of credit cuts (through banks) and commands to local governments to forbid new projects, and it sought to influence the sector by offering more narrow definitions of TVEs and by "stamping out" unsound practices. In 1990 several important regulations regarding this sector were introduced, such as "The Rules on the Contract Management Responsibility System of TVEs" (*The Corpus of TVE Laws of the PRC*, 1997: 260–263; *State Council Bulletin*, 1990, No. 10: 377); "The Regulations on Township and Village Collectively Owned Enterprises of the PRC" (*The Corpus of TVE Laws of the PRC*, 1997: 76–79; *State Council Bulletin*, 1990, No. 11: 387), which aimed at standardizing the operation of TVEs.

The year 1991 was the first year of the 8th Five-Year Plan (1991–1995), and the central authorities put forward a supportive policy for TVEs. The government realized that local governments were in too strong a position to impose irrational targets on collectively owned TVEs. Therefore, the State Commission for the Reform of the Economic Structure in a document entitled *The Key Points of the Reform of the Economic Structure in 1991* (issued on 25 April 1991) called for an improvement in the management responsibility system for TVEs and the introduction of "various ways to separate ownership from management appropriately." The commission also emphasized a general policy of support for TVEs that make export products and generate foreign exchange, as well as for the enterprises that produce famous brand products, especially high-quality products. The support should be realized in better state planning (indicative planning) to satisfy their need for raw materials (*State Council Bulletin*, 1991, No. 23: 825).

In sum, TVEs suffered in many ways from the overall recession in the economy and the austerity policies of the government.[20] As a result, there was a temporary falling off in the development of TVEs. However, the state was not able to gain stronger control over the local authorities due to the taxation and financial structures that gave local governments great autonomy (Ma, 1996).

THE MATURING OF TVEs (1992–1998)

Strong lobbying efforts from the coastal areas and fears of massive rural unemployment prompted the Chinese government to become more tolerant of nonstate enterprises. The renewed export drive during 1991–1992 also meant a new burst in TVE activities. These trends, coupled with Deng Xiaoping's call for greater market activity, sent TVEs into a new stage of their development (Zweig, 1992: 12). In 1991 the gross output value of TVEs topped ¥1,000 billion, reaching ¥1,162.17 billion. In 1992 the gross output value of TVEs rose to ¥1,797.54 billion with an annual growth rate of 54.67 percent (*China Statistical Yearbook 1994, 1994*: 346).

In 1992 the state in its economic work focused on the adjustment of industrial structures (*tiaozheng jiegou*) and the enhancement of efficiency (*tigao xiaolu*). One key policy in the economic restructuring in 1992 was to continuously develop TVEs. *The Key Points of the Reform of the Economic Structure in 1992* (State Commission for the Reform of the Economic Structure, 25 January 1992) stressed that the TVEs in the inland areas should find various ways to introduce funds, skills, and technology from the coastal areas and improve their management. The TVEs in the coastal areas should increase inputs and, enhance technology and product quality.

On 2 January 1992, the Ministry of Agriculture submitted to the State Council *Report on Furthering the Sustainable and Healthy Development of TVEs*, which signified an important development in state policies toward TVEs (*State Council Bulletin*, 1992, No. 8: 245). For example, governments at all levels should give necessary support and help with regard to the raising of capital, the financial departments should extend credit support for TVEs in accordance with the state industrial policies, the projects for new technology and new products in key collective TVEs should be included in the relevant state plans at different levels, personnel training of TVEs should be included in the state plans on educational development, TVEs with competitive strength should be authorized to handle their own foreign trade and cooperation, and the proportion of after-tax profits to be left in TVEs should not be lower than 60 percent (*State Council Bulletin*, 1992, No. 8: 245).

Seeing the inadequate TVE development in the middle and western parts of China, the State Council convened a meeting on 18 November 1992 to exchange experiences on accelerating the development of TVEs in the middle and western parts of China. In his speech (printed in *Peasants Daily [nongmin ribao]*, 30 November 1992), Tian Jiyun, vice premier at that time, attributed the swift development of TVEs to a good operational mode that is compatible with the market economy. At the beginning of 1993 the State Council made a "Decision on Quickening the Development of TVEs in the Middle and Western Parts," encouraging TVEs in the eastern part to help their counterparts in the middle and western parts. In February 1995 the General Office of the State Council wrote instructions on the "Pilot Project Scheme of the Cooperation between the TVEs in Eastern and Western Parts," submitted by the Ministry of Agriculture, and referred it to those concerned for implementation.

Because of the effect of Deng Xiaoping's talks during his southern tour and the 14th National Congress of CPC, clearly stating that China should establish a market economy (both important events happened the previous year), in 1993 Chinese TVEs scored the most splendid achievement ever with the growth rate of gross output value reaching 75.47 percent (calculated from *China Statistical Yearbook 1994*). Many provincial Party and government leaders realized that TVEs were the main hope for rejuvenating their local economies. For example, Zhao Fulin, Party Secretary of Guangxi Autonomous Region, said that only by developing TVEs could Guangxi rejuvenate itself; Lu Rongjing, Party Secretary of Anhui Province, said that it would be a historical mistake not to develop TVEs (*China TVE Yearbook 1994*: 5).

Good times did not last long. Starting from the second half of 1993, the national economy began to overheat again, and the macrotightening (*hongguan jinsuo*) policy was therefore enforced again. The growth rate of the TVE gross output value in 1994 dropped to 35.03 percent (calculated from *China Statistical Yearbook 1996*). In 1994 39,257 TVEs were closed or stopped, and 483,500 employees were forced to return to farmwork (*China TVE Yearbook 1995*: 5). However, Chinese TVEs began to mature. As before, they tried every possible means to seek a way out. Encountering difficulties in obtaining capital domestically, they started a lot of joint ventures with foreign partners. In 1995 alone, 9,372 new Sino–foreign joint ventures with TVEs on the Chinese side were set up, making a total number of 38,743; in 1995 alone, TVEs used $8.5 billion foreign capital, making the total amount of foreign capital used by TVEs reach $31.8 billion (*China TVE Yearbook 1996*: 6). In 1996 China continued to carry out the appropriately tight financial and monetary policies, and therefore inadequate capital input continued to be the number one difficulty faced by TVEs.

A major movement for TVEs in 1996 was organizing enterprise groups, and new group companies in that year reached 8,380 *(China TVE Yearbook 1997*: 3). However, the problem of small scale remained unchanged.

The most important event during this stage was that on 29 October 1996. The 22nd Meeting of the Standing Committee of the 8th NPC approved *The Township and Village Enterprise Law of the PRC* (*The Corpus of TVE Laws of the PRC*, 1997: 3–5), effective from 1 January 1997. The legislation of the TVE law started in May 1984, when 32 delegates proposed to formulate a CBE law at the 2nd Meeting of the 6th NPC. However, this proposal encountered many firm objections, mainly from economists, in addition to some people in the legislation organ. The representative figure was the famous economist Xiao Liang, who (Xiao, 1995: 5) believed that the concept of Chinese TVEs was something regional and nonagricultural that embraced diverse economic sectors; besides, the TVE did not constitute a complete, independent, and basic enterprise system. *The Regulations on Township and Village Collectively Owned Enterprises of the PRC*, issued on 3 June 1990 in the name of the State Council, was a temporary compromise. With the continued all-out lobbying efforts of the Ministry of Agriculture and its subordinate TVE Bureau, the TVE law eventually appeared on the stage.

The gross output of TVEs increased by only 21 percent (Ji, 1998: 32[21]) in 1996, and by only 18 percent in 1997 (Ji, 1998: 32). During his inspection tour on 20–22 April, President Jiang Zemin visited a number of TVEs in Jiangsu Province and exchanged views with local officials, enterprise managers, and technicians on the development of those enterprises. Jiang said that developing TVEs is an important strategy and a long-term, fundamental policy of China. He said that TVEs have played an important role in the modernization of agriculture and the industrialization of rural areas. The impressive performance of TVEs is important for China to attain 1998's goal for economic development, stabilize and strengthen agriculture, and press ahead with the reform of state-run enterprises as well. The president urged governments at all levels to attach great importance to TVE development and give them support in credit loans, export, financing, using foreign capital, and technical upgrading (*People's Daily*, overseas edition, 23 April 1998: 1).

OUTLOOK

From the examination of the history of TVEs it becomes understandable why, during the past and even now, the TVE was generally considered an appendage to rural agriculture, a supplement to urban industry, and small in scale. Yet nowadays China's economy is experiencing tremendous change, and the TVE will surely continue to evolve, possibly at a quicker pace. It is therefore meaningful to conclude this chapter with an attempt to identify several major trends in its future development.

First, the essential nature of the TVE will no longer be agricultural, as it is becoming an organic part of the industrial economy. At the beginning, the TVE was closely linked with agriculture: its capital relied on agricultural accumulation, its labor force derived from peasants, its raw materials were mainly farm produce. Nevertheless, in pace with the expansion of the scale of the TVE and the enhancement of its strength, bank loans are becoming its major source of funds; its labor force is being transformed from original peasants into purely industrial workers. As a result, the TVE is separating itself from agriculture and is constituting an organic component of the industrial economy.

Next, the operational characteristics of the TVE will not be of rural color, especially when the integration of rural and urban areas is taken into account. It is true that the TVE was born in the rural area, but having scored an astonishing achievement, it is increasingly far from the "rural" and increasingly close to the "urban." In the past some TVE entrepreneurs, due to various reasons, restricted their business to the rural area, but now they do business wherever there is a market, traveling between rural and urban areas and even going abroad. In some TVE-developed regions, small industrial districts equipped with a central supply of water, gas, and power have been constructed into small and medium-sized towns (an urbanization process), in addition to the fact that more and more TVEs are expanding into cities. It will be increasingly difficult to use the adjective "rural" to describe and cover the changing meaning of the TVE concept.

Last, "small size" will not necessarily be an indispensable feature of the TVE. In the past, once the TVE is referred to, people would subconsciously get the impression right away of its small scale, low-quality products, and its capability of producing only parts or components for the medium-sized or large-sized enterprises. But now, some TVEs are already of a considerable scale, and many more will expand their scale mainly by merger and acquisition, so as to realize the economies of scale.

It seems obvious that the Chinese TVE emerged under particular historical and contextual conditions, and its name has already changed once, from the CBE to the TVE, reflecting its different historical stages, namely, the stage of planned economy and that of planned commodity economy. I predict that in pace with the continuous development of the TVE, with the acceleration of the integration of urban and rural areas, especially with the genuine establishment and improvement of the market economy, the name of the TVE will be increasingly meaningless and therefore will gradually vanish.

NOTES

1. In China *nongcun fuye* (rural sideline production) refers to trades of most kinds except farming, forestry, animal husbandry, fisheries, gathering and hunting (*Ocean of Words*, 1979: 434). It includes processing of agricultural produce, handicraft industry, construction work, communications, transportation, commerce, and services.

2. On 25 September 1998 I paid a special visit to Zhang Yi. Zhang, who is now

retired, who was vice director of the TVE Bureau under the Ministry of Agriculture, and writes extensively about Chinese TVEs. He told me that a lot of statistics about CBEs are his calculation and that no official sources are available at all. However, the correctness of the figures provided by him is suspect, as I have found many obvious calculation errors. Errors of other kinds are unable to be detected as Zhang never gives the sources of his statistics in his writings. Therefore I always try to choose official statistics wherever possible, though being aware that they are not always accurate as well.

3. The general line for the transition period (put forward by Mao Zedong in 1953) was basically to accomplish China's industrialization and the socialist transformation of agriculture, handicraft industry, and capitalist industry and commerce over a fairly long period of time.

4. An elementary form of organization in agricultural cooperation, which consisted of two forms: temporary mutual aid teams and year-round mutual aid teams.

5. Short for elementary agricultural producers' cooperatives, in which distribution was according to the amount of work each member did and the amount of land he or she contributed.

6. Short for advanced agricultural producers' cooperatives, in which the land and other chief means of production were collectively owned by the co-ops, and the distribution system was based on the principle of "from each according to his ability, to each according to his work."

7. I guess the saying "eat from one pot" originated from the commune public canteen.

8. This was a system of payment in kind, once practiced in revolutionary wars and in the early days of the People's Republic and partly restored during the movement of the people's commune, providing working personnel and their dependents with the primary necessities of life.

9. Dazhai, a production brigade in Xiyang County, Shanxi Province, was made the pacesetter on China's agricultural front by the central authorities before the inception of reform.

10. Here "big industries" refer to the state-owned industries, most of which were (are) located in urban areas.

11. This *Decision* was approved by the 4th Plenary Session of the 11th Central Committee on 28 September 1979. The full text can be found in *Collection of Economic Statutes, Volume I* (1981: 56–79), compiled by the Department of Law, Zhongshan University.

12. Chengdu is the capital city of Sichuan Province.

13. Full text was printed in *China TVE Yearbook 1978–1987*: 432.

14. This Document 4 was entitled *Circular on Transmitting the "Report on Creating a New Situation for CBEs" Submitted by the Ministry of Agriculture, Animal Husbandry and Fishery, and the Party Group of the Ministry.*

15. The changes of the central authorities' attitudes toward CBEs can be seen in the three No. 1 Documents: Document 1 (1982) of the Party Central Committee and the State Council did not say a word about the development of CBEs, only mentioning that the existing CBEs should be protected, not dissolved or damaged; Document 1 (1983) mentioned that CBEs should be consolidated and strengthened; Document 1 (1984) greatly affirmed the significance of CBEs, urging that they should develop very swiftly. In Document 1 (1982) one sentence, in Document 1 (1983) one paragraph, and in Document 1 (1984) one part specially expounded the great significance of CBEs. In addition

to Document 1 (1984), Document 4 (1984) followed in three months, fully approving TVEs (all the Documents mentioned in this note can be found in *China Agriculture Yearbook, 1982, 1983, 1984*, respectively).

16. The national rural work conferences are annual occasions (mainly in December) that bring together the central and provincial decision makers in charge of rural work. "Document 1" of each year, an outcome of these conferences, is later approved by the Political Bureau of the Party Central Committee and given force as a circular of the Central Committee, in some years jointly issued with the State Council.

17. However, according to *China TVE Yearbook 1978–1987* (p. 31), the TVE total output value exceeded that of agriculture in 1986; instead of ¥474,310 million, the TVE total output value in 1987 was ¥476,430 million. This is just an example to show that even official statistics are not always consistent.

18. At the 7th Plenary Session of the NPC, the central government officially declared to fully carry out the policy of economic reorganization nationally from 1989 and spend two years or more to achieve this task, which meant that specific measures related to this policy had a restricted duration, until the end of 1991. The years of 1989 to 1991 were hence called the period of economic reorganization (*zhili zhengdun*).

19. According to *China Agriculture Yearbook 1990* (p. 43), the total output value in 1989 was ¥840,300 million (in 1980 fixed prices).

20. All of this might have something to do with the aftermath of the "4 June event" in 1989.

21. *China Statistical Yearbook 1997* does not provide the figure of gross output value. Yan (1995: 4) argues that though one can reflect from one aspect the speed of economic development, the growth of output value should by no means be regarded as a main index, which, instead, should be removed from statistical tables with the development of the market economy.

REFERENCES

Agricultural Economic Journal (nongye jingji congkan). (1981). A Report of the Forum on Whether CBEs Have the Problem of Squeezing the Big by the Small (shedui qiye youwu yixiaojida wenti zuotanhui baodao), p. 5.

Byrd, W., and Lin, Qingsong (eds.). (1990). *China's Rural Industry: Structure, Development, and Reform.* New York: Oxford University Press.

Chang, Kyung-Sup. (1993). The Peasant Family in the Transition from Maoist to Lewisian Rural Industrialization. *The Journal of Development Studies* 29(2), pp. 220–244.

Chen Xigen. (1989). Macro-Management of TVEs (xiangzhen qiye de hongguan guanli). In He Ciping et al. (eds.), *Macro-management of TVEs and Their Adjustment of Industrial Structure* (xiangzhen qiye hongguan guanli yu chanye jiegou tiaozheng). Shanghai: Shanghai Academy of Social Sciences Press.

China Agriculture Yearbook (zhongguo nongye nianjian) *1982, 1983, 1984, 1985, 1988, 1990.* Beijing: China Agriculture Press.

China Statistical Yearbook 1990, 1994, 1997. Beijing: MOFTEC.

China TVE Yearbook (zhongguo xiangzhen qiye nianjian) *1978–1987, 1994, 1995, 1996, 1997.* Beijing: China Agriculture Press.

Constitution of the PRC (zhonghua renmin gongheguo xianfa). (1985). *A Compilation of Laws of the PRC* (zhonghua renmin gongheguo falu huibian). Beijing: People's Publishing House.

[The] Corpus of TVE Laws of the PRC (zhonghua renmin gongheguo xiangzhen qiye fa quanshu). (1997). Beijing: Enterprise Management Press.

Huang, Daoxia. (1998). The People's Commune: From the Cradle to the Grave (Part 1) (renmin gongshe: cong dansheng dao xiaowang). *Fortnight Talk* (banyue tan), (10), pp. 30–33.

Ji Jinglong. (1998). The Current Problems Faced by TVEs and Their Solutions (dangqian xiangzhen qiye fazhan mianlin de wenti yu duice silu). *Economic Reform and Development* (jingji gaige yu fazhan) 2, pp. 32–36.

Lu, Xueyi. (1993). The Use of Chinese Rural Labor Resources and Its Implication on the Rural Environment. *International Sociology* 8(2), pp. 227–237.

Ma, Jun. (1996). Monetary Management and Intergovernmental Relations in China. *World Development* 24(1), pp. 145–153.

Mao Zedong. (1977). *Notes to "The Socialist Tide in China's Rural Areas."* Beijing: China Books and Periodicals.

Mao Zedong. (1979). *Selected Works of Mao Zedong, Volume 5* (Mao Zedong xuanji diwu juan). Beijing: People's Publishing House.

Morgan, S. L. (1994). The Impact of the Growth of Township Enterprises on Rural-Urban Transformation in China, 1978–1990. *Geojournal Library* (30), pp. 213–236.

Ocean of Words (ci hai). (1979). Shanghai: Shanghai Lexicographic Publishing House.

Peasants Daily (nongmin ribao). 30 November 1992.

People's Daily, overseas edition. 23 April 1998, 17 July 1998.

Putterman, L. (1997). On the Past and Future of China's Township and Village-Owned Enterprises. *World Development* 25(10), pp. 1639–1655.

State Council Bulletin (zhonghua renmin gongheguo guowuyuan gongbao). (1990). No. 10, 11.

State Council Bulletin (zhonghua renmin gongheguo guowuyuan gongbao). (1991). No. 23.

State Council Bulletin (zhonghua renmin gongheguo guowuyuan gongbao). (1992). No. 8.

State Council Rural Development Research Center. (1989). *Selection of Rural Policy Documents 1985–1989* (nongcun zhengce wenjian xuanji). Beijing: China Marxist University Press.

TVEB of Ministry of Agriculture, Animal Husbandry, and Fishery. (1986). Statistical Materials of TVEs (1978–1985). Mimeo.

TVEB of Ministry of Agriculture, Animal Husbandry, and Fishery. (1987). *Selection of Policies and Statutes concerning TVEs 1979–1985* (xiangzhen qiye zhengce fagui xuanbian). Beijing: Xinhua Publishing House.

Xiao Liang. (26 March 1995). On the Legislation of the TVE Law (yetan xiangzhen qiye lifa). *Economic Daily*.

Yan, Conghuai. (1995). On the development of TVEs (xiangzhen qiye fazhan lun). *Studies on TVE Economy* (xiangzhen jingji yanjiu) 1, pp. 4–7.

Zhang, Yi. (1990) *The Hard Course of Chinese TVEs* (zhongguo xiangzhen qiye jianxin de licheng). Beijing: Law Press.

Zhongshan University (Department of Law) (ed.). (1981). Collection of Economic Statutes, Volume I (jingji fagui huibian, diyi juan). Mimeo.

Zweig, D. (1992). Reaping Rural Rewards. *The China Business Review* 19(6), pp. 12–17.

Chapter 3

The Future of Private Enterprises in China

Wang Xueli AND Zhang Lijun

INTRODUCTION

"Private" has been a sensitive term in the economic system of China for a long time. On October 1, 1949, when Chairman Mao announced the founding of the People's Republic of China, everything in China became people-owned or, more concretely, state-owned. If anyone regarded something as private, he or she would be treated as being against socialism. During the heavy tide of socialist consolidation, many private enterprises in the most modern city of that era, Shanghai, were transformed into state-owned enterprises. During the great Cultural Revolution, families in the countryside were forbidden to raise hens and even had to cut off "those capitalist tails." It is clear that "private" was almost a synonym for capitalism in China before 1978.

After the historical conference of the Chinese Communist Party (CCP) held in 1978, what is today called "the reform process" began. The private sector reappeared in the economic system and performed an increasingly active role in the national economy. For instance, the growth rate of investment in fixed assets between 1981 and 1996 for state-owned enterprises was only 18.6 percent, while the rate for those individually owned was a much higher 23.5 percent, and for those collectively owned was the highest at 33.1 percent.[1]

It is not easy to find any research on the private economy of China before 1988.[2] After 1988 empirical surveys focusing on managers and case studies of certain enterprises increased steadily. Recently, due to the new strategic reconstructing of state enterprises, some small and medium-sized state enterprises were sold to individuals or private firms, causing a heated debate on property rights and the process of this transformation. One side of the debate claimed it resulted in the loss of state assets, since many of the assets were sold at surprisingly low prices to those who were top-level managers of the enterprises. Others disagreed on this point, referring to operational inefficiency of those assets. However, the rapid growth of the private sector during the transition to a market economy needs much more attention.

THE SIZE OF THE PRIVATE SECTOR[3]

It is quite difficult to find any official documents that give the size of the private sector. Here we try to estimate it conservatively and realistically based on the *China Statistics Yearbook 1997*. According to this source, the five major sectors—agriculture, industry, construction, transportation and communications, and commerce—accounted for 20.2, 42.4, 6.6, 5.1, and 8.1 percent of gross domestic product (GDP), respectively, in of 1996.[4]

Since the agricultural sector was the first one to employ market mechanisms, and private ownership is officially permitted, it is reasonable to estimate that market-oriented institutions in the agricultural sector are responsible for about 19 percent of GDP in China, and only a very small fraction of assets is produced by state farms.

Consider next the industrial sector, which accounted for 42.4 percent of GDP. This sector is composed four types of enterprises: state-owned, collective-owned, individual-owned enterprises in urban and rural areas, and a group of joint state-collective, joint state-private, joint collective-private, joint ventures with foreigners, and enterprises run by Overseas Chinese and by foreign investors. It continues to be dominated by state-owned enterprises with collective and individual enterprises performing rosily. These four types account, respectively, for 28.5, 39.4 (27.7% for township and village-owned), 15.5, and 16.6 percent of gross industrial output value. Collective enterprises may belong to local governments or individuals, and most township and village-owned enterprises are operated like private enterprises. To a significant extent, they are operated as profit-seeking enterprises similar to enterprises in a market economy. The fact that 71.5 percent of gross industrial output value is produced by the second, third, and fourth type of enterprises shows that perhaps about 59.8 percent (27.7% + 15.5% + 16.6%) of the industrial output in China, or 25.3 percent of GDP, is produced by enterprises operating somewhat like those in a market economy.

The construction sector, accounting for 6.6 percent of GDP, has three kinds of enterprises: state-owned enterprises, collective-owned enterprises in cities and towns, and rural construction teams. The corresponding gross output of these three categories was ¥416 billion, ¥369.5 billion, and ¥329.6 billion. In view of the fact that rural construction teams are usually owned by individuals, it seems plausible to count about 25 percent of gross output value of construction (1.65% of GDP) contributed by enterprises, with management incentives somewhat similar to those prevailing in a market economy.

The transportation, postal, and communication sector, accounting for 5.1 percent of GDP, is mainly owned by the state, although about 25 percent of total civil motor vehicles are private, and waterway transportation by private boats belongs to the market-oriented sector of the economy. Perhaps 1.27 percent of GDP can be included.

About 8.1 percent of the 1996 GDP originated from the wholesale, retail, and catering trade. More than 90 percent of the establishments in this sector are private or "private-like," and their sales account for nearly half of total sales. Based on these facts, 50 percent of total sales of this sector, or 4 percent of GDP, could be included as produced by the private sector.

Adding up the percentages (19% + 25.3% + 1.65% + 1.27% + 4%) of GDP produced by market-oriented units in the five sectors, we conclude that these units produced about 51.22 percent of China's GDP in 1996. That is the current size of the private sector in the national economy. "Private" in this context means that the actual ownership and operation of the economic units are not public. As we know, many units have a state-owned or collective-owned "cap on the head" for the various reasons, while the body is not in accordance with the head.

ENTREPRENEURS IN PRIVATE ENTERPRISES[5]

Information about this subject comes from a 1997 survey conducted by several scholars of the People's University, which questions about 600 private entrepreneurs located in the three largest cities in China—Beijng, Shanghai, and Guangzhou. Since managers' practices are a critical factor for enterprise success, we begin this section by putting together a rough picture of private enterprise managers who have either initiated the business themselves or purchased a state-owned firm.

Establishment of Enterprises

Only 5.2 percent of these businesses started before 1978, while an additional 7.1 percent, mostly in the countryside, started during the first stage of the reform (1978–1984). It seems clear that the reform policy was the guideline or a signal lights for these ambitious entrepreneurs. An additional 40.3 percent of the enterprises involved in the survey were established between 1985 and 1992. After Deng's "southern journey" in 1992, many managers apparently saw great opportunities developing, as nearly half of the managers in the survey founded their business after 1992. It was also possible to foresee a new tide of private enterprises' development after the 15th conference of CCP, which produced a new preferred policy with respect to private enterprises.

Experience of Managers Prior to Establishing Enterprises

A total of 33.5 percent of the entrepreneurs had their experience in the manufacturing industry, and many of them chose manufacturing as the focus of their

Table 3.1
Age Distribution of Entrepreneurs in Three Cities

City	19–29 yrs.	30–39 yrs.	40–45 yrs.	above 46 yrs.
Beijing	9.2%	34.2%	30.4%	26.1%
Shanghai	6.9%	20.2%	36.5%	36.5%
Guangzhou	35.9%	36.4%	15.1%	12.0%
Average	17.3%	30.3%	27.3%	24.8%

new enterprises. The second source was agriculture (12%), while 9.5 percent had experiences in education and research institutions, and 7.3 percent had been central or local government officials. The latter group brought with their valued resources for doing business in China—various connections (*guanxi* in Chinese) and better understanding of reform policies.

Generally speaking, more than half (56.6%) of these entrepreneurs were managers (middle- or high-level) of the institutions or enterprises where they had worked. This means they had management experience to a certain extent before they decided to establish their own business.

Demographic Characteristics

First of all, most of these entrepreneurs in the survey were male, while female managers were more common in the south. Second, young people under 40 were well represented in private enterprises (see Table 3.1). In addition, the difference between Guangzhou and Shanghai was quite interesting. In Guangzhou, the entrepreneurs were usually young and experienced but without good education backgrounds; in Shanghai, they were well educated and usually came from a higher position in management. Third, the widely held opinion that managers of private enterprises were poorly educated was not consistent with the survey findings. According to the survey, almost half of the respondents (45.5%) had at least a bachelor's degree or a college course, and those who had only primary school education accounted for only about 0.2 percent (see Table 3.2).

Another important, but not surprising, finding was that Beijing managers had the highest level of education among the three cities. The reasons are well known, such as Beijing's being the capital city of China and having the largest number of universities. We also find evidence of this in a survey organized by several government departments in 1997 called the "Investigation System on Chinese Entrepreneurs," which showed that managers of solely owned foreign and private enterprises had the highest education level.[6]

Table 3.2
Education Level of Entrepreneurs in Three Cities

Level	Beijing	Shanghai	Guangzhou	Average
Ph.D.	2.2%	0.5%	0.0%	0.9%
Master's	6.5%	1.5%	2.6%	3.5%
Bachelor's	50.0%	44.8%	41.6%	45.5%
Middle School	29.9%	35.0%	47.9%	37.6%
Primary School	0.5%	2.0%	4.2%	2.2%
Others	10.9%	16.3%	3.7%	10.3%

Types of Enterprises Established

Which industry did these entrepreneurs prefer to enter? The tertiary industry came out first. In the tertiary industry, manufacturing, wholesale, and retailing were the top three business sectors, 39.8 percent, 17.9 percent, and 16.7 percent, respectively. Another feature is that different cities had their own focus—Shanghai liked manufacturing, finance and insurance, and foreign trade, and Guangzhou preferred wholesale, retailing, and real estate, while Beijing concentrated on the information industry, consulting, and building. Most of the private enterprises were small, with no more than 20 employees. A lack of large-scale enterprise was a common phenomenon of the three cities and is analyzed later.

BOTTLENECKS DURING THE DEVELOPMENT OF PRIVATE ENTERPRISES

One of the advantages of private enterprises is management autonomy. This allows much-needed flexibility in decision making in the early stages of their development, which, in turn, permits response to changing market conditions. However, if the small private enterprise grows rapidly to a certain scale, it encounters some bottlenecks that make further development quite difficult. Interestingly, these problems often occur when the annual profits of the enterprise reach ¥1 million or the assets accumulate to ¥0.1 billion. In recent news was the Sanzhu Group's trouble in court (because one person died after drinking eight bottles of Sanzhu's famous product, a kind of nutrition food), and famous entrepreneurs Jiangwei and Shi Yuzhu highlighted this problem. It would be meaningful to identify and analyze the bottlenecks that seriously challenge the development of these enterprises.

The Decision-Making System of Private Enterprises Places Limits on Growth

Family business, without a formal system of decision making, is often the first mode of private enterprise. Usually, entrepreneurs make the choice based on their experience or expertise. However, no explicit strategy for managing growth is likely to be identified at the beginning or during the rapid growth phase, and the manager is likely to focus the business on an area that is familiar. Given this familiarity, the manager is not likely to discuss or seek approval of decisions, and any decision, once made, is final. Obviously, it is difficult under this kind of decision-making system to have a competitive strategy that adjusts to changing market conditions. That is why 50 percent of respondents from private enterprises in the official survey chose "wrong decisions" as the problem that most easily occurred in their business.[7]

Poor Quality of Products Damages the Overall Image of Private Enterprises

According to the results of a national survey on product quality in 1995, overall, 75.3 percent of the products tested met the standards, but few private enterprises (only 42.6%) met the standards. This was far below the results for the state-owned enterprises (79.6%) and joint ventures (80.2%).[8] The products of private enterprises usually are imitators of others' so that speed is more important than quality. The result is serious, as products made by private enterprises all equal "bad quality" in Chinese consumers' minds, which lowers the status of the whole private enterprise sector. For instance, shoes made by the private enterprises of Wenzhou (a city famous for its surprising development in the private sector and family businesses) were called "weekly shoes," since they copied the style and brand of some famous ones produced in Shanghai, but it was hard to wear the shoes for even a week.

Lack of Modern Human Resource Management and Inefficient Management Talent for Further Development

In many private enterprises, most of the management positions are assigned to the members or relatives of the family that owns this enterprise. Consequently, employees have to abide by the family law instead of formal regulations. In the same official survey, the most powerful constraints for managers of private enterprises are internal rules as well as national laws and regulations (both 85.7%).[9] There have been cases in which the employees of private enterprises were on strike because of "unbearable treatments." Furthermore, managers of private enterprises are often anxious to get full use of the talents of newly recruited managers, without consideration of training and development so as to reserve resources for the future. Not satisfied with family management and with no chance for further development, intellectuals often leave the enterprise. Without talented personnel in research and development (R&D), marketing, and management, it would be impossible for the private enterprises to implement a strategy to overcome the problems of growth.

Internal Conflicts of Interest among Family Members

Everybody dreams of becoming rich. What happens when it becomes true? Upstarts often spend large amounts of money on luxurious living with splendid villas, cars, or rebuilding the ancestral grave. All of these are typical for of the Eastern entrepreneurs, and little is left for the growth of the enterprise. Occasionally, family members have different opinions on the distribution of profits or further strategy of the enterprise, and the most serious consequence is the breakup of the enterprise. A hot topic of the media at the beginning of 1998 was the division of Hope Group (it had been referred to as the largest private enterprise at the time) among the four brothers of the Liu family.

Policy Discrimination of Private Enterprises Makes Raising Funds Much More Difficult

According to the statistics of the state banks, the credit loans given to private enterprises take only about 2.3 percent of the total, much lower than the percentage of private enterprises in GDP or than rate of growth.[10] Not only the volume but also the interest they have to pay for the loans is unequal to those of other ownership firms. In Shanxi Province, the interest charged on state enterprises is 7.2 percent, while it is 11.52 percent on private ones, even with certain mortgage collateral.[11] There are more restricted constraints on the private enterprises to list in the stock market. Without external financing channels, it is hard to obtain funds to invest in new equipment or prospective projects.

As can be seen, the bottlenecks that private enterprises face come from different sources. Some may be due to historical views of the policymakers on the position of private enterprises in the economic system; some may result from the special management style of the enterprises; or some may be the natural outcome of their current development stage. Anyway, no matter what the reasons, these bottlenecks have to be removed, so that private enterprises can make necessary changes.

WAYS TO ELIMINATE THE BOTTLENECKS

The 15th conference of CCP, held in 1997, was a milestone of economic reform, especially for private enterprises. For the first time in history, the government admitted that the coexistence of state-owned and private enterprises could be a way to contribute to the final objective of socialism, while before, the private sector was only a complementary part to the state-owned economy. This was the good news from the conference for private enterprises.

However, everything is double-sided. The other side is the forthcoming heated competition for these private firms. One of the groups of competitors connects with medium- or small-scale state enterprises, while the other connects with foreign companies. The strategic restructuring of state enterprises gave total freedom to the development of small-scale ones. These small enterprises have the advantage that private ones have only in their early stage—flexibility. Fortunately, this pressure will be likely to develop slowly as the whole restructuring process has just begun, and an alternative for these state enterprises is that they can be sold to individuals and become private ones. A more urgent threat comes from foreign companies. The high-tech private enterprises on the Zhongguan Village Street (the representative of the information technology industry in China) still remember the surge in employee turnover and the decrease of market share after the multinational corporations (IBM, Compaq, AST, National, etc.) entered China with their products and promotions. With further opening up of certain markets and industries to foreign investors, even large private companies have to face the challenge from these wealthy, experienced, and aggressive competitors.

Both government and private enterprises have to reconsider their policies or strategies for competition. From the perspective of government, the protection of private assets must be guaranteed by laws or regulations, in order to relax those entrepreneurs from "being concerned every day, worrying every day." The government should encourage combinations of small state enterprises and private ones under formal procedures and provide free and equal opportunity for the development of private firms as well. State banks need to give credit loans based on commercial considerations (such as profitability, security, liquidity, etc.) instead of ownership difference. In Hunan Province, Suining County is called "the oasis of private enterprises" because of the following: (1) the charges for private firms are the lowest of the whole country; (2) no management fees are charged; and (3) a special committee is working 24 hours a day and provides free services needed by private enterprises. Not surprisingly, the total output value of Suining County in 1996 was ¥1.21 billion, an increase of 134 percent over 1995.[12]

From the private enterprise's view, the first requirement is to have an explicit strategy. Without strategy for future development, any efforts are likely to become useless. The underlying assumption is that those entrepreneurs have to change their style from experienced decision making to scientific management.

Change is also needed in terms of employee commitment. Motivating employees in private enterprises requires more compensation and job satisfaction. In the famous private enterprise of the information industry, the Stone Group, there is a way called "Golden Ring," which means the corporation will divide its profits among all the employees, just like putting a golden ring on everyone's finger. It has been effective in solving the interest conflicts and gaining employees' commitment. In addition, private companies need to learn how to increase job satisfaction through training opportunities and empowerment. Maintaining current employees' commitment is as important as recruiting new talents for private firms.

An external orientation would also help private enterprises get good use of all resources and find their own position in the market. Entrepreneurs should take advantage of the ongoing state enterprise restructuring, and try to cooperate with some state enterprises and get mutual benefits. Moreover, more private enterprises should consider exporting to developing countries as part of their marketing strategy. A good example was a private firm that exported shoes to Romania without making shoes itself. The manager of this firm let some other enterprises make shoes for him according to the specifications of the orders, then sold them to the foreign market. In other words, the private enterprises should be good at utilizing all available resources (both internal and external). Only then will there always be a place for them to survive and develop.

Last but not least, the entrepreneurs of private companies should not be afraid of enlarging their business focus, but not be too ambitious either. Many failures of private enterprises result from unreasonable diversification. It is much more difficult and risky to withdraw funds from the wrong business than to invest in the right ones. Once again scientific decision making and control system in private enterprises are of great importance.

CONCLUSION

We should not ignore the large size of the private sector in China's economy. Indeed, we need to be concerned with the development of the most active actor in this sector, private enterprise entrepreneurs.

The entrepreneurs in private enterprises are admirable. They are experienced in management, manufacturing, and marketing. They usually have good education and engage in the tertiary industry. These entrepreneurs have created the outstanding performance of the private firms in their early stage.

Not everything goes smoothly. The private enterprises face several bottlenecks for further development. Family businesses that rely heavily on their own experience bring about a series of problems, such as wrong decisions, high employee turnover, conflicts of interest, and so on. Besides, some policy discrimination makes these private enterprises bear heavy burdens in terms of varied fees and lack of financing channels. Thus, private enterprises may lose motivation for further growth.

More heated competition for private enterprises is inevitable. These private firms need support and service from the government as well as improving their own management. Strategic thinking and scientific management are urgent. Smart use of all resources by private enterprises, especially cooperating with state enterprises, is a feasible way for them to reposition in the market. We suggest limiting diversification.

It is unnecessary to stop or slow down the wave of development of private enterprises. They need to improve themselves, they need freedom and equality. We are sure that private enterprises can be more productive and popular. They can become the merchants for creating new jobs, developing new products, adopting new management methods, and shaping a new picture of the market economy of China. In the end, they will become the glittering star in the sky and play a more and more important role in China's economy in the coming century.

NOTES

1. *China Statistics Yearbook 1997* (Beijing: MOFTEC).

2. 1988 was the year when the first regulations about private economy were passed by the state. The regulations included some clauses about private economy, and they subsequently have been added to the constitution of China.

3. All original numbers in this part are taken from *China Statistics Yearbook 1997*.

4. Most numbers in this part are taken from *China Reform* (newspaper in Chinese language), March 2, 1998, p. 7.

5. Investigation System on Entrepreneurs of China (1997), p. 120.

6. Ibid. p. 122.

7. Yangsheng (1998), p. 7.

8. Investigation System on Entrepreneurs of China (1997), p. 127.

9. Yangsheng (1998), p. 7.

10. Ibid.

11. Ibid.

12. The case is taken from homework of Tang Wentao, one of my students.

REFERENCES

Investigation System on Entrepreneurs of China. (1997). The Survey on Opinions of Current Managers of Enterprises on the Motivation and Constraints Issues. *Management World* 4, pp. 119–132.

Jie, Wei. (9 February 1998). How to Improve Internal Quality of Private Enterprises. *China Reform* (newspaper in Chinese language), p. 7.

Xueli, Wang. (1996). Reform of Large- or-Medium-Scale State Enterprises: Key of Transition from Central Planning to Socialist Market Economy. *Global Economics and Management Review* 2, pp. 127–154.

Xueli, Wang. (1997). *Reform of Large- or-Medium-Scale State Enterprises*. Macau: Macau Foundation.

Yangsheng, Yan. (16 February 1998). It is Time to Internal Check and Learn from Outside. *China Reform* (newspaper in Chinese language), p. 7.

Yanyun, Zhao, Qiyan, Zhao, and Zifang, Du. (2 March 1998). The Survey Report of Private Enterprises in Beijing, Shanghai, and Guangzhou. *China Reform* (newspaper in Chinese language), p. 7.

Part II

Outlook on Selected Industries

Chapter 4

The Structure and Development
of China's Financial Markets

Chen Baizhu AND Feng Yi

OVERVIEW

Financial reform has become one of the two most urgent tasks (with the restructuring of the state owned enterprises being the other) in the current stage of economic reform in China. Successful establishment of a modern financial market will provide an extremely important assurance that China's economic reform will continue; it will be instrumental in solving the dilemma of the state-owned enterprises through efficient allocation of domestic and foreign capital. To say that the ultimate success of the conversion of China's centrally planned economy to a market-oriented economy pivots on this single dimension—the financial market reform—is an understatement.

On the one hand, financial market reform will free economic activities from state control and help build a basis for civil society. On the other, recent developments, inside and outside China, have made Chinese policymakers especially cautious about the potential for financial crises to destabilize the national economy. It remains the top priority for Chinese policymakers to reform the financial system so that both market-driven and risk-reducing mechanisms, compatible with the evolving Chinese economy, may be established. International lending institutions, such as the World Bank, are also greatly concerned that the financial reform in China is successfully carried out.

Since 1978 the Chinese financial markets have been restructured to fit the needs of the economy. Between 1978 and 1984 the government established various financial institutions. Figure 4.1 indicates the major actors in China's financial structure, and Table 4.1 presents basic statistics for deposit-taking financial institutions in China. Of all participants in the financial markets, the most important one is China's central bank, the People's Bank. Of all deposit-taking financial institutions, the leading ones are state-owned commercial banks,

Figure 4.1
The Structure of China's Financial Markets

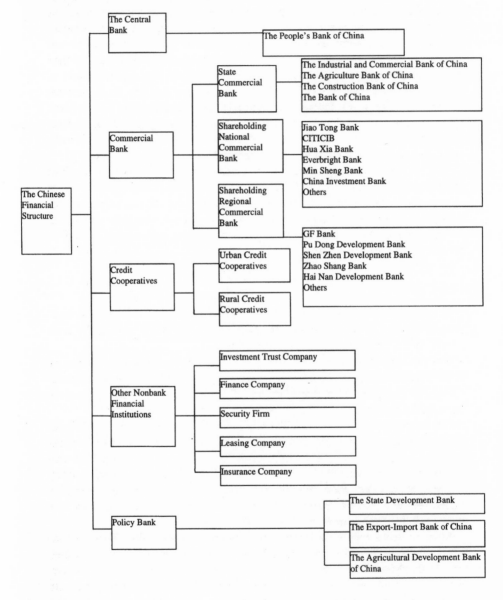

Table 4.1
Market Share of Financial Institutions, 1988–1995

	1988	1993	1994	1995
Policy Banks	0.0	0.0	5.6	6.8
State Development Bank	0.0	0.0	1.0	1.8
Agricultural Development Bank of China	0.0	0.0	4.6	4.9
Export-Import Bank of China	0.0	0.0	0.0	0.1
State Commercial Banks	85.3	84.2	79.8	72.7
Industrial and Commercial Bank of China	27.2	31.1	29.5	28.0
Agriculture Bank of China	14.6	16.8	14.0	11.1
Bank of China	27.1	19.4	20.6	18.1
Construction Bank of China	16.4	16.9	15.7	15.5
Other National Commercial Banks	6.2	5.8	4.9	4.6
Other Banks	0.2	1.1	1.6	1.8
Credit Cooperatives	8.2	9.0	8.1	13.7
Urban Credit Cooperatives	1.0	3.0	2.4	4.1
Rural Credit Cooperatives	7.2	6.0	5.7	9.6

Note: The numbers are percentages of the total of financial institutions' assets that exclude foreign banks and nonbank financial institutions. Data for these institutions are not available for years prior to 1995. For 1995 the commercial banks' share in total financial assets, including foreign banks and nonbank financial institutions, was about two-thirds.
Source: The People's Bank of China, *Quarterly Statistical Bulletin*, various years; China's Finance Society, *Almanac of China's Finance and Banking* (1996).

which sprang from the People's Bank. The following sections deal with the major components of China's financial framework and discuss their functions, problems, and prospects in economic reform.

RESTRUCTURING THE BANKING SYSTEM

Before 1979 the People's Bank of China was the only bank in the country. Its functions were typical of a central bank—for example, credit distribution, currency issuance, and foreign exchange reserve management. Additionally, it acted as a commercial bank by receiving deposits from households and firms, as well as making loans to and providing clearance services for business entities. In those days, the central planning economy just needed an accounting system to balance the books of various state-owned enterprises in pursuance to state planning.

Since 1978 economic reform has led to the expansion of nonstate sectors as well as an increase in the self-reliance incentives of state-owned enterprises. Consequently, the monobanking system became increasingly incompatible with the emerging economic system. Credit planning has become increasingly ineffective as a major way of adjusting fund flows on financial markets (Chang, Chen, and Li, 1999). On September 17, 1983, the State Council formally announced the transformation of the People's Bank of China into a central bank, effective January 1, 1984. Its commercial businesses were handed over to four state-owned commercial banks, which were established during the period 1979–1984. However, the People's Bank continued its commercial businesses, making loans to state-owned enterprises until after 1994, when comprehensive financial market reforms were initiated. Furthermore, the Central Bank Law passed in March 1995 banned the People's Bank from financing government budget deficits. In addition, it prohibited the People's Bank from making loans to various levels of central and local government agencies. Four state commercial banks— the Bank of China, the Agriculture Bank of China, the Construction Bank, and the Industrial and Commercial Bank—assumed the role of commercial banking business, which had been the role of the People's Bank.

Since 1986 shareholding, company-based commercial banks have been established at both national and regional levels. Concurrently, nonbank financial institutions have also grown. Additionally, parallel to the expansion of town and village enterprises (TVEs) and privately owned businesses during the 1980s, the number of rural credit cooperatives and urban credit cooperatives has been on the rise—5,217 urban credit co-ops and 50,219 rural credit co-ops had come into existence by the end of 1995. These rural and urban credit institutions provide liquidity and credit to facilitate the development of many town and village enterprises into major export-oriented industries. Furthermore, investment trust companies, securities firms, insurance companies, leasing companies, finance companies, and closed-end mutual funds have all emerged.

The four state commercial banks are the major players in the structure of China's financial institutions. For the average of the period from the first quarter of 1993 to the first quarter of 1997, the total assets owned by the state commercial banks were ¥4,310 billion. The total assets of the other four types of deposit-taking financial institutions—other commercial banks, rural credit cooperatives, urban credit cooperatives, and finance companies—amount to a little more than ¥1,200 billion. Thus, the assets owned by the state commercial banks were almost 3.6 times those of the other four types of financial institutions. Contrary to common belief, the rural credit cooperatives own more assets than the other commercial banks. In 1995 the market share for the former was 13.7 percent, and for the latter, only 4.6 percent, even though the rural co-ops did not own foreign assets, and the other commercial banks had on average ¥46 billion worth of foreign assets. The ownership of foreign assets by the financial company is small (about ¥0.01 billion), compared to the amount owned by the state-owned banks (¥328 billion).

Despite its dominance, the state commercial banks have experienced a reduction in their market shares: from more than 85 percent in 1988 to 72.7 percent in 1995. A similar pattern occurred for other commercial banks at the national level. By contrast, the market shares of both urban and rural credit cooperatives have been on the increase. Although the policy banks did not exist in 1988, their market share has risen to almost 7 percent.

In 1994 the requirement that state-owned commercial banks carry out policy loans to state-owned enterprises was discontinued. Instead, the newly established policy banks—the State Development Bank, the Export-Import Bank of China, and the Agricultural Development Bank—provided preferential loans to projects deemed important in view of the government's industrial and agricultural policies. Previously, these policy loans were issued by the state-owned commercial banks. The assets of the three policy banks as a percentage of the total assets of the financial firms have increased from zero before 1994 to almost 7 percent in 1995 (see Table 4.1). Notice that from 1993 to 1995, the asset share of the four state-owned commercial banks decreased by 12 percent. Half of this reduction is due to the relocation of the policy loan business to the policy banks.

Policy banks were established based on the rationale that the state needs to execute its industrial and agricultural policies. The Chinese government seems to believe that by allocating resources to key industries, it can better promote economic development. The legitimacy of applying the industrial policy hinges on whether there is a market failure and if the government can correct it. Experiences in past decades suggest that industrial policies have yet to provide convincing evidence that they can make industries competitive and successful.

Even though the asset share of the three policy banks had reached almost 7 percent by 1995, its fund remains inadequate, given the mounting task of supporting a large number of firms for policy purposes. As the interest rates on policy loans are much lower than the true cost of funds, firms have incentive to get themselves into the policy loan lists. Political influence and thus rent-seeking are inevitable in the decisions on policy loans. In addition to the funds directly obtained through state finance, the policy banks can raise funds by issuing bonds to financial institutions. As the bonds issued to financial institutions carry a higher interest rate than the interest rate on policy loans, this inevitably leads to a question of who pays for the difference.

In the midst of restructuring, the People's Bank adjusted its goal to the maintenance of price stability, in contrast to the multiple goals it pursued before. For a long time before the Central Bank Law was promulgated, the People's Bank was accustomed to pursuing monetary stability and promoting economic growth. As the operation of the People's Bank of China was not independent of the government, these two objectives were, for the most part, inconsistent with each other.

Government Bond Markets

As the result of government budget deficits that emerged after the economic reform in 1978, government bonds became an instrument to narrow the gap between government revenues and expenditures. Since 1978 the government has run a budget surplus for three years only. The budget deficit has increased over the years, and the bonds issued in each year have increased, too. The total value of bonds issued in each year as a percentage of total government expenditure in the same year increased from less than 5 percent in 1981 to more than 25 percent in 1996.

The total national debt expressed as a ratio to gross domestic product (GDP) steadily increased from 2.46 percent in 1984 to 6.10 percent in 1995. As GDP was about ¥5,826 billion in 1995, the total accumulated national debt was ¥355 billion in the same year. The central government finances its operations largely through government bonds. While the government bonds issued constitute 22 percent of total government expenditures, they make up more than 52 percent of the central government expenditure. As debt is accumulated, the interest payment becomes even larger. The interest payment of government debt in 1995 was ¥77.95 billion, or approximately 11 percent of government expenditures in that year.

Over the years, the variety of the government bonds has increased. The terms of maturity for government bonds vary from half a year to ten years. Short-term maturity bonds have been used increasingly by the government as an important financing instrument. In addition, financial bonds are issued to state commercial banks, other commercial banks, and nonbanking financial institutions.

The secondary bond market opened in 1988. To accommodate the exchange of bonds in the secondary market, bond-trading centers were set up in various localities. However, these bond markets were segmented, as suggested by the regional price spread of bonds deviating from the price of the same bonds traded in Shanghai (Li, 1998). Nevertheless, the price spread of bonds narrowed as soon as the Securities Trading Automated Quotations System (STAQ)—a system connecting securities trading in major trading centers—was started in April 1991.

Stock Markets

In the 1980s some firms started to raise capital by issuing stocks and bonds. The Shanghai Stock Exchange was inaugurated on December 19, 1990, and the Shenzhen Stock Exchange was established on July 3, 1991. Only eight stocks were listed when the Shanghai Stock Exchange started to operate. The number of listed firms, trading volumes, and total market capitalization have all increased dramatically since the opening of the exchanges.

China has deliberately segmented its stock markets, separating shares for domestic and foreign investors. In each stock exchange, there are two classes of shares traded. Share A, denominated in Chinese currency, is available to domestic Chinese residents only. Share B, denominated in U.S. dollars in Shanghai and Hong Kong dollars in Shenzhen, is open to foreign investors only. Almost all companies that have issued B-shares also have issued A-shares. The two classes of shares have identical voting rights. In order to open an account to purchase a B-share, one must satisfy two conditions: the buyer has to show proof of foreign residence and must have a foreign exchange account. Though the B-shares are reserved for foreign investors only, the rule is not strictly enforced. Additionally, some companies are also listed in Hong Kong (H-shares), New York Stock Exchanges (N-shares), or both.

In addition to these tradable shares, each listed company often issues nontradable shares. The nontradable shares include the state shares that represent state ownership and the legal entity shares that represent ownership by other registered companies. The ownership of nontradable shares can be transferred via negotiation. With permission, a small portion of nontradable shares can be traded in the nationwide electronic trading system: STAQ (Security Trading Automatic Quotation) and NETS (National Electronic Trading System).

Tradable shares can be listed in either the Shanghai or Shenzhen Stock Exchange. Dual listing is forbidden. Trading is conducted via an automatic, electronic, order-matching system. Orders are matched first by the price and then by the time. Since 1993 the Shanghai Securities Central Clearing and Registration Corporation has been responsible for registration, clearing, settlement, and depositary management. For A-shares, clearing and settlement take one business day (T+1), and for B-shares, they take three business days (T+3). The transaction costs are different between A- and B-shares. There are a stamp fee of 0.3 percent of the market value and a 0.1 percent transfer fee based on the par value for both classes of shares. However, the commission fees for A-shares and B-shares are not the same. The commission fee for A-shares is fixed at 0.6 percent of the market value. The commission for B-shares is not fixed; it usually remains below 0.6 percent of the market value for a large trading block.

Insurance Markets

In 1995 the Standing Committee of the 8th National People's Congress passed the Insurance Law of the People's Republic of China, which was the first insurance law in Chinese history. In accordance with the Insurance Law, the Chinese government merged the seventeen life insurance companies with the People's Insurance Company of China (PICC), as the latter had a joint ownership with the former. After the merger, the People's Insurance Company of China consisted of three subsidiaries: the People's Life Insurance Company, Ltd., the People's Property Insurance Company, Ltd., and the People's Reinsurance Company. According to the same law, the People's Bank approved two life insurance companies—Xinhua (meaning New China) Life Insurance and Shoukang (meaning longevity and health) Insurance—and three non-life insurance companies—Huatai (China's Security) Insurance, Yong-an (Forever Security) Insurance, and Hua-an (China's Security) Insurance. As of January 1997 China had six non-life insurance companies, two life insurance companies, and three comprehensive insurance companies, with a grand total of 140,000 employees, of whom 126,000 worked at the People's Insurance Company of China.

Premiums in 1996 amounted to ¥77 billion, of which ¥32.4 billion came from life insurance and ¥45.2 billion from non-life insurance (Di and Ye, 1998).

The insurance categories in China's insurance markets include property, life, liability, and agriculture. Property insurance consists of enterprise property, household property, transport equipment liability, cargo transport insurance, and others. Enterprise property insurance previously had a dominant share in property insurance. However, due to the expansion of property insurance into other property areas (e.g., transport equipment liability), the ratio of enterprise property to the total property insurance steadily decreased over the years. Take the People's Insurance Company of China (PICA), for example. In 1985 the percentage of the premium for enterprise insurance was 39 percent, the highest of all categories. In 1996 the percentage decreased to merely 12 percent.

By contrast, the percentage of the transport equipment liability premium has been maintained and increased over the years. Transport equipment liability includes liability on automobiles, tractors, motorcycles, bicycles, vessels, and airplanes. In 1985 the ratio of the liability premium to the total premium at PICC was 35 percent in 1996, it was 39 percent.

Industrial life insurance has made large strides in China's insurance markets. In 1985 the share of the life insurance premium in the total premium at the PICC was only 6 percent in 1996 it rose to 26 percent. The premium for industrial life insurance is relatively low. It normally does not require a physical examination, and the premium can be paid in monthly wage deductions. By contrast, the other two kinds of life insurance—pension and accidental death—amount to very little as a percentage of the total premiums, with both of them at about 7 percent in 1996 (estimated from the data from the PICC). The life insurance markets in China have massive room for expansion and deepening.

Other categories also experienced a gradual increase, followed by a leveling off. At the PICC, the premiums for household, cargo, and agricultural liability as a percentage of the total premium were 2 percent, 4 percent, and 1 percent, respectively. Before 1986 household insurance grew rapidly, at an average annual rate of 116 percent, eventually slowing. The number of households insured was about 30,000 in 1980 and increased to 52,570,000 in 1986 (Di and Ye, 1998). Similarly, cargo transport insurance started at low levels in 1980 and grew steadily up to 1988, with an average annual growth rate at 151 percent. Since then, the growth rate has been reduced. In 1981 the People's Insurance Company of China restored its business in agricultural insurance. However, since 1992, agricultural insurance has been on the decline.

Nonbanking Institutions

China's nonbanking industries consist of investment trust companies, security firms, finance firms, and leasing companies. By the end of 1996, China had 244 trust companies with total assets valued at ¥510 billion, 96 security firms with total assets at ¥159 billion, 64 finance companies with total assets at ¥6.7 billion, and sixteen financial leasing companies with total assets at ¥18.7 billion.

In 1979 China International Trust and the Trust Division of the Bank of China were established. Since then, a large number of trusts emerged across the country. By 1982 there were about 620 trust companies, among which about 520 were run by banks and about 50 by local governments (Di and Ye, 1998). In 1982 government branches were ordered to shut down their trusts. In 1984, however, another wave of trusts swept the country, adding to inflationary pressures. The government required that trusts not take any new transactions. From 1984 to 1994 banks and government departments set up numerous investment trusts. The multitude of trust companies resulted in an expansion of investment that competed with existing banks and caused financial instability. Specialized banks transferred funds into investment trusts as a way of avoiding control by the People's Bank. In 1996 the state commercial banks disowned their trust investment divisions; the branches of the People's Bank were also separated from their brokerage divisions. According to the audit of 206 trust companies by the People's Bank, the major problems of the trust companies lay in the inaccurate report of capital, a large number of nonperforming assets, and unlawful practice such as the use of high interest rates. As a result, a large number of trust companies incurred losses, and some of them went bankrupt (China's Finance Society, 1997:39).

Finance companies were the product of financial needs within the consortium of enterprises. The first finance company was established in 1987. The People's Bank approved the finance company for the Dongfeng Automobile Group. Since then, various finance companies were set up for such industry groups as chemical engineering, iron and steel, aerospace, textile products, energy, computers, automobiles, metallurgy, and electronics.

These finance companies have the potential of turning into commercial banks. However, as their performance depends on that of the industrial group, the risk is not diversified. The poor performance of the industry may result in and compound the problems of bad and nonperforming loans.

The concept of leasing was introduced in China in the 1980s. Currently, China has two kinds of leasing companies. The joint-venture leasing companies specialize in leasing equipment manufactured abroad. They purchase and lease equipment based on requests from customers. The other type of leasing company specializes in domestic transactions and is run by domestic enterprises, sixteen of which are financial leasing companies. The transactions of financial leasing companies include the lease of assets used in production, science and research, education, health, tourism, and transportation. Rules and regulations are generally lacking with respect to financial leasing companies, negatively affecting the development of leasing industries.

Credit Cooperatives

There are two types of credit cooperatives in China—rural credit cooperatives and urban credit cooperatives. While the former have in China since 1949, the latter started in 1979. Both have played important roles in savings and investments. They have made the loan process accessible to collectively and privately owned enterprises in both cities and the countryside.

Rural Credit Cooperatives

The guiding principles for rural credit cooperatives have been popular involvement, democratic management, and flexible operation. Since the 1980s the role of rural credit cooperatives has been enhanced to support the household responsibility system in the countryside. Though China's Bank of Agriculture supervised the credit planning of rural credit cooperatives, the latter had the power to make decisions on individual loans. In the past, the loans were made to the collectives but now are made also to individual households to start or expand production. The Bank of Agriculture also reduced reserves for rural credit cooperatives from 30 percent to 25 percent in 1985 and allowed the interest rates at the rural credit unions to be close to the market interest rate. It no longer paid subsidies to those cooperatives that incur losses, making rural credit cooperatives strive for self-reliance. In terms of management, the involvement of peasants has increased substantially, enhancing their incentives to increase deposits with the credit cooperatives. As of 1996 rural credit cooperatives had deposits of ¥879 billion and made loans of ¥629 billion. They took the deposits of ¥396.5 billion from the collectively owned enterprises and ¥291.5 billion from peasants. Meanwhile they made ¥561.9 billion in loans to agricultural production and ¥123.6 billion to town and village enterprises.

Urban Credit Cooperatives

The first urban credit cooperative emerged in 1979 as a response to urban economic reforms that led to an increase in collectively owned and privately owned enterprises. Due to the lack of these enterprises' access to funds, the branch offices of the People's Bank and specialized banks helped the setup of urban credit cooperatives to facilitate loans to them. Two factors contributed to the fast expansion of urban credit cooperatives before 1988. First, the entry cost was low, as the minimum capital for the urban credit cooperative was set at only ¥100,000. Second, during that time, the country still experienced tight credit control, particularly to collectively and privately owned enterprises.

The increase in the number of urban credit cooperatives was accompanied by high-risk loans, low quality of assets, and blind pursuit of the number and size of loans. In addition, some sponsors of urban credit cooperatives intervened in the operation of cooperatives and even used their funds and assets. In 1988 the People's Bank promulgated the Regulations of Urban Credit Cooperatives to remedy the problems mentioned, thus reducing the unhealthy expansion of the urban credit cooperative system. In 1996 there was a total of 4,630 urban credit cooperatives with total assets valued at ¥401.8 billion. Deposits were at ¥304.4 billion, and loans amounted to ¥196.4, with a loss of ¥7.3 billion.

CONCLUDING REMARKS

The future of China's economic reform lies in the reform of its financial markets. A critical issue for financial reforms is the role the central bank will play. The central bank should be allowed independence from unnecessary political and policy fluctuations. The Central Bank Law of 1995 failed to transform the People's Bank of China into a truly independent central bank capable of carrying out monetary policy without being influenced by government politics. According to the Central Bank Law, the People's Bank formulates and implements monetary policies under the supervision of the State Council (Article 3 and Article 7). The decisions made by the People's Bank regarding the money supply, interest rates, exchange rates, and other important matters must be approved by the State Council (Article 5). Inevitably, political considerations become an important factor in the formulation of monetary policies. For instance, some studies indicate that money supply in China tends to increase after each Party Congress (Xu and Ni, 1997).

With true political independence, the People's Bank should increase the use of indirect instruments for its monetary policy, including the discount rate, reserves, and open market operation. Though some of these indirect policies have been in use already, the People's Bank frequently resorts to direct administrative policy instruments. Applying direct administrative policy instruments can sometimes achieve the objective relatively quickly but may also result in heavier welfare losses and increased ineffectiveness. The central bank also should make sure that a sound system of financial supervision is established to reduce incentives that could lead to disorder and instability in the financial markets.

Interest rates remain largely undetermined by the market. In some markets—for example, the interbank markets and repo markets—market forces of demand and supply have a relatively large influence, but the determination of most interest rates is still a decision influenced by political considerations. Interest rates on loans to state-owned enterprises are set at a level to allow many loss-making firms to float, while interest rates on loans to private enterprises are set a higher level. Allowing some interest rates to be determined by the market while keeping other interest rates at a level incompatible with market forces may even exacerbate distortion in resource allocation.

State commercial banks should increase their capacity in risk control and management. They have not become economically efficient participants in the market. They secure the loans from the central banks at a below-market interest rate but lack accountability for investment performance. The structure and objectives of these banks are more compatible with making policies than with making profits.

Financial market reforms should be coupled with the restructuring of state-owned enterprises. China's economic reform is likely to slow down unless state-owned enterprises are reformed into profit-oriented economic agents. For a long time, state-owned enterprises have been able to secure preferential loans from

commercial banks without assuming risks and consequences for bad performance. This occurs in large part because state-owned enterprises are not institutionalized or structured to compete with other entities in the marketplace.
Therefore, financial market reforms should be devised to restructure the incentive system unique to state-owned enterprises.

China has a long way to go to become a modernized world financial center.
Before China can assume such status, it must open its financial markets to the
world, with the convertibility of its currency as a major policy change. However,
the recent financial crises that swept Pacific Asia have made China wary about
further opening up its financial markets. Devaluation pressure and financial instability have severely hurt countries with liberalized financial markets such as
Thailand and Indonesia. They are ensnared in a globalization process that is
fraught with forces out of their control. China will likely take a cautious stance
on further liberalizing its financial markets, even though an open financial system has been viewed as having such merits as the enhancement of market efficiency and the promotion of long-run economic growth.

REFERENCES

Chang, H., Chen, B., and Li, Y. (1999). Central Bank and Monetary Policy in China. In
    B. Chen, K. Dietrich, and Y. Feng (eds.), *China's Financial Market Reform:
    Progress, Problems, and Prospects*. Boulder, CO: Westview Press, pp. 124–141.
China Statistical Bureau. (1997). *China Statistical Yearbook, Volume 16*. Beijing: China
    Statistical Publishing House.
China's Finance Society. (1996). *Almanac of China's Finance and Banking, Volume 11*.
    Beijing: China's Finance Society Press.
China's Finance Society. (1997). *Almanac of China's Finance and Banking, Volume 12*.
    Beijing: China's Finance Society Press.
Di, W., and Ye, X. (1998). *The Reform and Opening of China's Financial Industry*.
    Beijing: Qinghua University Press.
Li, F. (1998). The Government Securities Market during the Economic Transformation
    in China. Working paper, Monash University.
People's Bank of China. *The People's Bank of China Quarterly Statistical Bulletin*.
    Beijing: Research and Statistics Department of the People's Bank of China. Var-
    ious years.
Xu, D., and Ni, J. (1997). China's Multiple Policy Goals and Business Cycles. Working
    paper, 12th Annual Conference of the Chinese Economists Society.

Chapter 5

The Different Behaviors of Chinese Automakers in Technology Introduction and Assimilation

Chen Jin

PROBLEM CONSIDERATION AND RESEARCH METHOD

This research analyzes differing competitive behaviors among modern Chinese corporations by the theoretical framework of corporate strategy. This study focuses on the auto industry, which is becoming an important element for the development of the Chinese economy. A realistic comparison is conducted on their various adaptation behaviors to environmental change and management resources, changes in organizational behavior, and the formation of development strategies for large enterprises and medium-sized and small enterprises that have poured into the car industry and are establishing mass production.

Concretely, this study analyzes the case of the Chinese auto industry from the perspective of corporate strategy theory. The subjects of this study are First Automotive Works Corporation (FAW), Dong Feng Motor Corporation (DFM), Shanghai Automotive Industry Corporation (SAIC), and Tianjin Automobile Industry Corporation (TAIC), the so-called Top Four in the current Chinese auto industry. This comparative research focuses on the introduction of car production techniques, the enlargement of production, and the implementation of development strategies and performance processes.[1]

This chapter mainly concentrates on the differing performance patterns and development speeds of each competitive automaker, especially former large-sized enterprises and small and medium-sized enterprises that are under almost the same environment conditions. How do these enterprises establish their development strategies? How do they compete? What are their competitive advantages? What are their main formation elements?

The reason I selected FAW, DFM, SAIC, and TAIC as the subjects of this study is that these four are not only the top automakers in the industry but also typical national enterprises. They have taken quite different paths on technology introduction along with environmental change since the 1980s. Important parameters, such as total profit, average productivity of each employee, and so on, have changed rapidly. Especially the former small and medium-sized and enterprises, such as SAIC and TAIC, have developed much faster than the former large enterprises. Research on this aspect is unknown outside China.

This chapter, focusing on the managerial strategy of a number of Chinese firms, examines how a firm under one economic system can overcome its existing organization inertia and formulate specific strategic capabilities when confronted by competitive market change. Theoretically, this research fills the space of an organization inertia study which has not yet been thoroughly discussed relating to the resource-capability view of the firm in management strategy. Practically, this research focuses not only on the development process of the Chinese automotive industrial technique level but also on the common ways in which all industries develop. Therefore, this research has great value to foreign firms concerned with their strategies of investment and technical assistance to China.

Due to the change of the economic management system, market needs shift from trucks to cars. This chapter presents an analytical framework relevant to strategy formulation and strategy implementation and the integration of strategy analysis and implementation process based on the actual performance of a firm's systematic reform. In addition, case analysis is based on the actual data of a field survey supported to the greatest possible extent by additional reference materials.

ANALYTICAL FRAMEWORK: A FIRM'S STRATEGY FORMULATION AND IMPLEMENTATION PROCESS RELATING TO ENVIRONMENTAL CHANGES

Research on Corporate Strategy and Organization Inertia

Corporate strategy consists of two relevant dimensions: strategy formulation and strategy implementation (Hofer and Schendel, 1978; Andrews, 1987). Strategy is generally defined as "a pattern in a stream of decisions" (Mintzberg, 1989).

In management strategy, a firm is regarded as a cluster of management resources or competences. Therefore, the research of the resource-capability view of a firm becomes very important.

Management resource and competence have the negative effect of organizational inertia, which inhibits innovation. Organizational inertia is deeply rooted in rationalized accomplishment of a firm's routine and coordination. New work has no defined routine; therefore, a firm's development is slower than environmental changes (Barton, 1992; Rumelt, 1995). Interaction with other different organizations has the great important function of destroying inertia and recon-ducting organization analysis. Furthermore, coordination with various organizations may produce more knowledge than a single organization.

The Formulation of a Market Economy and the Car Industry: A Reanalysis of Strategy

Auto production was controlled by a national planned economy system for 20 years till the 1970s. From the end of the 1970s, along with the market economy, firms have focused on the market and acted in accordance with principles of self-performance, self-responsibility for profit-earning, self-development and self-management. During this time firms' development consciousness became active. Meanwhile, together with financial reform, local governments implemented a policy of reorganization and enforcement of decision-making power for local firms. Additionally, the strategy orientation of foreign firms, which have poured into the Chinese market with capital and technology, also became an element that affected Chinese firms' performance. Therefore, from the end of the 1970s, firms not only had to meet their national plan goals but, faced with market opportunity and pressure, also had to "simultaneously fight" for their local government policy and foreign firm's strategy.

On the other hand, automakers' need transferred from trucks to cars from the 1980s. The need for cars grew from the early 1980s and increased rapidly in the mid-1980s. Passenger cars have been most required in the 1990s. Along with the increase in recent production, the car market has set more rigid requirements for quantity, specification, quality, and price.

Even within the same period, the pace of market change and the pace of national plan reform have differed since the 1980s. The reform of government plan and policy lags far behind market change. It takes even longer from a policy's specification to accomplishment. Therefore, it is possible for a firm to get approval from government, even though car production and technique introduction are in the restricted circles of the central government. A firm requires a new capability, that is, a strategy formulation capability, in order to select development strategies and upgrade strategy along with environmental changes.

Analytical Framework: Strategy Formulation and Core Elements

This chapter analyzes the attempts of Chinese automakers to overcome their former organizational inertia, such as the priority of national plan instead of market need, emphasis on truck production, focusing on quantity instead of quality, and productivity under the 30-year-planned economy, along with environmental changes.

A firm is active in changing its internal organization within a process of interaction with environmental changes. Each firm formulates its unique development strategy with a different degree of competitive success even within the same process, which is caused by different elements of strategy formulation and implementation process, including a firm's strategy formulation capability.

Environment Conditions

In contrast to foreign firms, national plan and local government policy are important elements. In addition, there are different speeds in the introduction of car technology at each firm, as well as specifications in resource of technology introduction of local government and conditions of foreign makers.

Resource Base

The resource base refers to management stock of resources in a firm. Organizational inertia also roots in a company's resource base. During its development, a firm attempts to utilize the upside and overcome the downside of its resource base.

Strategy Formulation Capability

A firm's *cognition capability* directly affects its acknowledgment of its external environment and internal resources, selection of achievable products, and market segment during strategy vision formulation and performance planning.

Resource input capability determines the enhancement of car production and achievement of mass production after strategy formulation and the technical introduction of car production. A firm must be capable of accommodating changes. The *accumulation capability of competitive capability* affects the elimination of the gap between a firm's manufacturing abilities and the car's quality specifications and technical regulations (especially among foreign makers), along with making market changes and enlarging the production scale after the introduction of technical aspects of car production.

As indicated in Figure 5.1, the resource base, cognition ability, resource input ability, competitive capability, and stock capability are core factors affecting the firm's specific strategy. These factors affect the performance of a firm's strategy by accounting for the interaction of external environmental conditions with reforms within an economic system and changes in market needs.

THE HISTORICAL DEVELOPMENT OF THE CHINESE AUTOMOTIVE INDUSTRY AND THE STRATEGIC FRAMEWORK OF CARMAKERS

Automobiles were first imported to and flourished in big cities like Shanghai, Tianjin, and Beijing between the 1920s and 1930s. To support this booming industry, automobile repair shops and parts manufacturers were established. In 1937 the China-Japan War took place. Newly established carmakers had to be moved to mid- or western China, as the Japanese army invaded the coastal areas. However, the Japanese also built up assembly and repair plants for military

Figure 5.1
Analysis Framework: A Firm's Strategy Formulation and Relevant Elements in the Chinese Automobile Industry

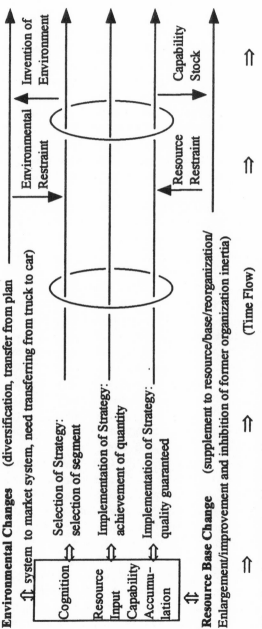

trucks in Shanghai, Tianjin, Jinian, and Wuhan. All of these plants declined after the Pacific War.

In the early 1950s the Soviet Union undertook 156 projects of technological and financial assistance to China, including the construction of one complex auto manufacturing works. Referring to the candidate cities, China considered Beijing, Xi'an, and Wuhan (which had parts production foundation). But finally, Changchun, in the northwest area and therefore near the Soviet Union, was selected, according to the suggestion of the Soviet Union. This led China to construct the First Automotive Works, which symbolized the start of the Chinese car industry. On the other hand, from 1957, due to a shortage of vehicles of all kinds except for medium-sized trucks, local government invested to establish small auto plants, most of which have not survived. The existing plants were primarily those with former repair and parts production foundations: Shanghai Passenger Car Plant, Beijing Jeep Plant, Nanjing Light Duty Truck Plant, and Jinan Large Truck Plant.

In the mid-1960s, the central government started to establish the Second Auto Corporation (DFM) for the production of medium-sized military trucks in preparation for war with the United States and the Soviet Union. This project was based on the FAW model and had a high degree of vertical integration, but it was constructed in an isolated mountain area with severe environmental conditions. Besides, from the late 1960s, along with the continuous development of former primary plants like Shanghai Passenger Car Plant, Beijing Jeep Plant, Nanjing Light Duty Truck Plant, and Jinan Large Truck Plant, some specially equipped (custom-designed) vehicle plants were established in local areas for local transportation needs. Started by the Beijing Jeep Plant, some local works like Tianjin Auto Works, Shenyang (Golden Cup) Auto Works, Guangzhou Auto Works, Wuhan Auto Works, and others began to imitate and trial-produce light-duty trucks and so led to an increase of light-duty vehicle makers.

From the late 1970s China adopted an openness policy. Due to the enlargement of the auto market and a supply shortage, the construction of local makers was inadequate. On the other hand, along with the opened market and the increase of car imports, the gap between Chinese automobile technology and that in developed countries became obvious. In order to reduce this gap, from the end of the 1970s the government pursued the policy of introducing of advanced techniques. At that time large corporations like FAW and DFM affiliated with the central government, concentrated on medium-sized truck model changes and the diversification of truck production. They did not pay attention to car production. The central government approved the joint-venture projects of Beijing Auto Industry Corporation and SAIC to increase the production technique level.

Due to the supply shortage of passenger cars and buses, from the mid-1980s car imports increased rapidly. The central government started to consider a new industry policy. Guangzhou Auto Industry corporation, which introduced the pickup technique, and TAIC, which introduced the mini-vehicle technique, had introduced car production techniques immediately from usual technique corporation partners. In May 1987, the central government held a "Chinese Automobile Industry Development Strategy Forum" at Dong Feng Motor Corporation, clarifying FAW and DFM as important car production groups and establishing a two-step development plan (DFM the first and FAW second). In fact, the DFM project was foiled because of the sanctions by the French government after the Tiananmen affair in 1989. In contrast, the joint-venture projects between FAW and Volkswagen (VW) led to a success. Later on, the central government increased import tariffs in order to protect the domestic car market and pursued a different tariff policy for domestic makers to import completely knocked down parts for the promotion of car localization.

The demand for cars increased rapidly, especially for mini-vehicles. Meanwhile, the productivity of SAIC and TAIC increased rapidly, and finally they ranked as the top two. In order to join the World Trade Organization (WTO), the central government pursued a new automotive industry policy on February 19, 1994, that led to the formation of a competition system among a few makers. Meanwhile import tariffs began to decrease, and the import license (I/L) system was canceled. Along with the market demands and government adjustment, car prices began to decrease and car production was diversified. A new competition system was beginning to be formed.[2]

THE FORMATION AND IMPLEMENTATION OF DEVELOPMENT STRATEGIES FOR SAIC AND TAIC

History of Cars and Auto Parts Production

In the first period of this century, Shanghai and Tianjin were the pioneer car-producing cities. Later, from the 1920s and 1930s, repair shops and parts manufacturing plants were built. Both became the most important parts production areas. During the Korean War of the 1950s, the rigid requirements for quantity, quality, and delivery dates for military truck parts promoted the standardization and specification in Shanghai and Tianjin.

Shanghai had the experience of technique introduction from abroad and auto assembly before World War II. After the war, the National Party's financial magnate purchased one auto corporation (Shanghai Car Plant, the prototype of Shanghai Volkswagen [SVW]) from an English business company to assemble, purchase, and repair Chevrolet and Austin serial cars. It was the biggest car assembly corporation in China at that time. Unlike in Shanghai, it was Japan's Toyota that introduced advanced automobile and parts production techniques to Tianjin. In 1938 Toyota established "Japan Toyota Automobile Corporation Ltd.—Tianjin Assembly Plant," which produced trucks and buses. In 1946, after the war, Toyota Tianjin Corporation started production of a small quantity of "Flying Eagle" vehicles based on a model of Japanese Daihatsu's three-wheel vehicle.

In the 1950s after the successful trial production of jeep and three-wheel vehicle trucks, Shanghai Auto Plant successfully produced the "Phoenix" passenger car based on the model of Poland's Polske and Germany's Mercedes Benz 220S. In 1964 "Phoenix" was changed to "Shanghai," with small production. During the Cultural Revolution, passenger cars were criticized as luxury transportation. Shanghai's capacity was only 5,000 till 1980, and its performance and quality didn't match those of Mercedes Benz. On the other hand, between the 1950s and 1960s, Tianjin auto works produced a number of vehicles that were copies of other areas' car models with less capacity. In the late 1950s many parts plants transferred to produce agriculture manufacturing products due to the government agriculture manufacturing policy. There was a serious shortage in the supply of auto parts and accessories. Later on, in 1973, TAIC produced a minicar based on Toyota's model for mass production, which was abandoned due to an adjustment of the central government policy. Therefore, how to increase technological level, engage in the mass production of autos, and develop their own products became the primary question for SAIC and TAIC. But till the end of the 1970s, both corporations were merely the administrative departments that assigned local government production tasks to their affiliated plants and supervised the completion of production plans. Moreover, they were only local medium-sized or small companies and so were much smaller than FAW and DFM in their production scale. They could not be supported and financially assisted by the central government.

The Formation of a Car Strategy Vision along with Environmental Changes

From the end of the 1970s, SAIC and TAIC clarified their models along with outside environmental changes. SAIC pursued a policy that focused more on the production of passenger cars and less on the production of trucks. TAIC conducted many market surveys and adopted a development plan for mini-vehicles based on the study of Japanese mini-vehicles.

Along with economic system reform, SAIC and TAIC were transferred from the administration department, which assigned local government's production task to their affiliated plants and supervised the completion of production plans, to economic corporate organizations with economic responsibility for production, construction, technology, and markets and direct control over personnel, finance, equipment, production, raw material purchase, and product market of affiliated plants. Meanwhile, Shanghai and Tianjin governments reorganized their local industrial structure in order to promote their automobile industries. The independent rights of SAIC and TAIC had been enlarged with contract and profit reserve systems. The central government's policy of "introduction of one passenger car production line and improvement of Shanghai car industry" led to the introduction of cars at SAIC. This policy was consistent with the idea of concentrated passenger car production at SAIC and, unsurprisingly, was supported by the Shanghai government. SAIC was active in the implementation of the central government policy. Besides, the purpose of the central government, local government, and SAIC was focused on the promotion of car production capability. Government and SAIC conducted a complete survey on introduced car models and foreign makers. In October 1984, SAIC introduced technology from VW and signed a formal joint-venture contract of car production with VW.

TAIC was active in the introduction of mini-vehicle production technology supported by the Tianjin government. The president of TAIC realized the importance of a common usage of parts between mini-vehicles and small cars when he visited Japan Daihatsu. The introduction of mini-vehicle technology may have promoted passenger car production. In March 1984 TAIC signed a contract to introduce the Hijet mini-vehicle with Japan Daihatsu. Along with this introduction, the Tianjin government imported 300 Charade passenger cars and distributed them to local taxi corporations, government, and large enterprises for follow-up survey. Moreover, a strategic vision for car production was formulated, and a base, including equipment, for small car production was prepared. During this period, however, the production scales of SAIC and TAIC were quite limited, with annual productivity of only 10,000–20,000 units.

The Enforcement of Car Production and Network of Formation of Parts Localization

From the mid-1980s, along with increasing market demand, car imports increased to a great extent. The Chinese government began to consider the policy of car technology introduction. Supported by the Shanghai government, SAIC, which had just signed a contract with VW, formulated a permanent plan with the capability of 30,000 cars in January 1985. From May SAIC conducted a long-term market demand survey together with Chinese General Automobile Corporation and VW. Furthermore, 100 experts spent ten months to complete a general report regarding the possibility of SAIC's producing 300,000 vehicles annually. Meanwhile, TAIC was producing small passenger cars along with minicars, as suggested by the government from 1984. In March 1986 the central government approved a "proposal item" of TAIC. TAIC signed a contract immediately with Daihatsu to introduce Charade car production technologies and establish a mass production system.

After the contract with VW, SAIC carried out a policy of independent fund raising supported by the Shanghai government. From 1987 the Shanghai government initiated a financial profit and tax contract privilege system for the local automobile industry. At the same time Germany-VW and the Chinese government concentrated together on the additional investment of SVW. TAIC had already prepared for small car production along with the establishment of a mini-vehicle production line. When opportunity came, it would transfer immediately to passenger car production. Later on, TAIC could not expect any investment from the central government or support from foreign partners. In order to adapt to changing markets TAIC adopted a "develop new by old" method for passenger car production, funds for which depended on the market profit of the earlier vehicle production of small trucks and mini-vehicles.

After the introduction of car production technology, SAIC reorganized its production structure and stopped its former production models. Production capability concentrated on car production, especially the Santana. Additionally, SAIC formed first the nationwide car parts supply network, which promoted the parts localization of passenger cars and contributed to the development of the Chinese automobile industry. In order to adapt to market demand, SAIC formulated a market system in order to increase its market share. Along with the rapid enlargement of the car market, SAIC undertook a series of strategy activities centered around investment in car production and parts makers. The capability of SVW was only 30,000 within its initial establishment period. But in 1996 its capacity reached 300,000, with annual production reaching 200,000. Along with the increase in production, sales volume, profit, and production efficiency of SAIC were increasing. From the early 1990s, it ranked No. 1.

After the introduction of mini-vehicle production, TAIC promoted new product development using the sales profit from former vehicle models. But primary investment was focused on car assembly rather than parts production due to the limitation of investment. Additionally, along with the increase of car production, TAIC was active in formulating a nationwide market system, pouring more power into the sales market. The capability of small cars of TAIC reached up to 60,000 in 1993 from the initial 10,000. In 1994 the central government made an additional investment for TAIC to establish a small car production plan with 150,000 productivity. In this way TAIC has developed into one of "the big three" companies in the auto industry by analyzing market demand orientation, adjusting models according to market change, and enlarging productivity like a "snowball," along with the outside environment change. It has been ranked as the No. 2 company by productivity and total profit of passenger car since the early 1990s.

The Process of Technology Assimilation and Capability Accumulation

The primary purpose for SAIC to establish a joint-venture corporation is to increase its capabilities by catching up to the advanced world's level. After the technological introduction of car production, a quality control (QC) system was formulated within the whole company. The formation of a rigid QC system is closely related to the management principle and management organization structure of Shanghai VW, which is the key assembly car corporation of SAIC. The managers of each management division who deal with parts makers in SVW are almost all Germans. The quality of parts supply is particularly emphasized. In addition, SVW established the quality control process of parts localization in parts suppliers, the same as the formation of QC system within SVW.

In 1988 SAIC formulated its QC "production zone" system within its Santana parts makers by the promotion opportunity of Santana parts localization. Advanced management methods were introduced and widely popularized by the introduction of an advanced production line instead of former manual operations, the organization of material circulation route and specified management, of production spot, color-mode management, and personnel training and operation inspection. In addition, SAIC studies and promotes Japanese lean production with the help of Japan Koito Manufacturing. In March 1997 SAIC signed a new contract with General Motors (GM), its second joint-venture opportunity with foreign makers. SAIC established an automobile technology center as its research and development (R&D) institute with GM, which emphasized its R&D ability together with car production.

The funds for TAIC's technology introduction and production development all come from the profit made from market sales. The adaptation to market demand and resulting profits determine the fortune of TAIC. In order to increase its productivity, TAIC is active in introducing and purchasing equipment instead of introducing software like production management and quality control. The technological training for its personnel is not enough either. The investment of TAIC is mainly on the assembly production of small cars and mini-vehicles instead of the technology innovation of its affiliated parts suppliers. The technology and equipment levels of most of its parts supplier are still quite low.

The Charade car, made by TAIC, is the most popular model in China. TAIC has tried many ways to get approval from the government and increase its productivity by a snowball rolling method. On the other hand, due to a supply shortage, the managers and personnel of TAIC have not paid much attention to quality. The former model of TAIC and the privilege of the mini-vehicle market have become out of date since the 1990s. In order to solve the primary Charade car market problem in the south, that is, an insufficient engine for air-conditioning, TAIC signed a joint-venture project with Toyota to establish a 1.3L engine plant in May 5, 1996. Meanwhile, TAIC frequently has assigned QC groups to Japan Daihatsu, which has led to an emphasis on quality control instead of just quantity.

THE FORMATION AND IMPLEMENTATION OF DEVELOPMENT STRATEGIES FOR FAW AND DFM

The Establishment of a National Project and Their Early Production Activities

The northeast and Hubei areas where FAW and DFM are located are the pioneer sites for auto repairing and trial production in China. But after the surrender of the Japanese army, almost all equipment in northeast car companies and parts makers was taken over by the Soviet Union and transferred to its own country, which did not have any relation with the establishment of FAW. While most car repair shops in the Hubei area were centralized in Wuhan, DFM was without foundation, as DFM built in the mountain area.

As new China's greatest "national project," FAW and DFM are regarded as the "first son" and "second son" of the Chinese automobile industry, with complete investment by the central government. During their establishment process, FAW and DFM received help from all over the country. Many engineers and technicians of SAIC and TAIC were assigned to FAW and DFM. FAW was established in the mid-1950s based completely on one set of blueprints introduced from the Soviet Union ranging from equipment to models, from production method to management method. Changchun, which was near the USSR and owned less manufacturing function, was selected as the company location at the suggestion of the Soviet Union. In contrast, DFM was a "Cold War project" that was built in the late 1960s in the middle mountain area of Hubei Province with severe environmental conditions, based on the FAW's model in the preparation for the war with the United States and Soviets.

The local content rate of their in-house parts of FAW and DFM was quite high from the beginning. Later, along with the enlargement of production, an increase in parts production was attempted. But due to the rigid corporate production system and insufficient environmental conditions, parts production was diffused very slowly. In addition, the products of FAW and DFM have been very simple for a long time, and most products are medium-sized trucks. In the late 1950s, FAW produced "Red Flag" luxury passenger cars with limited productivity by almost manual operations for central government senior leaders.

With the planned market economy, even though FAW and DFM are the top corporations in the Chinese automotive industry, they are merely manufacturing plants without management ability. Their enlargement is limited to productivity according to the national plan. The establishment and enlargement of productivity rely on investment by the central government. They depend on government plan and policy (i.e., government investment) and, to a great extent, are in a passive position that is limited by government as well as assisted by government investment. With the establishment of other makers, the market shares of FAW and DFM are decreasing. FAW and DFM regard their top position of productivity in the automotive industry with pride and as very important. Truck model changes and product diversification have become their permanent desire.

Promotion of Truck Diversification Related to Central Government Plan

From the end of the 1970s, along with the environment change, FAW and DFM have been confronted with crisis conditions. First, in 1975 the order for military all-wheel-drive trucks produced by DFM decreased rapidly, influenced by the alleviation of the Cold War. Military trucks had to be converted into ordinary trucks. From 1978 the primary product changed to the EQ 140, five-ton, medium-sized truck, a product competitive with FAW's "Jiefang." So the market share of DFM was increasing, while FAW confronted its first sales crisis from 1979. Truck inventory at FAW became serious, with the inventory at nearly one-third of production in 1985. In order to solve its dilemma, FAW did its first complete remodeling of the medium-sized truck. Later, for quite a long period of time, FAW and DFM competed with each other and undertook their own corporate strategies to maintain their top positions in the automotive industry.

With the introduction of the "profit reserve system" in 1980 and the "profit turnover increase contract responsibility system" in 1983, DFM had the capital with which to grow. Similarly, the changes in the medium-sized trucks at FAW depended on FAW's own profit reserves, depreciation reserves, and bank loan instead of government investment as in the past. In order to raise funds, FAW and DFM made great efforts. The central government treats FAW and DFM equally. With regard to distribution, the central government supported DFM first in its medium-sized trucks and supported FAW first in small trucks.

With the experience of hardship and financial difficulty, FAW and DFM learned to become active in obtaining government investment. In the early 1980s, in order to improve the unbalanced production of different models (i.e., the shortage of small and heavy-duty trucks), the central government proposed separate development policies for FAW and DFC. FAW was to increase its production of small trucks, and DFC was to increase its production of heavy-duty trucks. FAW and DFC obtained project investment and undertook their activities according to the truck diversified production policy of the central government. However, these two corporations did not prepare for the mass production of passenger cars until the car reform schemes of the central government occurred in the mid-1980s.

From the mid-1980s, along with the rapid growth of passenger car imports, the central government pursued a new industrial policy that encouraged DFM to produce 300,000 cars till 1995 and FAW to produce 300,000 till 2000. Influenced by this policy, the two corporations were eager to formulate their own development strategies for passenger cars. FAW especially hurried to propose a strategic plan of "unified planning, separate complement." It persuaded the central government to allow it to be the site of a "pioneer project" for introducing Dodges from Chrysler (later transferred to VW Audi). But because these two corporations' policies were formulated according to government plan, research on elements other than central government policy was not sufficient, which is verified by later challenges.

The Trouble of Technology Introduction for Passenger Cars and the Reconstruction of Organizations

FAW intended to increase "Red Flag" car production by 30,000 units with the introduction of the "Dodge 600" production technology after the introduction of "Dodge 600" engine. But Chrysler prices for "Dodge" production equipment were too high and so caused negotiation to stop. FAW had to choose VW for its technology introduction and regard VW as a joint-venture partner for its 150,000 productivity project, which included technological assistance from Audi car. Limited by foreign currency, FAW purchased old equipment from an American plant and selected the Jetta A2 passenger car (with 1.56L engine), released in 1983 as the model for mass production in the 1990s. The inflexibility of the old equipment brought certain technology risks to FAW that greatly restricted market competition and, later, product model changes.

In addition, FAW tried to engage in the diversification of truck production, especially for small trucks. Due to a conflict regarding profit distributions with local government, FAW invested a great amount of capital and time in the combination and purchase of local truck makers in order to guarantee a sales channel for the Dodge engine and increase its market share of small trucks. Because of the continuous truck combination, the capital of FAW became limited, which led to the cancellation of its new Audi (Little Red Flag) plan in the early 1990s. Although the sales of Little Red Flag kept growing, it was impossible for FAW to increase productivity to any great extent or cut costs down within the short period limited by its productivity. On the other hand, the mass-produced Jetta was confronted with a sales dilemma stemming from competition with SVW's Santana. Although FAW was ranked in the top position regarding total production by the growth of truck production in the mid-1990s, its production point was still restricted to truck production. Because of its backward car production, FAW's profit volume and production rate decreased.

After DFM was specified as the country's first passenger car production base according to government industrial policy, it began to look for a joint-venture partner. But due to the serious limitation of foreign currency over that time, the central government established quite restricted conditions for the DFM joint venture. DFM did not obtain any foreign currency from its own government, had to rely on foreign governments and bank loans, and was saddled with the condition of one-third assembly car exports. DFM made a great effort to get French government loans and selected Citroen as its partner. Unfortunately, in 1989 the Tiananmen affair led to project delays for several years because of French sanctions toward China. The mass production at DFM was completed more than one year later than at FAW.

In addition, the mountain area around DFM was unfavorable to passenger car production, especially to the distribution of parts makers, which forced DFM to transfer its passenger car production base to Wuhan. The production of car parts then spread to the Shanghai area from Wuhan, which cost DFM too much time. Meanwhile Citroen, as partner, doubted the development of China's automotive industry and did not set up a permanent development strategy and so influenced the development of DFM car production. Most importantly, from the mid-1980s, DFM had made a great achievement and occupied the top position regarding productivity by early adaptation of profit contract system and the enlargement of medium-sized truck production. DFM had never been confronted with the kind of crisis and pressure as SAIC and TAIC were now exerting. So since the 1990s, DFM has faced a management dilemma because of the decline of former markets and the slow growth of car production.

The Process of Technology Assimilation and Capability Accumulation

Influenced by the hope of achieving the "top position" in China's automobile industry, FAW and DFM were eager to obtain country projects and launched a competition for the top position, which delayed the development of car production. Within this period, competition for the passenger car market was intensified, and these two corporations had to compete with SVW-Santana. VW and Chrysler as joint-venture partners set strict rules for FAW and DFM regarding their trademark, quality, and parts control. The central government also demanded that FAW and DFM enforce quality control, increase function, improve models, and lower costs.

Confronted with increasingly intense competition, FAW introduced a QC system for its car production, assisted by Audi and VW. The affiliated parts makers also introduced foreign technology and equipment or established joint-venture corporations with foreign makers in order to promote their technology ability and management level. The Japanese lean production introduced in some plants was carried out in car and parts makers from the 1990s. But due to the insufficient capital and production cost management, they started to confront severe capital shortages in the mid-1990s, when they obtained a great amount of investment.

DFM began to adjust its strategy because of the intensified competition, by developing its small truck for market competition in order to increase its market share. Then with the privilege of new model improvement with Citroen, new cars with 1.3L and 1.6L stroke volume engines were released to compete directly with Shanghai's Santana and FAW's Jetta. In addition, DFM established a joint-venture corporation for engine production and marketing by half-and-half investment with Honda, when French Peugeot withdrew from Guangzhou in November 1997. The joint venture was supposed to supply engines for the Guangzhou-Honda Accord passenger car (with 2.3L stroke volume engine) in autumn 1999.

In order to overcome car production disadvantages, FAW and DFM enhanced their product development ability independently and by joint venture with foreign makers. Additionally, they attempted to obtain government policy and capital support and coordinated local government and foreign makers, as well as released their stock in order to overcome the insufficient capital problem. They also promoted car diversification in order to increase car market share.

THE FORMATION AND IMPLEMENTATION OF
DEVELOPMENT STRATEGIES: A COMPLEX COMPARISON

Resource Base and Major Issues

From the 1950s, SAIC and TAIC, which are located in China's most developed manufacturing industry areas, began to produce cars and small trucks based
on a foundation of auto repair and parts manufacture, but they were not paid
much attention by the central government due to their medium size and the
political Cold War. Therefore, they were limited to manual operations with small
production volumes. From trial production to the end of the 1970s, their development was slow due to the closed market. Their technical levels were low with
no model changes. Quality was stagnant. In this way, the most preferred issues
for SAIC and TAIC are the selection of their own unique models, establishment
of mass production, and improvement of car production technique.

FAW and DFM were the largest one-set firms established as a "national
project" with the founding of the People's Republic of China, invested in by
the central government, which introduced equipment, car model, mass production, and management system directly or indirectly from the former Soviet Union. Construction sites were selected among areas with a less developed
manufacturing foundation. The rate of part localization was quite high from the
very beginning. Production models were simple, and medium-sized trucks dominated. FAW and DFW are now chasing the top position in auto industry as
"first son" and "second son." Due to the development of other makers, however, the market share of these two makers is decreasing. They have tried to
maintain their top position with a strong desire to increase productivity, change
truck models, and keep a full-product line for many years.

Cognition Capability and Strategy Formulation

Comparing the strategy formation process of the car technology introduction,
we find that SAIC and TAIC introduced car models from foreign makers, conducted market demand surveys, and pursued specified strategy vision much earlier than FAW and DFM. In contrast, FAW and DFM promoted truck production
diversification according to the central government's plan. When confronted
with an intensified car market, FAW and DFM rushed to pursue their car development strategy by adapting to the central government's car policy. Due to
insufficient research, which left many problems and had to be improved much
later, we may conclude that in spite of the great change of market to the mid-
1980s, FAW and DFM concentrated merely on the truck market competition
for their own top position instead of focusing on the passenger car market.

From the perspective of management resources and competition capability,
along with environment changes from the early 1980s, these four corporations
determined their own development direction by the logic of overcoming the

disadvantage of existing resources. If direction is consistent with environment change and management resources, a successful strategy may be formulated. Otherwise, it will be unsuccessful. Actually, from the mid-1980s, along with the rapid growth of imported cars, the key point of the central government industrial policy has been an increased emphasis on passenger cars instead of trucks. FAW and DFM occupied privileged positions in model change and diversification regarding truck production, but they missed the opportunity to pour into the car market.

Resource Input Capability and the Enlargement of Car Production

SAIC and TAIC transferred their focus to passenger car production, adapting to environment changes after their introduction of car production technology. Especially at SAIC, investment is focused on "one-point concentration," assisted by the central government, local government, and foreign makers. FAW increased its car production rapidly, closely followed by increases in market need. Even though TAIC is assisted by its local government, it is not supported by the central government and foreign makers. Therefore, TAIC increased its production by "support new by old." The more rapid growth of passenger cars of SAIC and TAIC, rather than Beijing Automobile Corporation or Guangzhou Automobile Corporation, depended on their successful enhancement of car production.

Compared with SAIC and TAIC, the passive cooperation attitude of local government, environmental limitations, and the strategic adjustment of foreign makers influenced the development of car production of FAW and DFM. But what is more important, FAW and DFM were blinded by their former focus on truck diversification and so spent most management resources in truck production. Consequently, their car production fell behind a lot. A strong desire for the top position exists in FAW and DFM. We may find that in spite of the possibility of falling behind in car production, organizational rigidities that concentrate on increases in current production continue to exist deeply in FAW and DFM.

The Accumulation of Competitive Capabilities by the Upgrading of Managerial Techniques

From a comparison of the promotion process of technology and management abilities, we find that the potential capability of management know-how of these four corporations differs a lot. Though restricted by serious environmental conditions, according to its strategy of enhanced car production by different steps, the quality of SAIC Santana has received favorable comments not only within China but also from the VW group. In contrast, TAIC has concentrated only on low-level market demand. Even though productivity has increased, its quality control and production development have not been improved at all. Therefore, TAIC has become weak in confronting intensified competition. On the other hand, in order to improve disadvantages in car production, FAW and DFM have pursued QC systems in their assembly plants and parts makers as well as increased their own development ability for car diversification in order to adapt to intensified competition and increase their car market share.

During this process, TAIC introduced only foreign makers' technology by technological cooperation, while SAIC, FAW, and DFM established joint-venture corporations or reserved their former trademarks, which destroyed the former organizational rigidity of underestimating quality and so has promoted improvement. In contrast, TAIC missed its organizational improvement opportunity, and so its organizational rigidity of enhancing productivity and underestimating quality has been enforced. Additionally, SAIC and FAW have long experience in car production. SAIC has been especially distressed about its quality problem for a long period, which directly led to the introduction of management know-how from developed countries. In other words, during the same rapid development period of car demand, different corporations have behaved differently within specified environments based on their own historical experience and different research and competition consciousness due to market pressure.

Conclusion

A comparison among the four makers concludes that SAIC and TAIC have developed their cognition ability and resource input ability to a different extent regarding environmental changes. SAIC maintains its dominant position due to environmental changes. TAIC lags behind because of its former organizational inertia. On the other hand, regarding cognition ability and resource input ability, FAW and DFM were even further behind SAIC and TAIC, influenced as they were by preexisting organizational inertia up to the mid-1990s. Even though FAW and DFM dominated their top positions in truck production, their car production lagged behind, and profit-earning and productivity decreased. Therefore, FAW and DFM are now trying to take know-how and destroy the inertia accumulated from earlier managerial systems. These four firms are eager to overcome their former downside and cope with environmental changes. They act according to the common logic, but SAIC and TAIC as medium-sized and small firms take priority.

THE FUTURE OF THE CHINESE AUTOMOTIVE INDUSTRY

First, foreign automakers are active in the strategic performance of car production in China. During the mid- and late 1980s, when the Chinese auto industry had just begun to develop, European automakers, especially VW, were actively involved in China, while American and Japanese makers were rather passive. From the mid-1990s, American and Japanese automakers began to participate in car production in China. During the negotiation of the "second project of technique introduction of car production" with SAIC, GM, Toyota, and Ford all competed seriously. Finally, GM obtained the chance, while Toyota transferred its efforts to Tianjin. Toyota first purchased a great amount of Daihatsu stock in order to make it a branch corporation (Daihatsu was the foreign technology provider for TAIC). In May 1996 Toyota then established a joint-venture car engine factory with TAIC, which paved the way for future joint car production in Tainjin. Additionally, Honda, GM's Opel, and Hyundai competed seriously in Guangzhou after Peugeot voiced its intention to withdraw from the Chinese market. At last, Honda and Guangzhou Automotive Corporation achieved a joint-venture agreement to produce cars in November 1997. Meanwhile, Honda undertook a project to jointly produce engines together with DFM. In order to participate in a competition for production of a Chinese mini-vehicle, GM purchased 10 percent of Japanese Suzuki (which produced minivans in China) in September 1998 and so became Suzuki's largest stockholder.

Second is *keiretsulization* (grouping) of suppliers. In line with the further development of parts localization by automakers, the rate of parts localization keeps increasing. Meanwhile, all automakers are active in introducing parts production techniques from foreign countries and established their own local parts supply network. Examples of this include FAW in Changchun, DFM in Wuhan, and TAIC in Tianjin. In this way, suppliers to assemblers have gradually formed their own *keiretsulization*. At the same time, in order to achieve a 50 percent local content rate for in-house parts as required by the Chinese government for the introduction of car production techniques, foreign automakers are active in establishing their own parts supply network, for example, Honda in Guangzhou and Toyota in Tianjin.

Third, in the future there will be more intensified competition in the Chinese car market. Due to the formation of production capability of automakers and the participation of foreign makers, the competition among different models of cars will become more and more intensified unrelated to increased consumer purchasing ability. After GM entered Shanghai, Shanghai GM's Buick and FAW-VW's Audi competed with each other over cars with a stroke volume over 2.5L, Guangzhou-Honda's Accord and FAW's Little Red Flag (Audi's transfer) compete with each other relating to cars with between 2.0 and 2.5L, and FAW-VW's Jetta, Shanghai VW's Santana, and DFM Citroen's Citroen ZX compete relating to cars below 2.0L. Toyota intends to release its Corona in Tianjin to participate in the competition. The competition of minicars below 1.0L is mainly among Japanese car makers Tianjin Daihatsu's Charade, Chongqi Changan, Suzuki's Alto, and Guizhou Aviation Fujijuko's Subaru. The venture involving GM and Suzuki is most obvious, as it may lead to the rapid development of Changan Suzuki and change the competitive ability situation of Chinese automakers.

NOTES

1. The writer made ten field surveys from 1990 to 1996, three each for FAW, SAIC, and TAIC and one for DFM. In addition, the writer visited the China National Automotive Industry Corporation in May 1991 and in August 1994, Beijing Jeep Corporation Ltd. in September 1994, and the Industrial Economics & Technical-Economics Institute of China State Planning Commission in September 1994, July 1995, and August 1996.

2. Enterprises are classified according to their productivity from the beginning of 1980, according to China's central government. Enterprises with productivity over 50,000 are defined as large size, 5,000–50,000 as medium size, and less than 5,000 as small size. According to this classification in 1982, FAW and DFM were classified as large size, and SAIC and TAIC were only medium and small size.

REFERENCES

Andrews, K. R. (1987). *The Concept of Corporate Strategy*. 3d ed. Homewood, IL: Dow Jones–Irwin.

Ansoff, H. Igor. (1965). *Corporate Strategy: An Analytic Approach to Business Policy for Growth and Expansion*. New York: McGraw-Hill.

Barton, D. Leonard. (1992). Core Capabilities and Core Rigidities: A Paradox in Managing New Product Development. *Strategic Management Journal* 13, pp. 111–125.

Chen, J., Lee, C., and Fujimoto, T. (September 1997). Adaptation of Lean Production in China: The Impact of Japanese Management Practice. Paper presented at MIT 1997 IMVP Sponsors Meeting, Seoul, Korea.

Chen, Jin. (1997). Corporate Strategy Performance of the Chinese Automobile Industry. *The Annual Bulletin of Japan Academy of International Business Studies*.

Fujimoto, T. (June 1994). Reinterpreting the Resource-Capability View of the Firm: A Case of the Development Production Systems of the Japanese Auto Makers. Paper Presented at Prence Bertil Symposium, Stockholm. Faculty of Economics, University of Tokyo, Discussion Paper 94-F-20.

Hofer, C. W., and Schendel, D. (1978). *Strategy Formulation: Analytical Concepts*. New York: West.

Lee, C., Chen, J., and Fujimoto, T. (June 1996). Different Strategies of Localization in the Chinese Auto Industry: The Cases of Shanghai Volkswagen and Tianjin Daihatsu. Paper presented at MIT 1996 IMVP Sponsors Meeting, Saõ Paulo, Brazil.

Lee, Chunli. (1997). *The Chinese Automobile Industry: Manufacturing System and Technological Strategy* (in Japanese). Tokyo: Shinzansha Press.

Marukawa, Tomoo. (1994). Relation Formation in Chinese Corporations—Case of Automobile Industry. *Asia Economics* 35(9), pp. 37–51.

Mintzberg, H. (1989). *Mintzberg on Management*. New York: The Free Press.

Oshima Taku. (June 1995). Development of the Chinese Automobile Industry and the Strategy of Modern Japanese Automobile Parts Makers. Josai University, *Bulletin of the Department of Economics* 14(1), pp. 13–25.

Pisano, G. n.d. The Dynamic Capabilities of Firms: An Introduction. Working Paper, University of California, Berkeley, and Harvard University, WP-94–103.

Rumelt, R. (1995). Inertia and Transformation. Reproduced from *Resource-Based and Evolutionary Theories of the Firm* by Cynthia A. Montgomery. Amsterdam: Kluwer Academic Publishers.

Chapter 6

The Oil Dragon's Move: What It Means for China and the World

Deng Shengliang AND Xu Xiaojie

INTRODUCTION

On March 10, 1998, the Chinese National People's Congress approved an ambitious restructuring program. The program called for a major overhaul of the country's government organization and restructuring of some giant, state-owned enterprises. Market-oriented competition and revitalization of the economy are top goals of the program. Future economic development is dependent largely on whether both the government and state-owned industrial giants could regenerate their strategies to fit new challenges, ranging from energy to cereal to land to environmental concerns. The petroleum industry is slated for the overhaul program, requiring capital restructuring and business refocusing. The international energy community is gauging these changes and their impacts on the world. This chapter starts from an overview of the oil industry's past, present, and future. Our priority is given to the oil dragon's move and possible impacts in the next decade and beyond.

HIGH ECONOMIC GROWTH AND CONSTRAINTS: 1986–1997

China experienced high economic growth in 1985–1995 and leveled off at 8–9 percent in 1996–1997. The country faced serious inflation in the second half of the 1980s and economic bubble in the early 1990s. It took almost five years to realize its expected soft landing with 3 percent inflation rate in 1997.

However, behind the high economic growth and low inflation have been several looming pitfalls. To begin with, the 1.2 billion population creates huge demands for food and energy. Agriculture production has been constrained by shrinking agricultural resources (land and water) and outstripped by a growing consumption since the late 1970s. Meanwhile, high economic growth brought a growing demand for energy in 1986–1995 and made the country the second-largest energy consumer after the United States in 1993. Coal, accounting for 73 percent, dominates energy consumption and is blamed for considerable environmental pollution.

Chinese emission standards are higher than those of the developed countries. In 45 of 88 Chinese cities, emissions are higher than the state standard. China was the third-largest country in terms of carbon dioxide (CO_2) emission in 1990 and is now the second after the United States. Three of the ten most polluted cities are located in China (Beijing, Shenyang, and Xi'an). Under environmental pressure, an acceleration of gas and oil production is encouraged as a way to reduce coal-burn emission.

China's oil and gas outputs, accounting for 17.5 and 1.6 percent of primary energy mix, respectively, kept growing in the 1960s and 1970s and were slightly down after the mid-1980s due to inadequate reserves in place. An oil product gap between domestic output and demand appeared in 1993, and a crude oil gap appeared in 1996. Chinese oil import reached 59 million tons and netted 34 million tons in 1997, almost 60 percent of which is crude and largely coming from the Middle East.

OIL PITFALLS: 2000–2010

It was expected that China could maintain its economic growth around 8 percent till 2010 (CASS, 1997). Chinese gross domestic product (GDP) per capita would reach over US$800 in 2000 and US$1,500 in 2010. Meanwhile, population was estimated at 1.28 billion for 2000 and 1.42 billion for 2010, while the urbanization rate would be over 32 and 38 percent after the years 2000 and 2010, respectively.

Chinese food imports would average around 10 percent of demand in the next decade (CASS, 1997). At the same time, energy demands would soar and spike in 2010. The oil demand elasticity index is projected between 0.55–0.6, given GDP growth of 8–9 percent for 1995–2010, and 0.6, given GDP growth around 5 percent after 2010 (Xu, 1997a, 1997c). Compared with national demands, domestic supplies have lagged far behind due to natural resource limitation, infrastructure, and capital constraints.

Resource Constraint

The latest geological survey indicated that there are 424 basins with possible hydrocarbon deposits inside China. About 150 of them have been explored over the past four decades. As a result, about 14 billion-ton oil proven reserves (accounting for 3.7% of the world) and 30 Tcm gas reserves have been confirmed. Large oil deposits are found in such basins as Songliao, Bohai, Tarim, Uygur, Zhujiangkou, Pinghu (the East China Sea), and Yingehai (the South China Sea).

Chinese oil production grew rapidly from 0.12 million tons in 1949 to 100 million tons in 1978 and 150 million tons in 1997. China's oil reserves-to-production ratio (R/P) peaked in 1961 and declined thereafter. However, proven reserves have lagged behind requirements since the early 1980s. The R/P rate has decreased substantially in that newly added reserves failed to keep pace with high output rates. The gas R/P rate shows longer life than oil and presents a brighter future.

Western Dilemma

Currently, about 75 percent of crude oil production comes from the eastern part of China (called old oil). Unfortunately, eastern oil production has been declining and will continue to do so. The western oil (new oil) after 1985 has not grown at an expected pace to date. Xinjiang in west China is a backbone of a new hydrocarbon source. China National Petroleum Corporation (CNPC), along with foreign oil companies, has invested billions of dollars on exploration and production (E&P) activities on the region's three basins (Tarim, Junggar, and Tuha) over the past decades. The result, however, has been far from expectation. The goal for the region's oil output (40 million tons) for 2010 seems to be impossible, while the so-called pessimistic projection of 20–25 million tons is likely to come into reality. Moreover, Xinjiang demand for gas has been growing rapidly and will be the second-largest gas consumer inside the country after 2010.

Infrastructure Bottleneck

CNPC's oil and gas pipelines totaled 9,689 km and 9,112 km in length, with transporting capacity close to 135 million tons of crude oil and 10.5 billion cubic meters of natural gas, respectively, in 1996. The Petroleum Pipeline Bureau under CNPC carried most of the load of crude transport, completing oil transportation of 89.3 percent of CNPC's total crude oil transport turnover over the course of the year. The Sichuan Petroleum Administration carried 86.5 percent of CNPC's total gas turnover for the year.

Eight oil and gas trunk lines, 1,009.88 kilometers in length, were constructed during 1994–1996. Completed in 1997, the Shaan-Gan-Ning to Beijing gas pipeline (known as the Shaan-Jing gas line) is China's largest pipeline project in recent years. It is an 868-kilometer-long pipeline with a diameter of 660 millimeters and a maximum annual gas transport capacity of 2 billion cubic meters. International pipelines were suggested from western Kazakhstan, Turkmenistan, the Siberia, and Sakhalin Island. By 2010 Chinese gas supply will double. About 50 million tons of oil and 50-bcm of gas would be imported from neighboring countries.

Capital Constraint

For years, the majority of Chinese oil investment was planned and supported by the Ministry of Finance. In return, Chinese oil producers contributed a lot to the central government during 1965 through 1978. To stimulate oil production in the early 1980s, the government made an oil contract for 100 million tons and left CNPC an opportunity to sell its additional oil at world prices on its own. However, due to rigid planning and lower oil pricing, CNPC was under performance during 1988–1992, while government funding has been eliminated. In 1990s, CNPC turned to depend largely on its internal investment, while foreign investment declined from 16 percent to 5 percent. Currently, a growing thirst for major projects at home and abroad is posing great financial pressure on CNPC when it is facing increasing development costs. Future development requires a leap of internal cumulative and foreign financing capacities.

WHERE TO MOVE BEFORE 2010?

Industrial Strategy and Policy

Domestic Priorities

In order to maintain stable and gradual growth of supplies, China's oil strategy will continue to focus on indigenous E&P activities before 2010. East, west, and offshore are major suppliers at present and in the future. Oil production from east China, accounting for 75 percent, plays an important role in maintaining national supply. There remains a great potential to enhance production through tertiary recovery technologies and water conservation. Daqing, as the largest oil field, has kept its output over 50 million tons for 22 consecutive years and will continue to do so until 2010 by the earlier-mentioned proprietary expertise. Meanwhile, new added reserves of 100 million tons result from some mature and marginal areas annually. West China is taken as the country's strategic area and hot spot of the Chinese oil venture. Significant breakthroughs made in Tarim, Junggar, and Turphan-Hami basins have brought discoveries of productive oil fields. These discoveries have also occurred in the Qaidam and the Erdos basins, thanks to a better understanding of geology and expansion of exploration activities. Cumulative proven reserves in western China reached 675 million tons by 1996. A dramatic increase is expected for 2000. Having potentially huge hydrocarbon resources, Chinese offshore oil E&P activities have also been developed rapidly. Oil production increased to 16 million tons in 1997 with cooperation with foreign oil firms and self-operation. The latest calculation indicates that the offshore oil reserve is about 3 million tons. It is expected that, by the year 2010, both reserves and production will be increased with intensive exploration and development activities in Bohai and the South China Sea. The preceding illustrates that the country's domestic oil supply will be more than sufficient in the next decade.

Gas Development

An acceleration of natural gas development and utilization has been planned as a critical strategy to release oil supply tension, protect the environment, and optimize energy consumption. In the past decade, giant and medium-sized gas discoveries have been seen in basins like the Erdos, Sichuan, Tarim, Junggar, and the Qaidam as well as the South China Sea as a result of concentration on natural gas exploration activities.

From 1991 through 1996, 602.4 bcm of gas has been added to recoverable reserves. Gas resource offers a solid base for further development and utilization in the next decade. Production in 2000 was predicted to be 25–30 bcm. By 2010, output may be over 60 bcm.

It is certain that the gas industry in China has entered a steadily growing period promoted by growing demand from gas-fired generation, residential and commercial consumption, and gas replacement of oil projects. Sichuan and coastal provinces' quests for the clean energy source are rising. To balance demand and supply, some gas pipelines and downstream facilities have been built and more will be built. As a result, gas consumption will be over 5 percent of primary mix, according to a pessimistic approach. Again, an acceleration of natural gas development and utilization will not only release the tension of supply but also improve the living standard and air quality in most Chinese major cities. It will be of great importance for Chinese sustainable development in the future.

Energy Conservation

An appropriate utilization of hydrocarbon resources with higher efficiency is one of the key policies to balance the country's oil and gas supplies. In addition, to increase oil production, energy conservation has been a top priority of the Chinese government. Although China has improved its energy conservation, utilization efficiency remains lower than that of the developed countries. Now the country's economy is in transition from an energy-intensive way to energy-saving one. The force will create an energy saving-based industrial structure and new consumption pattern that will reshape future economic structure and effectively improve efficiency.

Open Policy

The petroleum industry has been international from its early stages onward. The Chinese petroleum industry can't do without international cooperation and transfer of technology. Commenced in 1978, Chinese open policy was extended to the petroleum industry. It was well known that the China National Offshore Oil Corporation (CNOOC) has conducted four round bids starting from 1982, when it was incorporated. Up to October 1997, 126 contracts and agreements with value of US$5.38 billion had been signed with 67 companies from eighteen countries. Promoted by foreign investment and self-operation, offshore oil pro-

Figure 6.1
Business Division of China Oil Sector

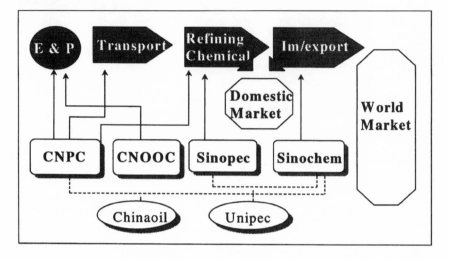

duction has grown 39.6 percent since its onset. China has and will benefit from foreign advanced technology and an effective management to propel its energy modernization.

Onshore oil bids started in 1985, when China opened its eleven southern provinces and autonomous regions to foreign investment, followed by ten northern provinces and regions in 1992, which made the total available areas for cooperation up to 2.5 million square kilometers. Thirty-seven contracts valued at US$1 billion have been signed for onshore international cooperation over the past decade. About US$5 billion foreign credit loans have been extended for the expansion of production capacity and the completion of some refining and petrochemical facilities. The advanced and appropriate technologies and equipment have improved the integrated technical strength. It is apparent that China has been a major and emerging market for international investors that is more and more open to the outside world.

Oil Industrial Overhaul

In the early 1980s, the Chinese oil industry started to face competition. The early reform of the industry in the 1980s led to a division of upstream, downstream, and offshore oil businesses. The former Ministry of Petroleum was replaced by nonintegrated oil companies (see Figure 6.1). Additionally, China's regulatory system was complex and in disorder (see Figure 6.2).

The industrial overhaul in March 1998 aimed at industry-wide restructuring and reorientation of oil strategy. The regulatory framework was considered by a newly established government agency, the State Petroleum & Chemical Bureau

Figure 6.2
China Oil Ownership/Regulation

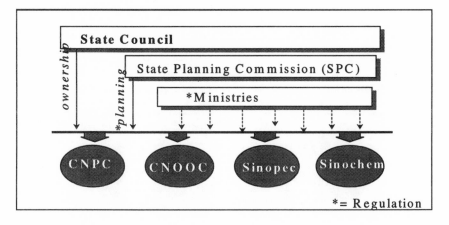

(SPCB), which plays the role formerly occupied by the State Planning Commission and CNPC. The organizational change was initiated by an oil asset swap between CNPC and Sinopec (see Figure 6.3).

CNPC has refocused its businesses on northeast, northwest, and Sichuan gas basins in the southwest part of the country. Sinopec, at the same time, has also been moved up to oil E&P areas in eastern and southern China. In addition, the chemical sector under the former Ministry of Chemical Industry and local oil distribution system run by provincial governments involved are subject to the overhaul program. As a result, CNPC has become a fully integrated oil firm while Sinopec is backed by both domestic and foreign oil sources. CNOOC and Sinochem maintain their structures. While the government meddling in the industry is muted, domestic competition has been seen in the north and southwest regions and the coastal line within the country. Petroleum regulatory function is simplified (see Figure 6.4). But there remain some doubts about SPCB's position as an appropriate agency to regulate and oversee the oil industry.

Overseas Expansion

Chinese oil imports reached 59 million tons in 1997, almost 60 percent of which are crude oil, mainly coming from the Middle East. To satisfy soaring domestic needs, CNPC unveiled a plan in late 1996 aimed at finding and developing 300 Mt of oil equivalent by 2010, one-third of which is planned from outside China. To reach this end, China has to turn its overseas entry strategy into expansion strategy for additional hydrocarbon resources. The year 1997 presented a milestone when CNPC signed seven oil contracts with foreign energy firms and governments. So far, the Chinese oil flagship has won fourteen contracts with extractable reserves of 400 Mt; more than half has come into

Figure 6.3
Oil Asset Swap

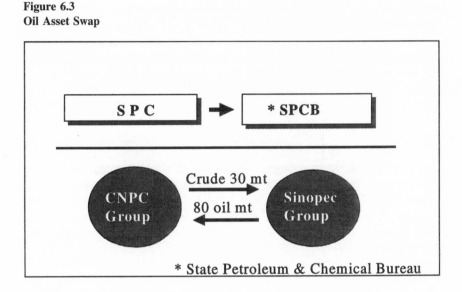

operation. Its E&P projects in Iraq are waiting for the lifting of the United Nations (UN) sanction. It is unanimous that China's overseas priority is given to neighboring regions, including east Siberia, Central Asia, and the Middle East. Of course, China has to harmonize oil and gas sources with East Asian and Southeast Asian consumers as well. Among several transportation options are gas pipelines from Russian eastern Siberia and its Far East region, oil and gas pipelines from Central Asia, and several oil and liquefied natural gas (LNG) sea-lanes. China prefers neighboring pipelines such as from western Kazakhstan to Karamai in Xinjiang, signed in September 1997. It may be China's hope that oil supplies both from Chinese Xinjiang and Kazakhstan could be increased to 30–40 million tons to make the Central Asia pipeline economically feasible. Moreover, it is highly likely for China to extend its Central Asian land routes from Kazakhstan and Turkmenistan down to northern Iran to reach the Persian seaports. Also, the country would be willing to join a pipeline from Kazakhstan to the Russian European part or join E&P activities in Russian Siberia for its expected gas stake from east Siberia and Russian Far East. Chinese E&P activities and probably imports of LNG from Southeast Asia have drawn wide attention and create debates on the risks the country has to bear.

LONGER VIEW BEYOND 2010

Global Trends

Since 1967, when world oil output reached 40.4 percent of the world's energy consumption (1.8 billion tons), higher than that of coal (38.8 %), oil has dom-

Figure 6.4
New Oil Industrial Structure

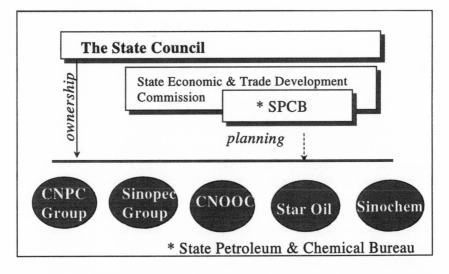

inated the world energy picture (*BP*, 1997). However, up to 1995, 243.6 billion tons of the world's ultimate reserves (457.2 billion tons) have been used. It was forecast that the world oil output would peak at 4 billion tons annually around 2020 and decline to 3 billion tons in 2050 and 1.3 in 2100 (Wan, 1996). With the world's natural gas reserve at 554 tcm, gas output will be paramount at 4 tcm in 2040 and declining to 3.7 tcm in 2050 and 2.5 tcm in 2100. Natural gas, as a cleaner-burning fossil fuel, is considered a "bridge fuel" to a nonfossil fuel time for the global economy.

There are several ongoing debates on a potential oil crisis around 2030 among petroleum economists and geologists (Compbell, 1996; Lynch, 1998). It is reasonable to project that the world oil price would be up, promoted by growing demand and shortfalls of resources. So far, the world oil extraction has outstripped two-thirds of the world's ultimate reserve. The world oil exploration and production (R/P) rate reached 40 years, 15 years level for the industrialized countries and 10 years for international oil majors, even though we can't ignore that the former Soviet Union (FSU), the Middle East, and Latin America regions present ample potential in hydrocarbon resources. The huge traditional demands from industrialized countries and emerging economies create great concerns over shortfalls in the coming decades. An imbalance of demands and supplies makes regional energy linkages more critical than ever.

The Oil Dragon's Rise

It was projected that China's economic growth will decrease below 8 percent after 2010. GDP per capita will reach nearly US$3,000 in 2010, over US$4,000 in 2030, and US\$4,777–7,639 in 2050. Meanwhile, population natural growth will peak at 1.58 in 2030 and fall to 1.55 in 2050, while urbanization rate will be over 50 and 60 percent in the years 2030 and 2050, respectively.

Oil production will decline around 2020. China's role as a consuming dragon will be overwhelmingly influential on its future oil policy. Energy conservation, environmental protection, and overseas expansion may be emphasized when its domestic oil and gas facilities mature. It is notable that gas production will be at its height. Overseas expansion will unfold fully.

Scrambling for Central Asian oil and gas sources seems to be a key to penetrate in the outside world in the twenty-first century. As the largest emerging market and land bridge in the Far East, China will play an important role in linking resources suppliers in Russia, Central Asia, and the Middle East. We believe that China, Turkey, and Iran will form a triangle backed by an outer triangle among the West (principally the United States), Russia, and China. China is positioned in an intersection of the two triangles, where it could interface with both Russia and the West. China would compete with the United States because of quests for both oil and gas from the Middle East and Central Asia. China's input in Central Asia will also balance Sino-Russian partnership in future transportation and distribution (Xu, 1997b).

Chinese oil diplomacy in Central Asia, Russia, and the Middle East should follow an integrated approach and become more aggressive to promote maximum market penetration. To this end, China prefers to promote a balance of power. China and Russia could work together to counterbalance and confront the Western involvement in Central Asia. It is important to prevent the West from exerting strong influence on the region and the South China Sea, where China is less advantaged. Or, it is possible that China might enhance its political ties with the West and lower its energy cooperation slant with Russia if the West can handle Eurasian issues more appropriately.

CONCLUSIONS

China, as a big dragon, will play a more important role in the global economy and politics. Its strong economic momentum has drawn worldwide attention. As a case in point, the Chinese oil industry—the oil dragon's past, present, and future—has been described above. The dragon's move was gauged in many respects, including domestic priorities, open policy, and overseas expansion. The messages in this chapter are clear:

• Oil consumption will overtake production when the country moves to its economic goal in 2010 and 2050. To bridge its demand and supply, China is slated to accelerate domestic exploration and production. Open policy serves as a by-product of domestic priorities before 2010.

• Considering environmental pollution and living standards, China's gas industry is rising. However, market imbalance is a main problem the country has to overcome. China's future gas supply can't operate without international cooperation.

- As flagships, both CNPC and Sinopec have been reorganized as commercialized and integrated company groups. This is the last attempt to overhaul the Chinese oil industry in this century. Clearly, there has been a bigger space for market competition inside the country. Looking forward, the regulatory system will be reconstructed. It was recognized that a relatively independent regulatory body would be indispensable and replace government agency(ies) in the future.

- To satisfy its social-economic needs, China has to move to overseas expansion for additional resources. Its overseas priority will be given to its neighboring hydrocarbon provinces, including the Middle East, Central Asia, and Russian Siberia as well as Southeast Asia. The Sino-Arabic corridor, new Silk Road, and Sino-Russian energy partnership will play a complementary role in securing its overseas energy linkages. Also, China has to bear risks and uncertainties when it enjoys its benefits from overseas ventures. It is wise for China to get closely involved in cooperation with the other countries and reconcile with the other powers. In turn, the world should reevaluate China's economic and geopolitical role.

In short, future oil and gas supply deficits will loom large and create an unprecedented challenge for the country's sustainable development. It is predicted that domestic priorities and the importance of an open policy will be emphasized in the next decade. Major change would occur around 2020, which will be a milestone for the country.

REFERENCES

BP World Energy Statistical Review. (1997). London: British Petroleum plc.

CASS (1997): *Chinese Economic Development with Projection to 2050.* Beijing: CASS Research Report (unpublished report, in Chinese).

China National Petroleum Corporation (CNPC). (1997). *Annual Statistics 1997.* Beijing: CNPC.

Compbell, C. (1996). *The Coming Oil Crisis,* Vienna: Multi-Science.

Hu, C. (October 1997). *China's Natural Gas Integrated Development to 2020* (in Chinese), a study report. Beijing: Petroleum Economic Research Center, CNPC.

Lynch, M. (1998). *Facing the Elephant: Oil Market Evolution and Future Oil Crisis.* Boulder, CO: International Research Center for Energy and Economic Development.

Simmons, M. (1997). *China's Insatiable Energy Needs.* New York: Simmons.

Xu, X. (June 1997a). *Asian Oil and Gas: Megatrends, Balance and Geopolitics.* CBA Energy Institute, University of Houston.

Xu, X. (Winter 1997b). China Reaches Crossroads for Strategic Choices. *World Oil;* reprinted by *PetroMin,* April, pp. 22–27, and *IAEE Newsletter,* pp. 10–14.

Xu, X. (January 1997c). China's Looming Oil Crisis and Ways of Avoiding It. *OPEC Bulletin,* pp. 7–9.

Wan, J. (June 1996). *Chinese Oil and Gas Production and Future Development.* Unpublished paper.

Part III

Competition, Cooperation,
and Capitalism

ences into a proper context. MNCs' involvement in China has gone through different phases, as shown in Figure 7.1.

- During the first ten years of economic reform, MNCs were basically quite tentative about China. They were not sure of the long-term implications of Chinese reform. Most were not willing to make major equity investments, and those who wanted to participate in the Chinese market chose to do so by licensing their technology to Chinese companies or by product imports. At that time, most of the "foreign" investment came from Overseas Chinese, firms located in Hong Kong, Taiwan, and Southeast Asia.
- MNCs' interest in China picked up markedly after 1992, fueled in a major way by Deng Xiaoping's pronouncement in Shenzhen of China's need to commit to economic reform. The Chinese leadership recognized that opening the economy to foreign investment would be critical to China's future growth. During the several years following, many MNCs scrambled to enter China, as many of them feared that they would miss out on the world's last great economic frontier.
- After several years of feverish entry into the country, MNCs began to learn about the challenges of operating in China. The reality and complexity of doing business in China began to hit home for many MNCs. China turned out to be a very difficult market in which to operate because of the changing regulations, different business practices (compared to those in the West), and the economics of Chinese output, which are often very different from what MNCs originally anticipated.
- Today, many MNCs have accumulated substantial experience in China—good and bad. Different industries had evolved in different ways in terms of regulations, supply and demand, competition, and business systems. While some MNCs have decided to divert or reduce their investments in China, many more continue to invest in China or have plans to achieve long-term profitable positions in China. In general, MNCs are finding that operating in China is very challenging and that in order to be successful, they will need to adopt a rigorous and practical approach. Also, MNCs are readjusting their expectations.

Despite past experiences, many MNCs continue to recognize the importance of China, either as a short-term market, as a long-term strategic imperative, or both. Many MNCs are, in fact, integrating their business systems with their operations in China because of the advantages that China can offer. For many MNCs, emerging markets are a key driver of their growth and China represents a very high, if not the highest, potential. This implies that China is often on the chief executive officer's strategic agenda. As many MNCs begin to enter their "second generation" in China—after setting up their bases of entry—they continue to look for the best ways to move ahead in China. Past experiences of MNCs in China can help new entrants to reflect what they should do to go forward.

START BY UNDERSTANDING CHINA'S REGULATORY CONTEXT

Company managers should understand the Chinese government's imposed regulations in each of these industries. Regulation drives the industry evolution

Chapter 7

Challenges of Competing in China for Multinationals

Edward Tse

INTRODUCTION

Many mulitnational corporations (MNCs) are attracted by the immense size and potential of China, and since the economy has opened up, MNCs have been investing heavily in the Chinese market. However, the experience and performance of MNCs in China have been mixed to date. While there are many success stories, a large number MNCs have found that their operations in China have not met their original expectations.

MNCs' involvement in China has gone through several stages over the last 10 to 20 years. While most MNCs were foreign to China 10 years ago, some have now become quite experienced and entrenched in the business landscape. Of course, many others are still neophytes to China. MNCs' experience also varies by industry. In those industries where the regulations have been relaxed, many MNCs have found that the industry dynamics have changed substantially in the past several years. In many highly unregulated industries, there is plenty of competition, if not overcapacity. Prices of products in many industries have dropped as a result. Developing a strong product market strategy and establishing an effective and efficient value delivery system are critical to success in China. On the other hand, many industries in China are still highly regulated, or even closed to foreign participation. MNCs have few, if any, degrees of freedom to operate in these areas. Many MNCs that had hoped to tap into the booming Chinese market have come away disappointed, often because they did not fully understand the reality of the operating environment in China. As a result, MNCs in China have had widely diverging experiences. In order to synthesize the lessons learned for others, it is important that we put these experi-

Figure 7.1
China Has Entered a New Phase of Foreign Investment

1978±	1989-1992	Late 1994	1996	Now

CHINESE PERSPECTIVES

Opening up of Chinese economy

"Crossing river by touching stones"

Marketization of economy
• Foreign investment key

Market size, growth not sufficient to attract foreign capital

Gaps in legal, investment infrastructure obvious

How far to open economy, political system, markets?

FOREIGN PERSPECTIVES

Questioned long-term success of the reform process

Unwilling to make major equity investments

Overseas Chinese pioneers

Multinationals scramble to enter

Great fear of "missing the China opportunity"

Reality hits home
• Regulations
• Business practices
• Economics

Prospects and experience in China vary by industry, by company

Readjust expectations as market and regulations change and companies' own knowledge improves

Figure 7.2
Few General Rules Apply in China; Context Varies by Industry/Sector and Is Primarily Driven by Regulations

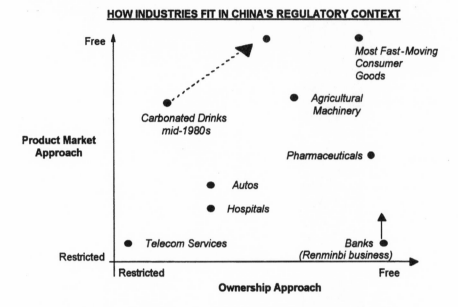

HOW INDUSTRIES FIT IN CHINA'S REGULATORY CONTEXT

and hence impacts the industry structure, competitive intensity and dynamics, and the degrees of freedom for companies operating in China. Therefore, company managers must put their businesses in China into a useful context to determine what regulations apply to their particular industries.

Regulations can be measured by two dimensions: product market approach and ownership approach. The product market approach applies to companies' product offerings and market activities. Typical attributes include what products companies are allowed to make and sell; where the products can be sold; what controls exist on pricing; and how the goods can be distributed. The ownership approach refers to the ownership type and structure that companies use to set up subsidiaries in China. Depending on the industry, various ownership approaches are possible for foreign companies such as wholly foreign-owned enterprises, equity joint ventures with various equity structures, and cooperative joint ventures.

To comprehend the importance of understanding regulations by industry, consider the regulatory differences among these industries (see Figure 7.2):

• The majority of the fast-moving consumer goods industry is the most liberalized in China. There are relatively few regulations on product mix, market approach, and ownership structures except for restricted products such as tobacco and liquor. This industry is very competitive and crowded with participants, including multinational companies, Overseas Chinese companies, and local players. As a result, these players are competing primarily on their capabilities.

• At the other extreme, however, is the telecommunications operations industry, which is officially closed to foreign companies. Some foreign companies have found ways to enter the market, but it's one of the most highly regulated sectors in China.

• The auto sector lies between these two extremes. Foreign carmakers are required to form joint ventures with an upper 50 percent limit on foreign ownership. All joint ventures must be approved by the central government, which controls the number of Sino–foreign joint ventures. The product market approach is semirestricted. The car model must first be approved. The joint ventures can in theory sell products throughout China; however, in reality, local favoritism exists. Pricing is set and controlled by the Chinese government. As a result, the financial performance has been variable. Before being granted a new joint venture, foreign companies invest significant resources in order to position themselves with the right government officials, ministries, and local carmakers. After securing the sought-after joint venture, companies continue to work with the authorities to resolve issues regarding local favoritism and pricing while at the same time build real capabilities along the entire value chain to ensure competitive product and service offerings.

Besides different regulations applying to different industries, China's regulatory context also varies over time. For example, when China opened its carbonated drink business in the 1980s, foreign companies such as Coca-Cola and PepsiCo were not allowed to hold majority equity positions in their joint ventures. Joint-venture partners were assigned by the Chinese authorities, and the number of joint ventures was controlled by the government. Today, foreign carbonated drink companies can have majority ownership in their joint ventures up to a certain maximum, and they can choose their own joint-venture partners.

Using this framework, we can explain the competitive dynamics and the need for partnership for foreign companies in their specific industry and draw some implications for determining the sources of competitive advantage in China. See Figure 7.3, which is merely Figure 7.2 turned 45 degrees. The right-hand corner of the square indicates the most liberalized end of the industry spectrum in China. The industries at this end are already very competitive; for instance, in consumer durables, the competition is already very intense. In this liberalized condition and highly competitive environment, companies need to bring or develop their capabilities to effectively compete. The need for partnership with local Chinese enterprises in the liberalized industries, therefore, is driven by the need for building specific capabilities that will help them win in the Chinese market. Increasingly, however, foreign companies in the liberalized industries find that they either already have the capabilities required to compete in China or can acquire the required capabilities themselves. Therefore, more foreign companies prefer to form their own wholly foreign-owned enterprises (WFOEs) or "virtual WFOEs," that is, joint ventures in which the foreign company holds the great majority equity and hence management control. At the other extreme, in which industries are highly regulated, competition is still generally low, if

Figure 7.3
This Regulatory Context Has Direct Implications for the Competitive Behavior of Industry Participants

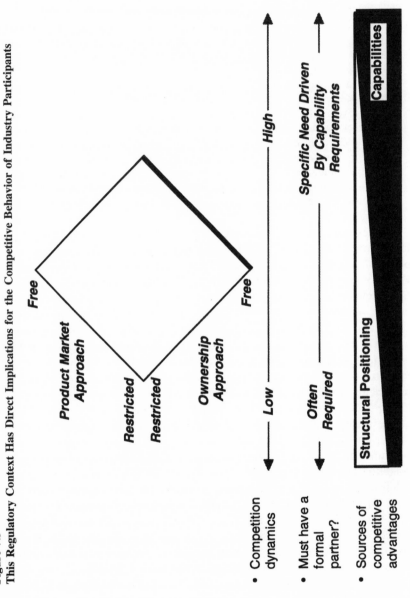

not prohibited, for foreign companies. In this case, foreign companies need to derive their competitive advantage through a combination of positioning with the relevant local players and building effective capabilities. Here partnerships are often required by regulations or are deemed necessary by foreign companies to help better position themselves within the industry.

The previous examples illustrate the diversity in the evolution of various industries in China, driven primarily by Chinese regulations. Without putting the industries into the proper regulatory context, it is very difficult to appropriately sort out the various experiences of companies operating in China. Over-extrapolation from one regulatory state to another and from one period to another can be very dangerous.

AVOID COMMON PITFALLS FACED BY MULTINATIONAL COMPANIES IN CHINA

Given the complexity of operating in China because of its vast size, regional diversity, poor infrastructure, and shortage of skills, many multinational companies have made fundamental mistakes in managing their businesses. Initially, multinational companies held a simplistic view of the Chinese market and lacked a real understanding of the market. In the consumer product industry, for example, companies—especially during the early stage of multinational companies' entering China—proclaimed statements such as: "There are 1.2 billion Chinese, and if each person buys x number of products per year, then our market in China will be this large."

However, the needs and characteristics of various market segments differ greatly. Vast diversity exists among major urban centers such as Beijing, Shanghai, and Guangzhou and among large cities, small cities, and rural areas within the same geographic region. For example, the official household income level of the top three urban centers is seven times greater than that of surrounding rural areas. In addition, the cost to serve and the nature of competition often vary by market segment. As a result, the real market size can be very different from that originally anticipated (see Figure 7.4). Some companies have re-trenched from this broad-brushed approach, focusing instead on a few markets.

Many of these initial segmentation approaches were rudimentary and did not reflect China's real situation. Some consumer product companies used income as a parameter for segmentation, which intuitively should be right. However, reported income often neglects much of the underground economy that is substantial in China's big cities and means that high-income consumers setting consumption trends were being overlooked.

Too often, multinational companies focus only on existing consumer demand. In an emerging market like China, however, policy, regulations, income, and consumption patterns can change rapidly. Companies that can anticipate these changes can turn them to their advantage. For example, Procter & Gamble created the perception that dandruff—traditionally a nonissue for the Chinese—is

Figure 7.4
The Actual Consumer Market Size Was Often Smaller than That by Simple Assessment But Often Offset by the Rapid Rate of Income Growth

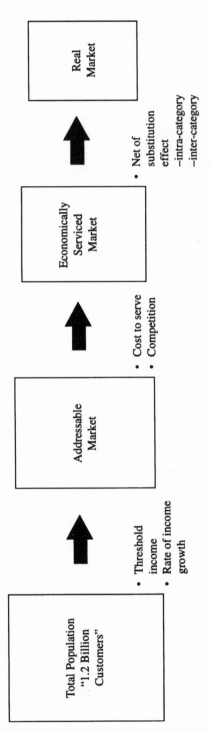

a social stigma and offered Head & Shoulders antidandruff shampoo to "solve" the problem. Today, Procter & Gamble controls over half of the total market share of the urban shampoo market. Along the same lines, Ting Hsin, a Taiwanese company, anticipated the need for more convenient and hygienic fast food and was the first to offer instant noodles packaged in a bowl. This package format became very popular, and Ting Hsin captured more than a 50 percent share of the instant noodle market in China.

A more common pitfall, however, is the lack of understanding of the real drivers of demand for different segments of Chinese consumers and how these drivers may change. For instance, a household cleaning products company found that product sales in major cities were substantially lower than initial predictions, using a "threshold income" approach. This analysis suggested that a significant segment of households had already crossed the threshold income line. However, further investigations revealed that generally poor living conditions (especially in Shanghai, where shared kitchen and bathroom facilities were common) created a disincentive to purchase cleaning products, irrespective of income levels. Instead, consumers preferred to spend their disposable income on products and services that provided instant value such as televisions, white goods, or a family dinner at McDonald's.

In the household cleaning products example, a recent decision by China to develop an affordable housing program may lead to tens of millions of Chinese households moving into new dwellings over the next several years. Focus groups have suggested that consumers would be willing to spend money on household maintenance; hence, there could be a potential surge in demand for "modern" household cleaning products. The challenge for companies is to anticipate the magnitude and timing of new demand by product and by geographic location.

Ineffective Sales and Distribution

China's distribution system has undergone major changes since economic reforms were unleashed in the 1980s. In the past, products were distributed in a rigid, tiered, category-specific system in which distributors were responsible only for physical distribution. They were not responsible for any commercial value-addedness, and direct sales by manufacturers were almost nonexistent. As the economic reforms began to emerge, the distribution system began to disintegrate, and the tiers and category-specific constraints broke. Some manufacturers, especially multinational companies, chose to go direct. However, the structural change did not bring a consequent change in the overall distributors' skills, at least to a level required for effective distribution in the new business environment. While the overall distribution skills are improving, the quickly evolving business requirements often outpace them. This mismatch has caused many problems for multinational companies in China.

For consumer products, the situation is complicated by the fragmented nature of the retail structure in Chinese cities. In a typical city there are dozens of major department stores, hundreds of supermarkets, thousands of "grocery stores," and tens of thousands of mom-and-pop stores and kiosks. Ensuring effective coverage and penetration is challenging.

As a result, many multinational companies have problems managing their sales and distribution. Often they find that the coverage and penetration of their products are ineffective. At points of sale, merchandising and shelf management are often not handled appropriately. Collection is often a problem, and logistics is a major headache.

There are plenty of root causes. Many multinational companies did not develop an understanding of the distribution and retail structure in their markets. Many of them did not understand the relative share of sales per type of account, the cost to serve, and the service requirements by account type. Often, there was not a clear evaluation of when direct sales would make better sense than using distributors, and vice versa.

In addition, many multinational companies face the challenge of building a skilled sales force in China. Some multinational companies inherited "salespeople" from their joint-venture partners; however, many of these people were from the old generation and did not have the skills to be effective in a market economy.

Operational Inefficiencies

Today, many multinational companies tend to focus their efforts on marketing and distribution. However, in doing so they often neglect the important operational aspects of their businesses. When many companies first entered China, they thought local costs were low and did not pay attention to managing efficient operations. However, the actual costs of operating in China can be unexpectedly high. Local labor and management costs have increased over the last several years, and expatriate costs are often higher than expected.

Manufacturing and sourcing costs can also be high. Companies are beginning to localize their supplies. In some cases, the comparatively low labor productivity, inadequate inventory management skills and systems, and suboptimal quality control (often leading to refit) can contribute to operating costs higher than expected. In one fast-moving consumer goods joint venture, the unit manufacturing cost in China was, at best, at par with other plants around the world, and for some products it was more than 30 percent higher.

Inappropriate Ownership Approach

Many Sino–foreign joint-venture relationships became problematic. Multinational companies found that the local partners did not meet their requirements. Some multinational companies thought they had to enter China with a joint-venture partner, which could bring the right *guanxi* (connections) to their business. While joint-venture partners sometimes are necessary or required in regulated industries, the old notion of *guanxi* became largely irrelevant in de-regulated industries.

Often, foreign companies and local partners have conflicting objectives. While foreign companies are often willing to absorb initial financial losses and to position themselves for longer-term success in China, many state-owned local partners are less willing to accept these losses. A key reason is that local government bosses of these Chinese enterprises are often evaluated by their short-term performance.

Another common reason for unsatisfactory partnership experience in China is the local partner's inability to increase investment in the joint venture. Raising the investment in a joint venture often happens after the relationship is well established and when the foreign partner wants to expand in China. However, in many cases, the local partner is not willing to contribute, claiming that it does not have the money to invest, the proposed expansion goes beyond its own geographic or product boundary, or it needs to channel its funds back to its supervising organization.

Yet, another typical reason is that the foreign and local partners disagree on strategic and operational issues for the joint venture. Brand focus and product focus are usually two of the most common areas of contention. The foreign partner naturally wants to push for its own brand in China, while the local partner often wants to do the same with its own local brands.

Thus, the experience of many Sino–foreign joint ventures in China has not been very positive. S. C. Johnson and Jahwa, a Shanghai household cleaning product manufacturer, terminated their joint-venture relationship, with Jahwa buying back its local brands.

CAPTURE CHINA'S GROWTH POTENTIAL

Capturing China's growth potential is very challenging. Competition is intensifying, especially in liberalized industries. Many multinational companies have made significant investments in China. In some industries, such as personal computers, audio equipment, white goods, and daily chemicals, top local players are quite competitive. Overcapacity is already evident in industries such as automobiles, audio equipment, white goods, and beverages.

Consumer preferences are also changing. Drivers of change are plenty: higher income, household formation growing at a faster rate than population growth, more available consumer information, more products, and more channels.

The liberalization of distribution channels in China provided more choices for suppliers, but the distributors' skills vary a great deal, thereby making the selection of distributors very critical. Retail channels are also changing quickly. New retail formats such as chain stores and supermarkets are emerging. Manufacturers need to develop sales skills that are commensurate with the requirements of the different sales channels.

ARTICULATE AND COMMIT TO A CHINA VISION

While the potential of the Chinese market is sizable, the timing and the path required to realize the potential vary by product market sector. The evaluation of the opportunity of each product market is a function of not only the threshold income but also other enablers. Threshold income may well predict the first take-up of "basic necessity" consumer products, such as refrigerators and washing machines, but as households possess these products, consumer choices shift to more discretionary products. Products of different categories may compete for the "share of the wallet" purchase. Purchase of big-ticket items such as passenger cars by consumers is limited today. Furthermore, opportunities in a well-penetrated urban market may be very different from those in a "virgin" suburban or rural market. The Chinese situation is too complicated to draw a simple, overall picture of the product market opportunities. Companies need to carefully evaluate the opportunities on a specific product market basis.

Companies should decide their objective in China and understand the resulting implications of their decision. Do they want to have broad-based product offerings in China or focus on a niche product? Do they want market share or immediate financial return? Do they want to build up the critical mass of their business now or later? Do they want to focus on major cities or penetrate a broad geography? The answers to these questions vary by company and by product. Companies must discern these differences and be careful not to over-extrapolate data and experience from one industry to another.

Against this backdrop, companies should decide the speed at which they want to develop their business and their desired product market positioning and coverage in China. Each strategic option has an associated set of implications on the competitive risks and the resources required. A company's strategic intent, therefore, must be commensurate with the resources it's willing to invest. However, there have been many cases in which multinational companies that want to quickly dominate the China market have not committed a team of managers with commensurate size, skills, and experience. For many companies, this has been a key cause for their inability to achieve their business objective in China.

BUILD A STRONG LOCAL ORGANIZATION

Successful companies in China are the ones that can build strong local organizations. Given China's operating environment and its rapid change, companies should be able to learn, adapt, and adjust. Managing in an emerging market like China is very different from managing in developed economies. Managers need to be entrepreneurial, be willing to accept ambiguities, and be sensitive to local business practices and culture and have a nose for capturing broad trends. Managers also need to maintain open and effective communications with the rest of the company, especially the headquarters, in order to set the right level of expectations for the China operation and to communicate the challenges of doing business in China.

Some well-performing multinational companies have found that while localization is the right long-term goal, complete localization in China will remain difficult for the next three to five years given the near-term imbalance in the supply and demand of capable and qualified local managers. Companies should take a dual approach to building their local organizations. At the entry and middle management levels, companies should put priorities on recruiting and developing local talent. Company managers should make the building of a local team a major, if not top, priority of their management objectives. More local talent with the right basic qualities is emerging in China. Companies should identify and recruit such people and equip them with the right skills.

While capable local managers are also emerging, complete turnover of the senior management to a local team is too premature for most companies. Some well-performing multinational companies continue to rely on expatriates who have the right experience and skills, together with the right outlook and commitment to continue to play an important role in the leadership of their local companies. In fact, local leadership of a multinational company in China typically requires the effective handling of multiple, distinctive roles that require different sets of skills and experience such as communications, management of the headquarters, building the local organization, and understanding the local market and competitive environment.

Some companies have found that instead of assigning a single person for all three roles, creating a core team of local and expatriate managers to share these responsibilities is better. At the same time, these companies require their expatriates to make the planning and development of local successors a key objective.

INSIGHTS AND FLEXIBILITY

In an emerging market like China, organizations should develop the capability to be insightful and innovative, and to establish institutional mechanisms for ensuring that these elements are captured. For instance, developing superior insights into the consumer is critical in any consumer market, but it's particularly important in an emerging market such as China. Indeed, the minds of the Chinese consumers are not yet "filled" nor "fixed." While there is substantial volatility in the market, there is also a lot of potential to build brands and market access.

Moreover, as the Chinese consumer market develops, more stratified market segmentation will inevitably emerge. Companies should capture consumer information as a core capability within their China organizations. In China traditional research approaches such as focus groups, interviews, and surveys work well. Many Chinese consumers are willing to talk about their consumer preferences.

Procter & Gamble, for example, captures Chinese consumer information using a 30-plus person market research team. Leveraging the tools and frameworks from Procter & Gamble's global research organization, this team coordinates the collection of market information to gain insights into Chinese markets. However, in a rapidly evolving market like China, a large, formal organization is not necessarily needed to collect useful consumer information. A multinational company making disposable products can collect and institutionalize market and competitor information through regular trade visits by its marketing managers.

Companies should study Chinese consumption behavior to understand fundamentals such as the key demand drivers, how these demand drivers may change over time, and how people may select one product substitute over another. Companies should identify the appropriate parameters to measure and focus on understanding them. Furthermore, companies should focus not only on understanding consumer demand but also on uncovering latent demand. Doing that requires creativity in the research approach. For some categories, benchmarking consumer behavior evolution in other Chinese economies such as Hong Kong, Taiwan, and Singapore can often shed light on potential developments in China.

Because of the fast pace of change in China, speed in collecting information is critical. Companies must focus quickly on the real fundamentals and get enough data to make business decisions. All too often, companies focus on ensuring statistical significance and sometimes focus on the wrong set of measurement parameters. In every situation, companies need to trade off between being approximately right and perhaps precisely wrong. However, there have been quite a few situations where by the time the rigorous research process was completed, plenty of changes had already occurred.

LOOKING FORWARD

China will continue to evolve rapidly, and the market and competitive landscape will continue to change. Regulations will also evolve. To capture market leadership, companies need to continue to focus their organizations on their vision in that market, consistent with the headquarters' expectations as well as the realities of the local operating environment. Companies need to develop and adopt a rigorous, capability-based, integrated approach to competing in the Chinese market. This will not be easy, but if successful, it will be financially, organizationally, and intellectually rewarding.

In addition, more multinational companies will integrate their China operations with the rest of their global business systems, organizations, and capability deployment mechanisms. For globalizing multinational companies, this integration should be a key item on their chief executive's agenda that merits a thorough evaluation, deep understanding of its impact on the global competitive dynamics, and forward planning of the appropriate strategy.

Chapter 8

Project and Location Selection in China: Lessons for Foreign Companies

Luo Yadong

CONCEPTS AND IMPORTANCE

Project Selection

A host government indirectly influences foreign direct investment (FDI) flow through the granting of subsidies for certain types of projects and the imposition of restrictions on others. Policy preferences are reflected in differentiated rules and regulations being applied to different categories of projects. Although the actual categories may vary across countries, a broadly defined classification may distinguish between those that are oriented toward technological advancement, exports, domestic markets, import-substitution, or infrastructure. Faced with the need for foreign exchange earnings, product and process innovations, and infrastructure improvement, most developing countries provide preferential treatment to technologically advanced and export- and infrastructure-oriented ventures. Macroeconomic priorities are reflected not only in tax policies, foreign exchange provisions, financing, and access to other production factors but also in variable market entry barriers.

A multinational corporation's (MNC) selection of technologically advanced or infrastructure-oriented projects is of the utmost importance. This is especially true for those ventures that pursue market growth, risk reduction, and economic efficiency. An export-oriented strategy is a major means for achieving cost minimization and efficiency, while domestic-oriented and import-substitution strategies are ways to accomplish local market expansion.

Export-oriented foreign invested enterprises (FIEs) tend to have an internal strategic orientation. They attempt to lower their manufacturing cost through exploiting lower labor or other direct costs in the host country. Their market focus is not on the local market but rather on home or international markets.

This manufacturing-export pattern of operations emerges in many FIEs operating in newly emerging market economies. These internally oriented FIEs emphasize high-capacity utilization, low advertising and promotion, low product research and development (R&D) efforts, and low manufacturing direct costs in the local market. They utilize the host country as an export platform to manufacture a product for resale outside the host country.

Local, market-oriented FIEs tend to have an external strategic orientation. They value product innovations meant to improve their output. They are less critically concerned with manufacturing expenses or relative direct costs. They put their focus on local market expansion rather than on home or international markets. Large market share, great market power, and high market growth in the host country are the long-term strategic goals of these FIEs.

Technologically advanced FIEs tend to have a dual-emphasis orientation. They maintain a stable domain wherein they not only operate with efficiency but also identify emerging opportunities through market scanning and research. In other words, dual emphasis-oriented FIEs seek benefits accrued from business opportunities in the local market and their efficiency-generating competencies gained through either market expansion outside the network or business integration within the network. In general, such FIEs emphasize output improvements and differentiation through product, process, or managerial innovation. Businesses that combine efficiency with improvements or innovations may have levels of return higher than the industry average. There is no strictly limited market focus for dual-emphasis FIEs. They can sell in the local market or export to home or third countries. Rather, the clear-cut feature of this type of FIE is the high intensity of R&D in product, process, and market. In order to attract a greater number of technologically advanced FIEs that are not solely focused on the local market, host governments of emerging economies often provide them with preferential treatment. This is of great value to their overall performance.

Selecting the type of project is important for both parent firms and FIEs. The project type can influence efficiency, risk reduction, local market growth, and cost minimization of both parent firms and their overseas subunits. Previous studies have suggested that the host market environment influences the incentive effectiveness. For example, Guisinger (1985) concluded that commodity-based incentives, such as tariff and quota protection, were of dominant importance to 24 out of 36 domestic, market-oriented investors surveyed in his study. In contrast, only one export-oriented investor out of a total of twelve was influenced by commodity incentives; financial incentives were far more important. Similarly, Reuber (1973) concluded that protection of local markets in a developing country was critical to market development and government-initiated projects. Tax preferences may be more important for export-oriented investors because they are searching for an export platform from which to manufacture for resale outside the host country. In recent years, Rolfe and White (1992) and Wells (1986) have further confirmed that export-oriented investors are more likely to be influenced by tax holidays and reductions than are host market-oriented investors.

In China, after expiration of the terms of income tax exemption and reduction, export-oriented and technologically advanced ventures are levied an income tax at half the rate stipulated for other types of projects (e.g., domestic-oriented and import-substitution). In addition, export-oriented FIEs are exempted from paying import duty on inputs used to produce exported products. Since a large amount of product value in export-oriented manufacture is made up of imported components, incentives related to import duties can be very important. Moreover, according to the new Chinese Turnover Tax law, which took effect on January 1, 1994, the value-added tax (17%) paid by FIEs is refundable if the final goods are exported to foreign markets.

Income or turnover tax preferences and import duty exemptions appear to have a strong effect only when a majority of the nontax factors (e.g., infrastructure quality) are also favorable. If none of the nontax factors are favorable, it is unlikely that tax holidays and import duty exemptions can alone attract foreign investment. Although technologically advanced projects also receive tax preferences, this treatment is likely to be offset by the disadvantages of non-tax factors. As the National Council for U.S.-China Trade (1990) reported, despite recent improvements, many U.S. investors still complain about the poor quality of the Chinese infrastructure.

Operational dependence on the local environment leads to greater exposure to uncertainties and risks. FIEs established to exploit the local market and take advantage of cheap labor are subject to uncertainty in both the local input and product markets. Export-oriented operations, on the other hand, can be run independently of local markets; their exposure to country-specific risks is kept at a minimum. Discrepancies between actual investments and what host governments desire also expose FIEs to uncertainty and risk.

In accordance with Chinese industrial policy, foreign investors are encouraged to invest in (1) high export ratio projects; (2) new equipment or new technologies that correspond to domestic needs; and (3) energy, transportation, telecommunications, and other infrastructure-related industries. FIEs investing in these types of projects are provided with further preferential treatment, including (1) reduction in land-use fees; (2) exemption from the profit remittance tax; and (3) priority in obtaining water, electricity, transportation, and communication services. Thus, other things being equal, FIEs investing in projects favored by the government have a higher performance in terms of risk reduction than do FIEs investing in other projects.

Different types of projects carried out by MNC foreign subsidiaries have varying market performance (Kobrin, 1988). Despite higher risks and uncertainty, domestic-focused and import-substitution projects benefit from more opportunities in local market growth than do others. Many developing and transitional economies have a high demand for imports. This fact will lead to greater opportunities for import-substitution when the government tightens import control as the result of a foreign exchange shortage. Developing and transitional economies also present more business opportunities than do developed markets. Opportunity does not guarantee venture success, however. An FIE's experience in the host market, ability to reduce local risks, and bargaining power vis-à-vis local authorities are all necessary for achieving and maintaining market power and growth.

Location Selection

Foreign manufacturers must also consider location characteristics. Transaction cost theorists view production site specificities as fundamental to choosing where to invest. The interaction between location-specific factors and investor competence as a source of competitive advantage has recently attracted research interest (Rugman and Verbeke, 1993). In general, the optimum location of production depends on plant economies of scale, transportation costs, tariff and nontariff barriers, relative production costs, and presence of long-standing customers in the foreign market. Friedman, Gerlowski, and Silberman (1992) also demonstrate that the local market conditions are significant factors affecting location choice.

Production location in the FDI literature is usually defined in terms of national markets. However, conditions also vary widely within national borders, especially in large or less developed countries or in the presence of transitional economics. Luo (1997) has provided evidence that the location decision within a country is significantly influenced by the host government's policies and preferences toward foreign direct investment. Indeed, in many newly emerging open economies such as China, different regions and even different areas within a region have varying treatments in tax, foreign exchange, and tariffs and have different local market conditions. Many developing countries have designated special areas as open economic zones to encourage or facilitate FDI operations. These zones benefit from better facilities, privileged policies, an international business atmosphere, and better investment infrastructure, which positively affect FDI performance. Region-specific and zone-specific locational strategies thus constitute important means for achieving risk reduction, cost minimization, and efficiency.

For FDI in newly opened market economies in transition, location strategy is even more crucial to venture success. It has been found that, in this context, cultural distance, business atmosphere, government policies, foreign business treatment, stage of economic development, and degree of openness vary substantially across different regions and between open economic zones and other areas.

The influence of cross-region location on FIE performance is an environment-specific issue. In fact, neither the level of economic development nor the stage in the economic reform process is even across different regions in China. The open coastal cities and open economic regions have historically been more de-

veloped economically and contain better infrastructure (transportation, communication, production and business service, etc.) than do other areas. Moreover,
the open areas have been provided with greater autonomy and authority to conduct their economic affairs. Open areas generally provide more Western-style
business facilities and a cultural atmosphere conducive to international activities.
Finally, FIEs located in open areas benefit from preferential treatment in terms
of income tax and other fees. For instance, income tax on FIEs established in
the open cities along the coast is levied at the reduced rate of 24 percent; ventures located in nonopen areas have a rate of 33 percent. Besides, FIEs in open
areas are exempted from paying the Industrial and Commercial Consolidation
Tax (ICCT) for their (1) imported production equipment, business facilities,
building materials, and vehicles; (2) raw materials, spare parts, components, or
packing materials imported for producing export products; and (3) export products. In sum, the open areas are likely to be perceived as less risky and more
efficient locations than nonopen areas.

According to the National Council for U.S.–China Trade (1990), investors
from the United States and other Western countries are more likely to locate
their operations in open areas than those from Asian territories and countries
(Hong Kong, Taiwan, Singapore, Thailand, etc.). For instance, until 1989, 95
percent of U.S.-origin FDI flowed into China's targeted metropolitan and major
cities of open coastal provinces, with the remaining 5 percent establishing operations in nonopen areas. In contrast, about 43 percent of Asian investment
was located in inland provinces and nonopen regions or small cities in coastal
provinces. The major factor contributing to this lack of symmetry is the greater
cultural affinity among business people from the Asian sphere, particularly from
the other Chinese commonwealth and their local counterparts. The Chinese commonwealth area nurtures a network of entrepreneurial relationships and an array
of political and economic systems that are bound together not by geography but
rather by shared tradition. Since less open areas in China are generally more
tradition-bound, Asian investors may experience less difficulty in adapting to
these environments. Another major factor contributing to this distribution pattern
of FDI is the sectoral difference between investors from Asian areas other than
Japan and those from the United States and European countries. In recent years,
many production bases for traditionally labor-intensive industries such as textiles
and light industries have shifted from coastal areas to inland regions or from
large, open cities to small, nonopen areas. This movement reflects the need to
control costs in these industries, where Asian investors have had a dominant
presence. The key profile of each major location is detailed in Table 8.1.

One of China's most remarkable efforts to attract FDI was the promulgation
of the Provision to Encourage Foreign Direct Investment (''the 22 Articles''),
initiated by the State Council in October 1986. In addition to offering a series
of preferential policies, this provision encouraged each region, down to the
county level, to set up one Economic and Technological Development Zone
(ETDZ) in its territory. Hence, any geographical region can generally be divided

Table 8.1
Major Locations at a Glance, 1993

Province	Population (millions)	GDP (¥ billions)	Imports ($ millions)	Exports ($ millions)
Heilongjian	36.4	103	1,001	1,831
Jilin	25.6	67	640	1,307
Liaoning	40.4	181	2,230	6,210
Hebei	63.0	18	360	1,990
Beijing	11.0	85	1,380	1,700
Tianjin	9.3	50	5,900	6,600
Shandong	86.4	270	1,520	5,900
Jiangsu	69.6	276	2,741	5,959
Shanghai	13.0	151	16,950	13,980
Zhejiang	43.4	170	2,410	4,320
Fujian	31.5	95	4,042	5,825
Guangdong	66.0	314	19,900	27,000
Inner Mongolia	22.3	46	550	650
Shanxi	30.1	65	203	634
Henan	89.5	158	559	1,366
Anhui	59.0	98	324	964
Jiangxi	39.7	70	228	884
Shaanxi	34.4	62	500	990
Hubei	56.5	108	1,340	1,686
Hunan	62.5	115	739	1,610
Guangxi	44.4	9	726	1,325
Hainan	7.0	20	1,667	902
Ningxia	5.0	10	32	111
Gansu	23.5	35	200	280
Sichuan	112.5	187	1,266	1,650
Guizhou	34.1	41	118	245
Yunnan	38.0	66	317	523
Qinghai	4.5	11	14	90
Xinjiang	16.0	48	417	495
Tibet	2.6	3	80	20

Source: *China Statistical Yearbook 1994* (Beijing: MOFTEC).

into two parts: the ETDZ and the rest. The ETDZ is often located near a harbor. It is designed to provide the basic infrastructure for the establishment of new ventures. ETDZ emergence became a magnet for FDI over the past few years. In these zones, FIEs benefit from preferential treatment on various taxes and fees such as the Enterprise Income Tax (EIT), Customs Duties, the Industrial and Commercial Consolidation Tax (ICCT), and land rent. For instance, EIT is 15 percent for FIEs in ETDZs while 24 percent in other locations, unless the enterprise is export- and technologically oriented. Consequently, FIEs located within ETDZs are in a better position to achieve profitability than are FIEs located outside ETDZs.

According to the Provisions for the Encouragement of Foreign Investment, FIEs in ETDZs can attain further preferential treatment if they produce either technologically advanced or export-oriented products. The Instrument of Ratification Needed for Joint Venture, Cooperative Ventures, and Wholly Foreign-Owned Ventures promulgated by Ministry of Foreign Trade and Economic Cooperation (MOFTEC) on June 16, 1986, stipulates that if a firm fails to conform to this policy, all the privileges based on its location in an ETDZ and the type of projects will be revoked. This suggests that a firm's zone location is correlated with its type of project. In other words, among FIEs in ETDZs, those investing in export-oriented or technologically advanced types of projects are in a better position for cost reduction than are those investing in other types of projects, other things being equal.

GOVERNMENTAL POLICIES

Locational Policies

In July 1979, Guangdong and Fujian were granted special policies and flexibility in their foreign economic activities by the central government. These include (1) increased local power to invigorate their economic development; (2) more flexibility in opening up economically, developing international business and trade, attracting foreign investment, and introducing technology, under the guidance of state planning; and (3) more financial support, with the two provinces free to utilize most of the added revenue over the next ten years.

In August 1980, the Standing Committee of the National People's Congress approved the establishment of four special economic zones (SEZs), namely, Shenzhen, Zhuhai, Shantou, and Xiamen. In April 1988, the 7th National People's Congress at its first session approved Hainan as China's largest special economic zone. The local government of these SEZs are granted provincial-level power in economic administration. There are specific favorable policies, such as increased credit loans, retaining all newly increased revenues, including those from foreign exchange earnings, for a certain period of time and exemption from tariffs for materials needed for construction within the zones. To be more specific, FIEs located in these five SEZs enjoy (1) a reduced 15 percent rate on corporate income tax; (2) exemption of income tax for the first two years and a 50 percent reduction of income tax during the third to fifth years, starting from the first profit-making year, for manufacturing FIEs with a term of business over ten years, upon approval by tax authorities; (3) an extended three-year, 50 percent reduction on corporate income tax for FIEs using advanced technology; (4) a reduced rate of 10 percent of income tax for FIEs exporting their own products, if their yearly export volume reaches 70 percent or more of the total output value; (5) exemption from export tariffs and value-added tax on export products manufactured by FIEs; (6) exemption from import tariffs and value-added tax on imported equipment or raw materials needed in the manufacturing of exported products by FIEs or office equipment for use by the FIEs themselves; and (7) favorable rates for land usage.

In April 1984, fourteen port cities were opened and granted more autonomy to attract FDI. These cities include Tianjin, Shanghai, Dalian, Qinhuangdao, Yantai, Qingdao, Lianyuangang, Nantong, Ningbo, Wenzhou, Fuzhou, Guangzhou, Zhanjiang, and Beihai. FIEs located in these coastal cities are entitled to the following preferential treatment: (1) a 24 percent corporate income tax levied on manufacturing FIEs in general; (2) a 15 percent corporate income tax for those FIEs that are technologically intensive, have a project with over $30 million in FDI, and are infrastructure-oriented or state-encouraged; (3) a 50 percent reduction of the 24 percent corporate income tax if 70 percent of output is exported; (4) manufacturing FIEs with a business term of over ten years are entitled to a two-year exemption from and a subsequent three-year 50 percent reduction of the corporate income tax, starting from the first profit-making year; (5) JVs investing in port construction and having a minimum fifteen-year business term are entitled to a five-year exemption from and a subsequent five-year 50 percent reduction of the corporate income tax; (6) FIEs are exempt from tariffs and value-added tax for equipment and materials imported for production and exempt from value-added tax for their exported products.

Since 1984 the State Council has approved the establishment of 32 national-level ETDZs. They are located in Dalian, Qinhuangdao, Tianjin, Yantai, Qingdao, Lianyuangan, Nantong, Caohejing, Minhang, Hongqiao, Ningbo, Fuzhou, Guangzhou, Zhanjiang, Weihai, Yingkou, Kunshan, Wenzhou, Rongqiao, Dongshan, Shenyang, Hangzhou, Wuhan, Changchun, Harbin, Chongqing, Wuhu, Xiaoshan, Nansha, Dayawan, Beijing, and Urumqi. FIEs investing in these ETDZs enjoy the following privileges: (1) a 15 percent corporate income tax for manufacturing FIEs. If the project will be over ten years in duration, it enjoys a two-year exemption from and a subsequent three-year 50 percent reduction of corporate income tax; (2) a 10 percent corporate income tax for FIEs with 70 percent of output exported, after a stipulated term; (3) a 50 percent reduction of the 15 percent corporate income tax for an extended three-year period; (4) exemption from tariffs and value-added taxes for imported materials, equipments, parts, and accessories that are used in production and operations; (5) exemption from export tariffs and value-added tax on export products.

In February 1985, the State Council approved the establishment of open coastal economic regions, including Pearl River Delta, Yangtze River Delta, and South Fujian-Xiamen-Zhangzhou-Quanzhou Delta, covering 51 cities and counties. In March 1988, the state further approved Liaodong (East Liaoning) Peninsula, Shandong Peninsula, and several cities and counties in other coastal regions as open coastal economic regions. This makes almost all coastal cities and counties open to foreign investment. The following preferential policies are applicable to FIEs in these regions: (1) a 24 percent corporate income tax; (2) a 15 percent corporate income tax for those FIEs that are either technologically advanced, have over $30 million in FDI, or are infrastructure-oriented; (3) favorable corporate income tax, tariffs, value-added tax, and other benefits for export-oriented and technologically advanced FIEs.

In April 1990, the State Council opened the Pudong New Area of Shanghai, which is a triangular area to the east of the Huangpu River, southwest of the Yangtze River mouth, and next to downtown Shanghai. The area covers 518 square kilometers, with a population of 1.38 million. Bordering on the East Sea and nestled against the Yangtze River to the north, the Pudong New Area is situated at the juncture of the so-called golden seacoast and golden waterway of China. The central government gives Shanghai greater power to approve the formation of FDI projects. FIEs in the Pudong New Area have the following privileges: (1) a 15 percent corporate income tax in general and two-year exemption and a subsequent three-year reduction by 50 percent of the tax rate if the project duration is over ten years; (2) a five-year exemption from and a subsequent five-year reduction by 50 percent of the corporate income tax when investing in energy and communication projects such as building of airports, harbors, railways, highways, and electric power stations; (3) FIEs are allowed to set up tertiary-sector projects such as department stores and supermarkets; (4) FIEs are allowed to set up financial institutions such as banks, accounting and auditing firms, and insurance firms. International trading companies are also permitted to be established and conduct import and export business; (5) no tariffs or value-added tax on imported machines, equipment, vehicles, materials, and the like used in production and operations; (6) the land use right can be transferred within the area with up to a 70-year grace period; and (7) all the income obtained by the government in the area will be used for further development and improvement of the area's infrastructure.

In May 1988, the first of China's New and High-Tech Industrial Development and Experimental Zones was established in Beijing. Emulating the "electronics street" of Zhongguanchun in Beijing's Haidian District, this industrial park, also called China's "Silicon Valley," covers an area of 100 square kilometers. China has since approved the establishment of over 50 more High-Tech Zones. FDI projects in these zones enjoy even more favorable treatment than those in ETDZs, according to the Interim Regulations on Certain Policies of the State New and High-Tech Industrial Development Zones, issued by the State Council, and Taxation of the State New and High-Tech Industrial Development Zones, regulated by the State Tax Bureau.

China has also approved fourteen bonded areas in Pudong (Waigaoqiao Bonded Area), Tianjin, Futian (Shenzhen), Shatoujiao (Shenzhen), Dalian, Guanzou, Qingdao, Zhangjiagang, Ningbo, Fuzhou, Zhuhai, Hainan, Shantou, and Xiamen. Bonded areas serve mainly to initiate entrepôt trade and offer export services such as processing, packaging, storage, and exhibition. FIEs located in these bonded areas are allowed to act as agencies for other FIEs in the same area that need to import raw materials or parts used in their production. FIEs in these areas are not required to obtain import or export licenses or permits for imported machines, equipment, and materials necessary for the construction of infrastructure facilities and production. These imported items are also free from tariffs and value-added taxes.

Project-Related Policies

Project orientation affects the FIE's eligibility for preferential treatment from the government and its vulnerability to governmental intervention. An export-oriented project is defined by MOFTEC as one that exports at least 70 percent of the total product manufactured in China. The definition of "technologically advanced project" is, however, obscure. In practice, foreign investors need to check with the local authorities about whether or not their technology is considered advanced before making any commitments. If less than 70 percent of total output is exported but sold domestically in the Chinese market, it is considered by the government as a local, market-oriented project. Infrastructure-oriented projects, in general, refer to those invested in energy, transportation, telecommunications, power generation, and other infrastructure-related sectors that bring in new technologies. Import-substitution projects are those that produce products within China that previously had to be imported to meet domestic demand. These products are generally sold in China in foreign currency instead of renminbi (RMB). In recent years, the number of import-substitution projects has been decreased drastically as a result of the rising quality of goods now produced by many local firms and FIEs.

MANAGERIAL ADVICE

Finding a Home

A recent survey reveals that Shanghai and Shenzhen are home to China's most profitable first-generation American joint ventures, with returns on investment at 16.2 percent and 13.6 percent, respectively. Western companies in the inland cities seem to be less profitable than those in eastern coast provinces. Nearly half of the executives reporting on inland investment projects responded that their joint ventures had not met expectations due to poorly developed infrastructures and transportation networks and uncertain raw material supplies (Stelzer et al., 1991).

Nevertheless, being in an inland town or province with a committed municipal or provincial leadership can have some unusual benefits. Because there are fewer ventures in many inland cities, FIEs there can get more personal attention and support from the provincial governor or mayor. Closer personal interactions with top local decision makers can be more frequent. These interactions have become increasingly important during the past decade as the Chinese economy has become decentralized, shifting substantial power to local governments.

There are many cases where foreign ventures in some small inland cities have managed to overcome mounting obstacles due to direct involvement by local governments. This is not normally expected from the municipalities of big cities. Many local officials are zealous supporters of Deng's reforms and are eager to attract foreign direct investment. In order to compete for foreign investment with coastal areas, some of them adopt aggressive policies to offset their disadvantages in terms of geographical location. Commitment from local governments is often indispensable to the success of a foreign business in China.

Foreign investors in China have access to a broad range of special incentives, depending on the location of their venture, the nature of the project, and how the FIE project is classified. As noted earlier, FIEs located in different areas and with different project types are treated idiosyncratically by the Chinese government. Any foreign investor looking at opportunities in China needs to understand exactly which preferential policies may apply to a particular project. However, getting a firm handle on this is not always easy. Local government officials who are eager to entice foreign investment may exaggerate the incentives in a particular locale. In recent years, the explosion of "special areas" has left many investors wondering how to choose one locale over another. Foreign investors should check out whether or not the "special area" is approved to offer preferential investment policies. If so, they should find out what level of the government (central, provincial, or city) holds the authority to implement these policies. A thousand ETDZs at various levels have been established, ranging from state-level ETDZs to county- or even township-level small ETDZs. In general, preferential policies offered by low-level ETDZs are very unstable. In fact, many of these small, lower-level ETDZs have been recently shut down by the central government.

Geographic affinity represents an important factor contributing to the phenomenal growth of FDI initiated by investors from Hong Kong, Taiwan, Macau, and Singapore. Hong Kong and Macau are adjacent to Shengzhen and Zhuhai, both among the first four special economic zones opened in 1979. Similarly, Taiwan is just opposite Xiamen, another special economic zone located in Fujian Province. Although Singapore is not as close to China as Hong Kong and Taiwan, it enjoys strong geographic advantages, due not only to its proximity to the mainland but also to its international air and sea routes, which straddle the time zones of Asia and Europe. It is at the heart of the economically dynamic

Asia-Pacific region. These geographic advantages reduce transportation costs and turnaround time for mainland production, obviously crucial in vertically integrated manufacturing.

The opening of China coincided with the emergence of severe labor shortages in Hong Kong, Singapore, and Taiwan and the need for restructuring within these three economies. There has been a large-scale movement of export-oriented, labor-intensive industry from Chinese community territories, particularly Hong Kong, to such mainland coastal areas as Guangdong, Fujian, Jiangsu, and Zhejiang. In addition, although international investors from Hong Kong, Taiwan, Singapore, and Macau are the major source of FDI in China, in a broad sense they are moving relatively labor-intensive activities into China in an attempt to escape rising labor costs and space constraints at home. Many Chinese community investors, particularly those from Hong Kong and Taiwan, have been operating in such labor-intensive industries as textiles, garments, electronics, electrical goods, metal, plastics, and toys. As the tightening labor market has raised wage costs in their home territories, and economic expansion has made factory sites more and more expensive, moving production to China, where wage levels are fundamentally lower, becomes immensely attractive. Today, it is rare to find a single Hong Kong-owned electronics company that does not have at least one factory in Guangdong, the huge province that borders Hong Kong.

In the past, foreign companies, whether from Asian territories or from the Western world, have mostly gone to coastal areas, where they were attracted by preferential tax policies, easy access to trained labor, and the region's rapidly developing infrastructure. To encourage FDI in the interior regions, the central government has recently introduced measures to enhance border trade, open inland infrastructure and oil and gas projects to foreign participation, and improve tax incentives for foreign investors in major inland cities, among others. These changes have already made the interior more attractive to foreign investors and may generate even better investment opportunities in the future.

The Chinese government, well aware that further disparities between coastal and inland economic growth rates could pose long-term risks to social stability, has prescribed a number of policies to give the inland economy a boost. First, the government has extended the open city concept to selected locations in the interior. Some inland cities are now able to offer the same or even better investment incentives than in SEZs, ETDZs, or coastal cities. Local governments have been given broad discretionary authority to enact legislation to encourage foreign investment. As a result, thousands of cities all over China are vying to attract FDI.

Second, China has opened up sectors or areas previously off-limits to foreign investment. For example, foreign companies can now pursue offshore oil- and gas-drilling opportunities in the Tarim Basin and other inland areas. Moreover, central authorities have sought to encourage trade between inland provinces and countries on China's borders by reducing tariffs and reestablishing transport links.

Third, China announced in April 1994 that the three specialized banks would prioritize loans and allocations of funds to the interior. As the State Planning Commission recognizes that the inflow of foreign capital to China will be insufficient to fund all of the country's infrastructure needs, China's new State Development Bank plans to focus on the inland provinces, leaving the wealthier coastal areas to rely on commercial funding sources. It is reported that the bank will prioritize loans to four sectors: infrastructure such as railways, highways, and communications; raw materials industries such as steel, coal, chemicals, and oil; new industries such as electronics; and agriculture and forestry.

Fourth, foreign investors in inland regions such as Changchun, Changsha, Chengdu, Chongqing, Guiyand, Hefei, Hohhot, Lanzhou, Kunming, Mudanjiang, Nanchang, Nanjing, Shenyang, Shijiazhuang, Taiyuan, Urumqi, Wuhan, Xian, Xining, Yanchun, and Zhengzhou now enjoy a 15 percent tax rate for general enterprises, with a full or partial tax holiday of three to ten years. FIEs established in remote, economically undeveloped areas can also qualify for a further 15–30 percent tax reduction for an additional ten years.

Lastly, more than 25 high-technology zones, mostly in the interior, are allowed to offer technologically advanced projects tax advantages similar to those provided by the SEZs. These high-tech zones are located in Changchun, Changsha, Chengdu, Chongqing, Fuzhou, Harbin, Hefei, Lanzhou, Nanjing, Shijiazhuang, Weihai, Wuhan, Xian, Zhengzhou, and Zhongshangang. FIEs in these zones are eligible for a reduced tax rate of 15 percent. EJVs with terms of over ten years, designated as high-tech enterprises, are also entitled to a two-year tax holiday, starting with the first profitable year.

At present, the interior's major strengths are its low land and labor costs and proximity to natural resources. Foreign companies looking to set up enterprises utilizing low-to-medium technologies and requiring a considerable labor force will find the interior most suitable. As the infrastructure and available labor skills in the interior improve, medium- and high-tech industries will also find suitable investment sites there. Even if a prospective foreign investor prefers the coast, he or she should examine the inland areas to see how they compare before deciding on a final project location.

To summarize, foreign investors should consider at least five aspects of location before making a decision. First, prospective foreign investors should find out about all the local policies relevant to FDI project approval, taxation, financing, land use, infrastructure accessibility, and industry priority. They should also consult MOFTEC's list of officially approved special industrial zones or ETDZs to avoid getting caught in an unofficial, "pseudo economic" zone. In early 1994 the State Council closed 1,000 of the 2,700 special industrial zones that had been set up by local governments to attract foreign investment.

Second, as noted earlier, prospective foreign investors should thoroughly examine infrastructure conditions. For example, lack of deepwater ports in certain regions can pose a problem for import or export. FIEs located too far from a railroad terminal may have high transportation costs. Foreign investors should also ensure that the existing water supply, electricity grid, and telecommunication systems can meet the needs of the proposed plant.

Third, foreign investors should consider local living conditions and the influence on the expatriate life of their staff. Important factors may include housing, transportation, communication networks, health care facilities, international schools, and cultural distance.

Fourth, foreign executives should evaluate the local government and find out if municipal and provincial officials will be accessible, whether they are inclined to provide assistance, and how efficient they are.

Finally, investors should study the accessibility and quality of production factors such as local labor, capital, natural resources and raw materials, and technology. Labor skills and the ability of local firms to absorb new technologies are particularly influential to venture success.

Location selection is often interrelated with such decisions as project selection, industry selection, timing decision, and partner selection. For instance, export-oriented projects should be located in areas that supply superior labor skills, transportation conditions, and the local materials needed for production. Projects in capital-intensive or technology-intensive industries might be better situated in cities with a strong infrastructure and absorptive capabilities. The first mover in a newly opened sector should choose a site that is developed economically, has connections with the Western business culture, and is promoted by the government. Late entrants already familiar with the Chinese market may consider an interior area where market demand is high and industrial competition is weak. A foreign investor launching a joint project with a local partner who already maintains superior organizational and technological skills and relationships with external stakeholders (such as suppliers, customers, distributors, and government officials) is not limited to coastal regions.

Choosing the Right Project

Recently, some researchers examined the effect of project type selection on FIE performance based on the analysis of the data collected from Jiangsu Province (Luo, 1997, 1998). The primary findings suggest that there exists a systematic association between project type and FIE performance; different project orientations influence FIE performance idiosyncratically. FIE success hinges on a good fit between the strategic objectives of the parent firm and the strategic orientations of its overseas projects. Maintaining market orientation flexibility and contributing distinctive competences are imperative for overall success.

Export-oriented projects are found to favorably influence FIE risk reduction. Most export-oriented FIEs are satisfied with their export growth. Indeed, export-oriented projects in a global environment can enable FIEs to accomplish their strategic tasks by taking advantage of the internalized transnational networks of MNCs. This internalization advantage effectively assists FIEs in achieving economic rents derived from comparative advantages across national boundaries.

Today, country-specific comparative advantages in certain factors are not quickly dissipated due to the existence of trade barriers across borders and mobility barriers within the border. Under these conditions, globally integrated networks can enable the internally oriented FIEs to take advantage of transaction costs economies and internalization advantages. Moreover, an internally oriented strategy can help the investor reduce operational risks and attain preferential treatments by the host government in emerging economies. It is hence advisable that export orientation is an appropriate strategic choice for those transnational investors who seek risk diversification, short-term financial return, global integration advantage, or production factors exploitation in host countries.

Local market-oriented projects are found to be significantly correlated with FIE sales growth but have high operational risks. In other words, FIEs seeking market growth in China appear to have accomplished their goals in local market expansion but have encountered high instability and uncertainty. By focusing on identifying and capitalizing on emerging market opportunities in China, local market-oriented FIEs help MNCs attain internationalization advantages by geographically expanding foreign markets and transnationally increasing product scope. With increasing familiarity with the Chinese environment, more and more MNCs have in recent years entered this market in pursuit of local market shares. Indeed, when government-instituted controls over industry supplies are lifted during transition, the explosion in the number of participants, both foreign and local, in newly competitive industries does not exhaust its potential. The rapidly expanding Chinese economy together with the existence of a pent-up demand spurs MNCs to search for local market growth using innovative, risk-taking, and proactive strategies. For large, diversified MNCs that are longsighted, technologically competitive, and adaptive to the local environment, external orientation would be a right choice for them to preempt emerging product or market opportunities.

Technologically advanced projects tend to have a dual emphasis. That is, their market domain is in both the Chinese domestic and international markets. This dual orientation is the only one of the three types of projects that positively relates to profitability. Market orientation flexibility (i.e., not focused solely on the local market) and advanced technological skills are major reasons a dual orientation relates to overall success. Market orientation flexibility not only mitigates an FIE's dependence on local settings, thus reducing the firm's business uncertainties, but also enables the firm to quickly respond to changing conditions in the host, home, and international markets. Additionally, keeping a certain degree of market orientation flexibility is commonly encouraged by host governments, particularly in transitional economies. This encouragement supports all major aspects of FIE performance. Another reason for the superiority of the dual-emphasis orientation lies in the fact that parent firms of this type of FIE contribute rent-generating competence (e.g., advanced technology) to the venture. While market structural potentials are a necessary condition for corporate success, distinctive competences are a sufficient condition for achieving sustained economic benefits.

CONCLUSION

The analysis also demonstrates that the relationship between project type and sales growth is moderated by investment size. Local, market-oriented projects with a greater investment size are more likely to succeed in achieving market growth than those with smaller investments. Thus, an appropriate fit between project type and investment size can contribute to high efficiency. Economies of scale and investment commitments seem important for market expansion in China.

To sum up, prospective foreign companies should consider several factors before choosing a type of project. First, they should check out the Chinese governmental policies regarding different types of projects. These policies include taxation, financing, infrastructure access, foreign exchange balance, local content requirement, and industrial regulations concerning entry barriers, regional restrictions, distribution channels, and partner selection. Second, prospective investors should integrate project selection with the strategic goals of the parent companies and corresponding orientations of the FIEs. Moreover, they should consider their own ability to reduce risks and uncertainty in the local context and their strengths in financial, technological, operational, marketing, and managerial arenas. Next, investors must be able to maintain an appropriate balance between the local responsiveness of their FIEs in China and the global integration requirements of their entire network. The density of interactions between their FIEs in China and other subsidiaries as well as the parent within the network should be viewed as crucial to project selection. Finally, prospective investors should opt for projects that are not only financially profitable but also strategically flexible. Strategic flexibility has been proved to increase both profitability and stability. Keeping the project flexible in terms of market orientation is particularly essential for projects invested in the highly uncertain and complex environment of China.

REFERENCES

Brecher, R. (May–June 1995). Considering the Options. *China Business Review*, pp. 10–19.

Friedman, J., Gerlowski, D. A., and Silberman, J. (1992). What Attracts Foreign Multinational Corporations? Evidence from Branch Plant Location in the United States. *Journal of Regional Science* 32, pp. 402–418.

Guisinger, S. (1985). A Comparative Study of Country Policies. In S. Guisinger (ed.), *Investment Incentives and Performance Requirements*. New York: Praeger, pp. 16–29.

Kobrin, S. J. (1988). Trends in Ownership of U.S. Manufacturing Subsidiaries in the

1980s. In F. J. Contractor and P. Lorange (eds.), *Cooperative Strategies in International Business*, pp. 129–142. Lexington, MA: Lexington Books.

Luo, Y. (1997). Partner Selection and Venturing Success: The Case of Joint Ventures with Firms in the People's Republic of China. *Organization Science* 8(6), pp. 648–662.

Luo, Y. (1998). Strategic Traits of Foreign Direct Investment in China: A Country of Origin Perspective. *Management International Review* 38(2), pp. 91–104.

National Council for U.S.-China Trade. (1990). *Special Report on US Investment in China*. Washington, DC: Department of Commerce.

Ness, A. (September–October 1995). Shifting the Center. *China Business Review*, pp. 43–46.

Reuber, G. (1973). *Private Foreign Investment in Development*. Oxford, U.K.: Clarendon Press.

Rolfe, R. J., and White, R. (1992). The Influence of Tax Incentives in Determining the Location of Foreign Direct Investment in Developing Countries. *Journal of the American Taxation Association* 13, pp. 39–57.

Rugman, A. M., and Verbeke, A. (1993). Foreign Subsidiaries and Multinational Strategy Management: An Extension and Correction of Porter's Single Diamond Framework. *Management International Review* 33, special issue, pp. 71–84.

Stelzer, L. et al. (November–December 1991). Gauging Investor Satisfaction. *China Business Review*, pp. 54–56.

Verma, S. (January–February 1995). Looking Inland. *China Business Review*, pp. 19–25.

Wells, L. (Autumn 1986). Investment Incentives: An Unnecessary Debate. *CTC Reporter*, pp. 58–60.

Chapter 9

The Internationalization of Chinese Enterprises: Evidence from the United Kingdom

Lu Tong

INTRODUCTION

Although the outward internationalization of Chinese enterprises[1] is recent and small-scale, there seems little doubt that major growth will occur in the future. In the years 1993 to 1995, China was the second-largest host country in inward direct investment flows, and there is active government policy interest in inward technology transfer (Young, Huang, and McDermott, 1996).

The objective of this chapter is to provide a contribution to the understanding of Chinese enterprise activity abroad, drawing on the results of a survey in the United Kingdom in 1997. The chapter highlights the parallels and lessons that can be drawn from research on state-owned multinationals (MNEs), general trading companies (GTCs), and developing country MNEs, and aims to provide a baseline against which studies in other host nations may be undertaken and from which the future development of Chinese enterprises may be charted and analyzed.

THE OUTWARD INTERNATIONALIZATION OF CHINESE ENTERPRISES

Outward direct investment, involving some of the large Chinese state-owned enterprises (SOEs), dates from the late 1970s. By the end of 1983 China had 61 affiliates in 23 countries with a total investment stock of US$90 million (World Bank, 1993). As of 1993, it is estimated that China had nearly 5,000 overseas affiliates in 120 countries, of which approximately one-quarter were nontrade subsidiaries. Thus, despite some high-profile overseas acquisition activity in manufacturing by a number of large Chinese SOEs (Young, Huang, and McDermott, 1996), the majority of foreign affiliates were small trade agencies with market-seeking objectives (Zhao, 1993). Initially, China's outward FDI was concentrated in developing countries, but in recent years, excluding Hong Kong and Macau, it is estimated that over 70 percent of Chinese affiliates were located in industrial countries (Zhang and Van Den Bulcke, 1996).

Chinese outward investors can be grouped into four main categories. The first are foreign trade corporations (FTCs) of the provincial and municipal governments (e.g., SINOCHEM, China Minmetals Group). The FTCs generally lost their former monopoly position in the 1980s and adopted a new corporate strategy that included internationalization; SINOCHEM, for example, was the first enterprise group selected by the government for an experiment in building a socialist transnational.

The second category comprises the large industrial enterprise groups, which were designed as a showpiece in respect of ownership and management reform and which were permitted to expand abroad with few restrictions (e.g., Shougang Corporation). In this group might also be included a number of foreign business-oriented companies or conglomerates that were set up by central and local governments in the early 1980s to develop into international business (Zhang and Van Den Bulcke, 1996). Although the categories are not completely distinctive, a third group comprises financial enterprises such as the Bank of China, the People's Construction Bank of China, and China International Trust and Investment Corporation (CITIC). While the Bank of China had branches in more than 20 countries before 1950, a number of other banks were formed or reconstructed only in the 1980s, with internationalization commencing in the 1990s. CITIC was set up in 1979 as the first national, nonbank financial enterprise, a highly international company, CITIC's activities are now widely diversified, and it is little different from some of the conglomerates and FTCs. Zhang and Van Den Bulcke (1996) identify a fourth group of small-scale Chinese outward investors, namely, the large number of smaller and medium-sized industrial enterprises, principally from Guangdong and Fujian Provinces. There is also evidence of the rapidly expanding township and village enterprises (TVEs) initiating investment outside China.

RELATED LITERATURE

State-Owned Multinational Enterprises

Some of the early literature on developing country MNEs identified the significance of state ownership in outward investment activities (Heenan and Keegan, 1979; Kumar and McLeod, 1981; Monkiewicz, 1986). SOEs were found to be active in natural resource industries, particularly oil, and to a lesser extent in services. The emergence of Eastern European multinationals was also recorded by McMillan (1987), from the mid-1960s marketing subsidiaries began to be established in the West by the countries' foreign trade organizations as part of an evolution of their trade policy designed to provide a direct link from the production enterprise to the market. The importance of the trade support function was confirmed by Hamilton (1986) and by Artisien, McMillan, and Rojec (1992) for Yugoslav MNEs.

McMillan (1987) established that initially the traditional East European affiliate abroad represented several home-based foreign trade enterprises. Subsequently, specialization took place (especially when technically sophisticated manufactured goods were involved), accompanied by investment in auxiliary functions relating to the modification, distribution, and servicing of the product; the foreign subsidiaries were also given a purchasing role on behalf of home country importers. Another trend was the diversification of commercial, banking, insurance, transport, and other services' enterprises to areas not directly related to the home nations' foreign trade, including third country trade transactions. The author related this to the increased autonomy of affiliates and a stronger profit orientation. However, in respect of Yugoslav enterprises, Artisien, McMillan, and Rojec (1992) did not identify much further evolution into production ventures in the West.

Writers on East European MNEs also observed the internationalization of banks and financial services companies. The banks' roles included the provision of channels to Western national and international money markets for trade financing, the investment of hard-currency funds in the West, and the provision of financial data and analysis on international monetary developments. In addition, the foreign operations enabled banking affiliates to gain expertise in international finance and helped ensure the privacy of foreign financial transactions.

It was concluded that the characteristics and behavior of East European state enterprises were little different from those of other firms in host countries, and their objective was to compete successfully within the rules of the marketplace. In addition, the potential of state management and control to provide greater economic power than could be exercised by equivalent private Western firms did not appear to be utilized. Analyzing the activities of state-owned MNEs from both developed and developing countries, Anastassopoulos, Blanc, and Dussauge (1987) provided a typology of enterprises based on the propensity to multinationalize and the propensity of the state to intervene. While a category of "unfair competitors" existed, the authors argued that success as an MNE required SOEs to forgo their primary mission of public service.

This issue of the competitive advantages of state-owned and controlled businesses is crucial, both for decisions over entry into and behavior in foreign markets and for the long-term security of foreign operations if and when privatization occurs. In theory, SOEs may not be required to earn profits or pay dividends: they have no fears of loss or bankruptcy, they may have preferential access to state financing and receive hidden subsidies, and they possess monopoly or monopsony power. All of these factors provide the potential for unfair competition. In an international business context, the possibility of earlier and more rapid internationalization becomes feasible. International business theory stresses the requirement for ownership advantages to enable the MNE to compete successfully in an unfamiliar foreign environment. But the SOE may be able to bear losses overseas and build ownership advantages through technology learning and technology acquisition.

The Chinese government, as with others, has recognized the crucial importance of multinational operations in a global economic era and has been actively promoting outward FDI. Anecdotal evidence exists of Chinese enterprises making speculative and unwise investments abroad, without the constraints that would operate for a private enterprise. For an SOE, it is possible to justify unwise investment decisions in terms of the lessons that may be learned for the future or the need to take a long-term view.

As with SOEs in other countries, critical issues in China concern the performance of these enterprises and their future. It was estimated that about 70 percent of Chinese SOEs were running at a loss in 1996 (*Financial Times*, 25 April 1997). Although the term "privatization"[2] is not used in China, "shareholding economic reform," in which SOEs are converted into shareholding enterprises, is a somewhat similar process (Ma, 1996): shares are issued to the state, enterprises (including foreign-owned MNEs), and individuals. While the process is still at an early stage, the pace of activity is likely to accelerate, allied to other initiatives such as the consolidation of enterprise groups and sell-offs of smaller SOEs (see *Financial Times*, 5 February, 25 February, and 28 April 1997).

Postulates regarding Chinese enterprise activity in the U.K.:

• Activities will be chiefly in services (marketing and financial services), reflecting the overall pattern of Chinese internationalization, and will involve SOEs.

• State ownership seems likely to accelerate the pace of internationalization in a Chinese context, and could therefore be associated with weak performance and poor prospects for the future and perhaps speculative ventures.

• U.K.–China trade is less important than that with some other European countries, thereby limiting trade-related activities; conversely, the city of London will prove important for financial services and allied services (e.g., shipping) companies.[3]

General Trading Companies

Potentially, much can be learned about the Chinese FTCs from the experiences of general trading companies elsewhere in the world economy, especially East Asia (Kojima and Ozawa, 1984; Balabanis, 1994; MacBean, 1996). The first Japanese trading companies, founded in the 1870s, had the European trading houses as a prototype, they were designed to handle all trading activities and overcome deficiencies in trade experience and lack of knowledge of foreign markets, languages, and cultures. These foreign trade companies tended to specialize in a limited range of products such as metals, machinery, textiles, or foodstuffs. One hundred years on, Japanese GTC strategies were emphasizing "third country trade, pursuing direct investment strategies, investing in R&D [research and development], expanding in energy-related business and adopting a long-term management plan" (Cho, 1987: 48). The Korean general trading companies were formed after 1975 to promote Korean exports, modeled on the Japanese GTCs, and other countries such as Brazil have attempted to apply the same template. This led to extensive analysis, especially during the 1980s, on the characteristics of GTCs, success requirements, and so on (Sarathy, 1985).

According to one author (Kim, 1986), the environmental factors that favored GTC formation included an underdeveloped infrastructure, an industrial base dominated by small and medium-sized enterprises (SMEs), standardized products, fragmented distribution channels, and a dependence on foreign traders.

Within such an environment, the GTCs operate as an intermediate type of cooperative organization between markets and hierarchies (Kojima and Ozawa, 1984). Although the Japanese GTCs are commonly used as a model, there are in fact many types of related organizations, offering the potential for different patterns of evolution and strategy over time. Kim (1986) suggested three international development stages (reminiscent of the internationalization process models—see Luostarinen, 1970; Johanson and Vahlne, 1977) characterized by increased product and geographical diversification and by a dilution in the relative importance of the trading functions, associated with a widening in the scope of activities to include financing and then production. Cho (1987) suggested eight generic strategies for GTCs ranging from complete specialization to diversification based on one or a combination of functions, product, and area.

In Western countries in the 1990s, such conglomerate activity has fallen out of favor (Hinterhuber and Levin, 1994). Many companies have recognized that they do not necessarily have value-added expertise and core competences in more than one area and have sought improved performance through strategic business units and strategic networks.

In respect of China, pre-1978 all trade was conducted through about twelve FTCs that had a monopoly over particular products. As part of the Open Door Policy from the end of the 1970s, authority to engage in international trade was decentralized, leading to a shift of FTC branches to provincial and township control and the creation of many new FTCs. By 1986 there were 1,299 FTCs, increasing further to a peak of 5,000 in 1988 (MacBean, 1996). Many of the new FTCs were ill equipped for their role, and problems led the central authorities to shut down around 1,400 FTCs by the end of 1988. Although direct trading rights were extended to the larger state-owned enterprises as part of the market reform and decentralization process, over 90 percent of imports and 80 percent of exports were handled by the FTCs in 1992.

Research by the World Bank (1993) and MacBean (1996) indicates that competition and efficiency in importing and exporting have increased significantly since the 1980s; and, along with other factors (Panagariya, 1995), the growing experience and professionalism of the FTCs have played an important role in China's export success. Some of the positive features of FTC activities include the following: active market search for export clients assisted by the development of their own information networks; the provision of medium-term finance to local firms; financing overseas trips for clients; assistance in training employees of local enterprises and, more generally, transfer of technology and know-how to local manufacturers; and international procurement of materials and machinery for domestic enterprises. On the negative side, however, a number of problems remain: foreign companies complain of protracted negotiations as staff refer decisions to supervisors; local firms accuse FTCs of withholding information or providing inadequate information; and some local enterprises have highlighted the advantages of direct trading such as informal technical assistance from foreign buyers and exporters, advice on standards and on production methods, new machinery, and so on.

One factor underlying these problems is the evidence of continued monopsony among many FTCs. Some products are still allocated exclusively to particular national or provincial FTCs; for example, SINOCHEM has exclusive rights to sell petroleum. Competition among FTCs is restricted by poor information flows across China; and by mid-1992 only 538 manufacturers could trade directly (World Bank, 1993). From their own perspective, FTCs complain of the multiple objectives set for them by government, namely not only profits but also foreign exchange generation and job creation (MacBean, 1996).

Postulates:

- Differing patterns of evolution of Chinese enterprises in the U.K. will be apparent, although diversification will be a common theme. Following the Japanese model would see the early signs of global conglomerate enterprises.

- Competition within China, with the growth in the number of FTCs and the possibilities for direct trading (for both Chinese and foreign-owned firms), will be affecting U.K. affiliates adversely both as exporters and as importers.

- London is a major center for commodities trading (foodstuffs, raw materials, and metals) and will prove an attraction for Chinese FTCs.

The Growth of Developing Country MNEs

The initial models of Third World MNEs concentrated upon the ability of developing nations to innovate and hence develop technological competences (ownership advantages) that could be exploited in neighboring countries. Tolentino (1993) has presented this as a developmental model in which the sectoral path of FDI evolves toward more technologically sophisticated manufacturing investments and support activities, allowing for independent technological development trajectories. Data emerging from studies of Third World MNEs suggest that there may be another component of the technological accumulation process, namely outward FDI, which is designed to acquire technology from abroad. Lecraw (1993), for example, found that the advantages of export-enhancing Indonesian MNEs lay in their access to low-cost natural resources and labor. The enterprises then used their capital to acquire management, technology, and marketing advantages through FDI; this led to a leapfrogging of the stages of internationalization. Within this stream of work, much less attention has been paid to developing country services' MNEs; although, for example, four Japanese banks opened branches in London between 1918 and 1924, and Moscow Narodny bank was established in London in 1919 (McMillan, 1987).

Young, Huang, and McDermott (1996) studied the internationalization process for five large Chinese SOEs and highlighted the importance of acquiring advanced R&D and manufacturing know-how and especially marketing expertise from acquisitions in developed nations. This supports the work of Zhang and Van Den Bulcke (1996), although the latter also focused upon the fact that most of their sample enterprises had established joint ventures with Western companies within China. These joint ventures facilitated the acquisition of large-scale production technology and skills and experience with different organizational structures.

Further research to understand the processes by which knowledge acquisition (especially from abroad) takes place is called for relating to Chinese enterprises set up both by acquisition and by new venture mode. The ability to manage successful operations abroad would provide some indication of the extent to which Chinese enterprises have been able to successfully apply their own or assimilate acquired ownership advantages.

One potentially important issue in this respect concerns business networks. A number of authors (e.g., Hamilton, 1996a) have argued that business networks in Chinese society are very different from those in the West: ''[N]etworks in the West consist of empirically and situationally defined interactional patterns that exist among individuals and explicit organizations. . . . In Chinese society, however, networks specify sets of people linked together in pre-defined relationships; these networks exist whether or not the linked individuals interact at all or interact according to the rules of their specific relationships'' (Hamilton, 1996b: 288). It is suggested that the Chinese are able to adapt to societies in which institutional supports for business are weak, as in Southeast Asia, by relying upon these personal networks and relationships. By comparison in the highly structured business environments of the West, the Chinese are considered to be at a disadvantage (Australian Department of Foreign Affairs and Trade, 1995).

Postulates:

- Most operations in the U.K. will take the form of new ventures at an early stage in the internationalization process. Manufacturing activities and acquisition entry will be little in evidence.

- The lack of business networks in the U.K. will prove problematic.

- Certain of the competitive advantages (e.g., large-scale, resources) possessed by enterprises in China may be transferable into a Western environment. Otherwise, with financial support from their parent companies, it may be possible to build competitive advantages in the West. In other cases, failure or divestment could occur.

- Among the longer-established Chinese enterprises in the U.K., there will be evidence of technology transfer back to China.

METHODOLOGY

Details of Chinese organizations in the U.K. were obtained from the *China–Britain Trade Review* (January 1997) (Hong Kong–based enterprises were not included in the listing since Hong Kong was a British colony at the time). The publication listed organizations under five headings: Chinese Embassy, Financial Sector, Service Sector, Import-Export Corporations, and Trading Companies from China's Provinces. The departments of the Chinese Embassy were omitted from the sample, as were Service Sector organizations such as the China Council for the Promotion of International Trade and the China National Tourist Office. Of the remaining organizations, a number could not be contacted and were presumed to have gone out of business, while several others (separately registered) were part of the same group. In total, 24 Chinese enterprises were identified, all based in the Greater London area. Enterprises were invited by telephone and letter to participate in both a postal questionnaire survey and a personal interview survey. Assisted by contacts and intermediaries in Beijing, 16 enterprises (67%) agreed to participate in the personal interview research (15 of these same enterprises and one other returned the self-completion questionnaires).[4] Interviews were conducted with the senior manager in the organization (managing director or chief representative) or his deputy and lasted between 45 minutes and two hours. A number of enterprises specifically requested anonymity in the presentation of the results. The structured self-completion questionnaires were analyzed quantitatively, while the semistructured and unstructured questions in the personal interview research were interpreted qualitatively.

EMPIRICAL RESULTS

Background

The basic characteristics of the sixteen Chinese enterprises in the U.K. are as follows:

- Fourteen were central government-owned, one provincial government–owned, and one a mixed ownership enterprise (which started as a private company but now has central and provincial government involvement).

- Seven operated in financial services and nine in trading and related activities including shipping; only one company had manufacturing as part of its portfolio.

- Except for one bank (Bank of China), which was set up in London in 1929 and had a number of branch offices around the U.K., the other banks had representative offices; the remaining enterprises had established subsidiary companies.

- Twelve of the enterprises were established in the 1980s or 1990s, and all had been established as new ventures as opposed to acquisitions.

- Most firms had other European (and other worldwide) operations. But, excluding Hong Kong and Macau, the U.K. represented the first international venture for ten of the sample enterprises.

- The average employment level was 31 (of whom seven were Chinese nationals), with eleven enterprises having 10 or fewer (mostly Chinese) employees.

The evidence is thus of recent and small-scale internationalization, as would be expected given the overall distribution of Chinese international business operations. Underlying this pattern are the economic reform process in China and the country's integration into the world economy through rapid trade expansion. Within the planning process for sectoral and geographical export targeting has been a recognition of the need for outward investment to support trade or bypass trade barriers. These influences are seen clearly in the annual reports of the sample enterprises, especially the trading companies. Emerging from decisions of the State Council in the early 1990s, the goal of building the enterprises into "first class transnational conglomerate[s]" with "global perspective[s]" through a strategy of "business diversification, industrialisation and internationalization" featured prominently in the annual reports of virtually all the trading companies. Among the interviewed banks, too, a typical comment was that "the Chinese government wants the banks to be international," although it was also pointed out that internationalization on the banking side was slower than among trading operations because "the central bank was concerned about losses on the Barings/ Sumitomo scale." The quantitative survey results provide confirmation of this finding: the top-ranked factor in Chinese firms' motivations for investment in the U.K. was "long-term strategic objectives of the parent company."

Considering the factors in the choice of a U.K. (and London) location more specifically, there are three broad categories of response, namely, knowledge/ information generation, trading opportunities, and market factors. These factors are linked quite closely to the nature of the enterprises that operate in financial services and trading; only two companies—in banking and insurance—service the 200,000-strong ethnic Chinese community in the U.K.

The mode of entry of the enterprises at date of establishment is as follows. The bulk of the firms set up representative offices initially; in the case of the banks, there was generally no option because of Bank of England rules (see also discussion following). But, in any case, the representative offices had the same functions of information and research on behalf of the parent or as part of planning for commercial operations: liaison with U.K. customers and suppliers (including correspondent banking) and organizing visits for delegations and training for headquarters' staff. For the few remaining firms, long-standing relations with and knowledge of the U.K. market enabled them to go straight into commercial operations with a subsidiary company.

Evolution of Chinese Enterprises in the U.K.

For the financial services enterprises the pattern of U.K. market servicing in 1997 had not changed as compared with the mode of entry. This was a highly controversial issue. All the representative offices had been established in the belief or understanding that the banks would be permitted by the Bank of England to upgrade to branch office status. The latter was regarded by the sample banks as providing the following advantages: facilitate commercial operations in the U.K.; borrow funds at low interest rates from the parent; no requirements to have bank activities audited; and valuable for staff training. All the banks were in continuing discussions with the Bank of England, which had expressed a number of concerns in respect of weaknesses in the Chinese central bank's supervisory and monitoring systems and in the fact that the parent company Chinese banks were excessively influenced by the Chinese government. A view was also expessed by the sample banking enterprises that wider issues relating to reciprocity and perhaps to China's application to join the World Trade Organization (WTO) were involved. The Bank of England had suggested that the representative offices convert to subsidiary companies in the U.K. However, this was not acceptable to the Chinese banks because it meant closer supervision by the Bank of England; higher costs of establishment and operation (e.g., legal, accounting, and auditing services); requirements for capital from the parent, thereby reducing the parent companies' capital base on their balance sheets; and a small U.K. capital base and hence limited lending capacity.

A number of related issues emerged in discussions around this controversy. A recognition of the need for reform of the Chinese banking regulatory system is shown in the research activities undertaken by the banks in London on behalf of the parent enterprises (see discussion following). The Federal Reserve in the United States appears to have similar concerns to those of the Bank of England and again has restricted the Chinese banks to representative office status. Three of the banks had recently set up representative offices in Frankfurt (with another currently considering this location): in part, this was due to more positive signals from the Bundesbank regarding branch licenses; on the other hand, there were concerns from the Chinese banks themselves about language issues and, more fundamentally, about their ability to generate profitable business in the relatively small German market. These same concerns must also exist in the U.K. because of the competitive situation, the limited trade between China and the U.K. (for servicing Chinese trading organizations), and the small size of the retail market already dominated by the Bank of China. Certainly, except for one responding bank, the enterprises did not yet appear to have identified potentially viable niche markets.

The pattern of evolution of the trading enterprises varied significantly. All had replaced representative offices by one or more subsidiary companies; but within the context of conglomerate parent company policies, there was evidence of a range of business strategies being pursued at a subsidiary level and with differing degrees of success. To some extent, the pattern is age-related, and thus the three most diversified enterprises were set up in 1979, 1986, and 1993, and they were the largest employers among the trading companies. One of these enterprises, with a core business in metals trading, owned a manufacturing business in building materials. It was formed in 1986 as a 50:50 joint venture with a British partner to manufacture a range of products that could not be delivered on time out of China; the Chinese enterprise increased its equity stake in 1988 and bought the remaining shareholding in 1992, when the British partner retired. Over time the warehousing and distribution function has expanded relative to manufacturing. Manufacturing competitiveness required investment in automation, which seemed to be resisted by the parent enterprise on the basis of comparisons with the labor-intensive techniques within China itself. The future of U.K. manufacturing is, therefore, in some doubt.

From the perspectives of strategic maturity and successful performance, the remaining two diversified companies (including SINOCHEM) provide interesting developmental models. The SINOCHEM strategy is closely modeled on the Japanese and Korean GTCs at both parent and subsidiary levels: with a core business in trading, subsidiaries were allocated specialist roles in the 1990s, and in the U.K. case the specialty was fertilizers; from this core, the strategy has involved wide-ranging diversification. Within the context of a charter from the State Council to pursue a conglomerate strategy, at U.K. level the policy of the shipping company has been that of controlled diversification into related business areas.

Of the other six trading companies, three were specialist traders—metal derivatives, metal physicals and futures, and commodity physicals (principally sugar). Their activities were conducted through the London Metal Exchange and London Commodities' Markets. These companies were very small employers, relying heavily on the skills of an individual trader. Although in theory the operations are locationally mobile, interaction with networks of brokers associated with the London markets and the development of trust are critical factors in tying the companies to a London base. To illustrate the point, one enterprise had two commodities' trading subsidiaries in London and New York, handling, respectively, physicals and futures, reflecting the specialties of the two markets. Employment expansion potential is limited, but the companies should continue to be successful, provided the specialist trading skills are not lost.

The final three trading companies were in a much more vulnerable position. With a decline in the traditional trading business of their parent enterprises due to competition, representative offices have been upgraded to subsidiary companies to build commercial business in the U.K. None of the companies had been given clear objectives by their parents and were still in the process of seeking profitable business, mainly linked to imports of consumer and light industrial goods from China, such as garden furniture, garden tools, brake pads, measuring instruments. Patterns reflect production difficulties in China associated with the inflexibility of SOE manufacturing, lack of concern over quality and delivery, and inability or unwillingness to design to customer requirements. Such factors led to marketing difficulties in the U.K., the latter being exacerbated by limited market research and more general marketing expertise and by price competition from other Chinese manufacturers. The future of these subsidiary companies is far from assured.

Technological Advantages and Technology Learning

Given the small sample size and the diversity of Chinese enterprise operations, it is not possible to draw general conclusions on the existence or nature of firm-specific advantages. As is apparent from the previous discussion, moreover, half of the sample enterprises were still investigating market opportunities, that is, methods of transferring parent company ownership advantages into profitable business in the U.K. Considering the results from the quantitative survey, the top-ranked competitive advantages identified by the sample were flexibility and adaptability, excellent customer relations, high quality of service, and servicing Chinese customers (i.e., captive market). Conversely, the main problems of Chinese enterprises in the U.K. were distribution networks, office costs, cultural barriers, quality of management personnel, and lack of marketing information.

The qualitative interviews permitted a wider discussion of these issues. Among the representative offices and the small importers, difficulties of accessing information and business networks in the U.K. were posing problems. As one company observed: ''The problem in China is corruption; here there is no corruption but we have no connections either.'' Such difficulties were accentuated on occasion by the inexperience of Chinese staff and rotation systems (see later).

At the other end of the scale, the two successful diversified enterprises were able to articulate clearly their competitive advantages. For the evolving conglomerate SINOCHEM, the latter were professional personnel, financial strength, buying power, knowledge of and support from the home market, and international presence and flexibility. For the shipping company, reputation (based on size, longevity, and international presence) and all aspects of nonprice competition (service, vessel scheduling, etc.) were stressed.

In the light of the evidence from the literature review, the advantages and disadvantages of state ownership were explored (see Table 9.1). Only a minority of companies were willing or able to respond on this topic. ''Reputation'' was the number one advantage mentioned, although it was stressed that it might be difficult to distinguish this from the reputation of U.K. management or reputation derived from an international presence. Nevertheless, even a company such as a metals trader argued that state ownership provided an impetus to the company in terms of financial support.

Table 9.1
Advantages and Disadvantages of State Ownership for Chinese Enterprises in the U.K.

Advantages

- Elimination of business risk ("risk is country risk," "can't see bankruptcies of state-owned financial enterprises")
- Reputation (linked to state ownership and security)
- Government as facilitator, including provision of finance
- Ensures independence of (small) company in U.K.[a]

Disadvantages[b]

- Limited investment support because of financial problems in China
- Increased bureaucracy and reduced flexibility
- Inadequate reward systems
- Emphasis on age rather than expertise in appointments/promotions

---

Notes:
[a] The insurance company noted that it was among the smallest firms in its sector in the U.K. and would be an acquisition target as an independent enterprise.
[b] Several of the largest established enterprises indicated that these disadvantages mainly applied to their operations in China itself. In the U.K. business was run in Western style ("no need for a hundred stamps"), and there was little interference or control from headquarters.
Source: Enterprise interviews.

The inefficiencies of state ownership associated with, for example, employment and management practices were still in evidence, but at the margin in the larger and longer established enterprises. These included policies of equal opportunities ("equal salaries"), underemployment of rotating Chinese staff ("floaters"), and the emphasis on age as opposed to expertise in appointments.

The literature on Third World MNEs, albeit relating chiefly to acquisitions abroad, has suggested possibilities for reverse technology transfer (from subsidiaries to parents). This topic was a major focus of both quantitative and qualitative surveys. In investigating the contribution of Chinese enterprise activity in the U.K. to the parent companies, the most important factors mentioned were strategic development, market expansion, and management skills; hence, the emphasis was on the implementation of corporate strategy. However, in response to the question on the benefits of the Chinese corporate presence in the U.K., management software, knowledge/experience, risk taking, attitudes, international marketing skills, and international network data all scored highly. It seems, therefore, that any reverse technology transfer that occurs is informal or, at least, has not been viewed in the context of technology learning or transfer.

This finding was confirmed in the qualitative research. There were only two

Table 9.2
Research Topics for Chinese Bank Representative Offices

- Management structures and activities of commercial banks in U.K.[a]
- New financial techniques/products (e.g., Smartcards)
- Financial developments in U.K./Europe (e.g., European Monetary Union, banking mergers, supermarkets as banks)
- Bank regulation/legal framework for banking[a]
- Banking failures
- Money laundering[a]
- Market opportunities for potential branch operations

Note: [a]Especially important for Chinese Central Bank.
Source: Enterprise interviews.

cases where a formal technology transfer process took place. The long-established Bank of China had set up a training center, running executive programs in association with U.K. universities for general manager-level bank staff from around the world; commencing in 1993, around 120 managers a year were trained in investment banking, coporate finance, and so on. Also the shipping enterprise had developed in-house training manuals, and the staff manual had been adopted at the head office; in addition, the U.K. operation was the first to attain accreditation, and staff had been sent to China to train home country personnel (this subsidiary had won the ''best overseas company'' award for the multinational group in 1993, 1996, and 1997).

Despite the inability to recognize reverse technology transfer or to formalize the process, the potential for learning was fairly significant, linked to information/knowledge generation, visits from delegations and external training, intragroup exchanges and meetings, and staff rotation.

Information/Knowledge Generation

This function was most obviously apparent among the bank representative offices. Table 9.2 summarizes some of the major research topics, which in most cases were those identified by the parent banks. Among the remaining firms, information generation had again been an important function during the enterprises' representative office phase but was less apparent among subsidiaries.

Visits from Delegations and External Training

Organizing visits for delegations from China was a common, if time-consuming and tedious, activity for most of the U.K. offices, especially where headquarters personnel were involved. Visits of suppliers, though less common, also did occur. Among the banks and a few of the trading companies, there was a regular, if small-scale, flow of staff for in-house training with, for example, correspondent banks; and one company had sent two staff for M.B.A. study.

Intragroup Exchanges and Meetings

Three of the groups operated with a European regional headquarters or a European holding company. The objective was to understand the market as a whole and prevent internal competition, but clearly there is a learning process through regular, usually annual meetings. In another two instances, biannual meetings of all overseas companies took place.

Staff Rotation

Many of the sample companies had a high proportion of Chinese staff. In four enterprises, Chinese senior managers had operated in the U.K. for many years (as when know-how was linked to a specific individual trader), but in general a rotational policy was operated, with two- to four-year terms being usual. Although a common feature of multinational management, in a Chinese context this policy was heavily criticized by virtually all respondents. First, it was argued that extended stays were necessary to achieve proficiency in English and to gain familiarity with the culture and business systems. Second and related, short stays generated short-term behavior and restricted the growth of firms. To quote one company: "In the first year you gain familiarity with the environment, in the second year you think of opportunities and in the third year you get ready to go home." By this view, a minimum five-year stay was required for planning purposes. Third, although rotation might be a general principle, on occasion no formal policies or timescales were in place. Executives might thus have their appointments extended on a year-to-year basis, creating uncertainty and problems for individual planning.

Despite these criticisms, there was a grudging acceptance that rotation could have "an important influence on managerial professionalism at head office." This was expressed in terms of Western management philosophy, style, and practices. Specific illustrations related to efficient time management, keeping appointments, speed of decision making within a system of formal investment appraisal, replacing inefficient managers, effective organization structures, operating an efficient service function, and so on.

The potential for technology transfer is thus very considerable, especially in a generalized sense of managerial competences as opposed to firm-specific capabilities.

Banking

The internationalization of banks for developing countries has a long history. Correspondent banking relationships appear to fail to provide the detailed institutional knowledge required for credit and market analysis and the necessary level of customer service. An initial step might, therefore, be the establishment of a representative office. Its role will include communication with customers and referring them to affiliates, banking branches, or subsidiaries, along with information gathering and assessment (concerning the host country's financial system, economic risks, local customs, and commercial possibilities for branch operations). A bank branch, a common subsequent step in internationalization, operates under home country control but can undertake all banking activities in the name of the bank. By comparison, a banking subsidy is a legal autonomous entity that is bound by host country law. Other modes of entry include joint ventures and consortium banking.

A feature of the banking industry is the continuing high level of government involvement: restrictions are imposed on market entry through, for example, the granting of branch licenses and, on continuing operations, through rules on capital requirements, liquidity, and so on.

In the case of Japan, Sumitomo Bank, Mitsubishi Bank, Mitsui Bank, and Yasuda Bank opened branches in London between 1918 and 1924. All were closed down at the start of World War II. The former *zaibatsu* (Japanese conglomerate) names were prohibited for the banks in the postwar years, but their successors opened representative offices or branches in the early 1950s. Thereafter, growth continued, and by 1985 25 Japanese houses were authorized to offer full banking services in the U.K. Concerns about over-representation of Japanese banks in London were linked to reciprocity issues and the reluctance of the Japanese authorities to allow more British financial houses to engage in securities business in Japan or to become members of the Tokyo Stock Exchange. While these were resolved, specific criteria, as laid down in the Banking Act, continued to be applied in considering applications for banking licenses. These concerned the quality and experience of management, proposed business activities, and so on. Moreover, in granting banking licenses, the Bank of England had to be satisfied that operations established in London would be adequately supervised by the home authorities in Japan. In any event, by November 1994 there were 47 Japanese banks in London.

The city of London is, of course, a major attraction for banking and other financial services companies of all nationalities as "the only true world centre." It offers a large and skilled labor market; a range of supporting services such as legal services, accountancy, telecommunications, specialized computing support, and a wide range of information providers; a well-developed legal, regulatory, and tax framework; and deep and liquid markets. Similarly, financial centers, especially London, rely heavily on reputation and a network of personal relationships. These agglomerative economics reinforce the position of financial centers like London and are not easily replicated.

Evaluation

A number of postulates were presented earlier derived from a range of streams of literature and existing evidence on the outward internationalization of Chinese enterprises. Evaluation of the survey data indicates the following:

P1   Activities were all in services (although one enterprise had a manufacturing arm also), a pattern that reflects early internationalization in support of trade and replicates both East European and indeed East Asian experiences. All enterprises were state-owned, apart from one "collective investing company"; the smaller, privately owned Chinese outward investors are more likely to share the characteristics of conventional Third World MNEs, focusing their activities upon neighboring countries.

P2   There was strong evidence of Chinese government "push factors" in internationalization and of long-term strategic objectives. However, at the level of the U.K. office or subsidiary company, a number of recent arrivals (mainly banks but also trading companies) had no clear plans and had not identified viable business opportunities.

P3   No data were available on the incidence of Chinese trade-supporting activities in other European countries; some enterprises suggested a much higher concentration of trade offices (in, for example, Hamburg). Interestingly, two of the three European headquarters/holding companies were located in Germany. However, the London commodities markets were a significant locational determinant for some trading enterprises, and certainly London was a major attraction for banking firms.

P4   Within the context of conglomerate parent strategies, longer-established trading subsidiaries were also diversifying. The most diversified sample enterprise specifically mentioned the Japanese GTCs as a model. There was still a strong specialist core trading activity within this latter firm, however, and a large shipping/transport conglomerate was pursuing a strategy of carefully controlled related diversification. Differing patterns of evolution were thus in evidence.

P5   Most of the trading companies noted growing competition and a loss of market share. This has mainly affected export business to China. Consequently, one of the diversification drivers has been the need to expand import activity and third country trade.

P6   Reflecting the observation under P3, a number of companies were involved in specialized trading activities—physicals, futures, and derivatives—through the London Metal Exchange and Commodities Markets.

P7   All operations took the form of new ventures as opposed to acquisitions and were wholly or principally involved in service industries. One company had mining and petroleum refining operations in the United States and was considering the potential for mining acquisitions or joint ventures in Central and Eastern Europe. Another trading enterprise had a manufacturing facility for motorcycles in Latin America and regarded joint-venture or wholly owned production in the West as a logical next step.

P8   The more recently established enterprises were facing difficulties in building business networks in the U.K., partly because of cultural differences, partly because of inexperienced personnel. Given the experience of the established operations, however, there is no reason to believe that differences in the concept of networks between China and the West pose a long-term barrier to business success.

P9   About half of the sample were still at an early stage of investigating ways of transferring parent company ownership advantages into profitable business in the U.K. Their firm-specific advantages included low cost, low technology manufacturing, and mass marketing allied to resources, whereas U.K. market opportunities are in higher value-added products and services and niche markets. It seems possible that a number of divestments may occur among such enterprises.

P10   The potential for technology transfer back to China is considerable. This mainly takes the form of "managerial professionalism," alongside characteristics of competitive advantage in service industries such as quality, delivery, customer service, and so on. However, in many companies the possibilities for learning have not been recognized in a formal sense, and there are considerable barriers to learning at parent company level.

The behavior of state-owned MNEs, of GTCs, and of Third World MNEs is thus helpful in understanding the early internationalization of Chinese enterprises. It is doubtful if a great deal more can be extracted from some of this allied literature, however, since the topics have not attracted significant research interest in the recent past. The literature on Third World MNEs has the strongest conceptual underpinning, although the mechanisms by which technological accumulation occurs have been explored to only a limited extent. There are suggestions of technology transfer evolution, beginning with inward transfer through equipment purchases, inward joint ventures, and so on and extending through to, say, acquisitions of R&D, marketing, or manufacturing companies in developed nations (Lecraw, 1993; Young, Huang, and McDermott, 1996). As this chapter suggests, attention also needs to be given to the processes by which successful new (green-field) ventures are established in developed countries and the contribution these may make to technological accumulation in the home nation. There are questions concerning the nature and extent of ownership advantages within the home-based enterprise and whether these are transferable into developed nations; whether state-supported companies can build ownership advantages *ab initio* within host industrial countries; and the characteristics, procedures, and processsses for technology transfer back to the parent company. Further conceptual development as well as empirical study is called for.

Brief mention was made of the literature on the internationalization process of the firm. These models have value in understanding the sequencing of Chinese operations abroad. To date, only limited evolution has been in evidence among the Chinese enterprises in the U.K. As the cases of the more mature enterprises revealed, nevertheless, future patterns of subsidiary development will be of major interest, especially in terms of choices among specialization/diversification and upstream/downstream, related/conglomerate diversification.

CONCLUDING REMARKS

Young, Huang, and McDermott (1996) suggested that Chinese MNEs (and Third World MNEs more generally) may seek direct capital involvement in developed nations at an earlier stage in their corporate evolution than has been apparent among equivalent enterprises in the past. This investment and the acquisition entry route commonly chosen would be aided by state ownership and a long-term strategic perspective on foreign activities. This study, based on a cross-section of Chinese enterprises, facilitates a broader perspective on Chinese internationalization. It is apparent that foreign activity has indeed been encouraged in the U.K. at an early phase of corporate development. In a significant number of instances, internationalization may, however, have been premature, with inexperienced management, a lack of planning, and vague objectives for the foreign operations; the long-term future of such operations is by no means assured. On the other hand, there is evidence too of parent corporation strategies of globalization and conglomerate development being implemented effectively at subsidiary level in a small number of sample enterprises (see also *Financial Times*, 14 August 1997). The strategic problems and dilemmas for such multinationals include those identified in the study of Young, Huang, and McDermott (1996). These include the "dual company" problem, especially that derived from Western management styles and practices versus management in state-owned Chinese bureaucratic enterprises; overly rapid expansion; and deficiencies in both the quality and quantity of experienced managers. For the successful future of such evolving conglomerates, profitable and competitive global activity is of paramount importance, if the companies are to manage the forthcoming shocks associated with enterprise reform within China.

ACKNOWLEDGMENT

The author would like to thank Stephen Young for his cooperation in conducting the research.

NOTES

1. Reference is made throughout to the "outward internationalization" of Chinese enterprises, rather than to "outward foreign direct investment" (FDI) and "multinationality." The reason for this is that a number of the ventures in the U.K. are representative offices that are not directly engaged in income-generating activity.

2. It is not possible to include a review of the very extensive literature on privatization. An interesting reference is Kumar (1993).

3. Space constraints prohibit a fuller discussion of host country influences on banking internationalization From the perspective of lessons from other countries, however, it is worth noting the concerns of the Bank of England regarding overrepresentation of Japanese banks in London in the 1980s. Specific criteria as laid down in the Banking Act are applied in considering applications for banking licenses. These concern the quality and experience of management, proposed business and income streams, and so on. Moreover, in granting banking licenses, the Bank of England has to be satisfied that operations established in London will be adequately supervised by the home authorities.

4. The questions in the self-completion questionnaire were structured, using a five-point scale. Although the tabulations are not presented here, reference is made at various points to top-ranked factors derived from these analyses. The quantitative results are available from the authors on request.

REFERENCES

Anastassopoulos, J.-P., Blanc, G., and Dussauge, P. (1987): *State-Owned Multinationals*. Chichester, U.K.: Wiley.

Artisien, P., McMillan, C. H., and Rojec, M. (1992). *Yugoslav Multinationals Abroad*. Basingstoke and London: Macmillan.

Australian Department of Foreign Affairs and Trade (East Asia Analytical Unit). (1995). *Overseas Chinese Business Networks in Asia*. Canberra: Australian Department of Foreign Affairs and Trade.

Balabanis, G. I. (1994). The Development of European Trading Companies along the General Trading Company Model and Antecedents of Their Export Performance. Ph.D. thesis, University of Strathclyde, Glasgow, U.K.

Cho, D.-S.(1987). *The General Trading Company: Concept and Strategy*. Lexington, MA: D.C. Heath/Lexington Books.

Hamilton, G. G. (ed.) (1986). *Red Multinationals or Red Herrings?* London: Frances Pinter.

Hamilton, G. G. (ed.) (1996a): *Asian Business Networks*. Berlin and New York: Walter de Gruyter.

Hamilton, G. G. (1996b). The Theoretical Significance of Asian Business Networks. In G. G. Hamilton (ed.), *Asian Business Networks*. Berlin and New York: Walter de Gruyter, pp. 283–298.

Heenan, D. A., and Keegan, W. J. (January–February 1979). The Rise of Third World Multinationals. *Harvard Business Review*, pp. 74–82.

Hinterhuber, M. H., and Levin, E. M. (1994). Strategic Networks—The Organization of the Future. *Long Range Planning* 27(3), pp. 43–53.

Jiang, Sou, and Lu, Juyong (1994). Strengthening the Management of Fixed Assets of Chinese Overseas Enterprises (in Chinese). *Multinational Corporation Studies*, No. 8.

Johanson, J., and Vahlne, J.-E. (1977). The Internationalization Process of the Firm—A Model of Knowledge Development and Increasing Market Commitments. *Journal of International Business Studies* 8(1), pp. 23–32.

Kim, C. W. (Summer 1986). The Diffusion of the General Trading Company Concept. *Sloan Management Review*, pp. 35–43.

Kojima, K., and Ozawa, T. (1984). *Japan's General Trading Companies: Merchants of Economic Development*. Paris: Organization for Economic Cooperation and Development.

Kumar, A. (1993). *State Holding Companies and Public Enterprises in Transition*. Basingstoke and London: Macmillan.

Kumar, K., and McLeod, M. E. (eds.). (1981). *Multinationals from Developing Countries*. Lexington, MA: Lexington Books/D. C. Heath.

Lecraw, D. J. (1993). Outward Direct Investment by Indonesian Firms: Motivations and Effects. *Journal of International Business Studies* 24(3), pp. 589–600.

Luostarinen, R. (1970). Foreign Operations of the Firm. Licensiate thesis, Helsinki School of Economics.

Ma, S.-Y. (1996). Foreign Participation in China's Privatisation. *Communist Economies and Economic Transformation* 8(4), pp. 529–547.

MacBean, A. (1996). China's Foreign Trade Corporations. In: J. Child and Y. Lu (eds.), *Management Issues in China: Volume II International Enterprises*. London: Routledge, pp. 183–200.

McMillan, C. H. (December 1980). The Rise of Eastern Bloc Multinationals. *International Management*, pp. 19–23.

McMillan, C. H. (1987). *Multinationals from the Second World*. Basingstoke and London: Macmillan.

Monkiewicz, J. (1986). Multinational Enterprises of Developing Countries: Some Emerging Characteristics. *Management International Review* 26(3), pp. 67–79.

Panagariya, A. (1995). What Can We Learn from China's Export Strategy? *Finance and Development* 32(2), pp. 32–35.

Sarathy, R. (1985). Japanese Trading Companies: Can They Be Copied? *Journal of International Business Studies* 26(2), pp. 101–119.

Tolentino, P.E.E. (1993). *Technological Innovation and Third World Multinationals*. London: Routledge.

World Bank. (1993). *China, Foreign Trade Reform: Meeting the Challenge of the 1990s*. Washington, DC: World Bank.

Young, S., Huang, C.-H., and McDermott, M. (1996). Internationalization and Competitive Catch-up Processes: Case Study Evidence on Chinese Multinational Enterprises. *Management International Review* 36(4), pp. 295–314.

Zhang, H., and Van Den Bulcke, D. (1996). International Management Strategies of Chinese Multinational Firms. In J. Child and Y. Lu (eds.), *Management Issues in China: Volume II, International Enterprises*. London: Routledge, pp. 141–164.

Zhao, Jingxia. (1993). Integrated World Economy and the Challenges and Opportunities for China (in Chinese). *Multinational Corporation Studies*, No. 8.

Part IV

The Lure of Chinese Management

Chapter 10

Chinese Small Business Management: A Tentative Theory

Siu Wai-Sum

INTRODUCTION

Research findings (e.g., Acs and Audretsch, 1990; Bannock, 1981; Birch, 1979; Bruch and Hiemenz, 1984; Hull and Hjern, 1987) generally conclude that small businesses contribute greatly to economic development. This assertion is also applicable to small firms in Hong Kong because they have played, for some time, an important role in the colony's economic growth (Brown, 1971; Owen, 1971; King and Man, 1979; Sit, Wong, and Kiang, 1979). In 1990 small and medium-sized firms (employing fewer than 500 staff) constituted 99.8 percent of the local manufacturing establishments, employed 87.03 percent of the total manufacturing laborforce, and contributed 82.85 percent of total sales (*1990 Survey of Industrial Production*, 1990). A longitudinal study (Sit, Wong, and Kiang, 1979; Sit and Wong, 1989) revealed that between 1978 and 1987 the contribution of small and medium-sized enterprises to employment and sales had increased, but the share by large firms had substantially declined. Given the importance of small firms in Hong Kong's economy, it is strange that no major research study has been conducted to examine exactly how and to what extent these Chinese small firms have managed to survive, grow, and succeed or, more specifically, how Chinese owner-managers formulate business plans, set corporate goals and objectives, manage employees, and make business decisions.

SMALL FIRM RESEARCH IN HONG KONG

To date, publications on small firm management in Hong Kong are few and scarce. Major research studies are based on economic perspectives such as town planning (Dwyer and Lai, 1967; Dwyer, 1971), urban development (Dwyer and

Sit, 1986), and economic development (Liu and Wong, 1992; Sit, Wong, and Kiang, 1979; Sit and Wong, 1989). Generally, it is concluded that factors such as the laissez-faire economy (Friedman and Friedman, 1980), sociocultural traditions (Topley, 1967; King, 1992), family networks (Wang, 1977; Redding and Hwang, 1986), psychological traits (Bond and Hwang, 1986; Bond, 1991), the entrepreneurial spirit (Redding, 1990; Siu and Martin, 1992), and marketing orientation (Siu and Kirby, 1995) are essential to the success of small firms in Hong Kong. However, management researchers have not provided a detailed analysis on the management practices of small firms in Hong Kong.

Moreover, further review of the literature reveals that the research undertaken has been generated in an ad hoc manner as a consequence of the general absence of a systematic approach, lack of a well-developed and grounded theory, and inadequate appreciation of the influence of the Chinese culture on management practices of small firms. In addition, much of the literature on small firm management has adopted the Western management paradigm. Though researchers such as Kindle (1982) and Waldie (1981) have pointed to the importance of using traditional cultural values in understanding Chinese management decisions, no major study of Chinese small firm management adopts this approach. Thus, this research redresses this imbalance by comparing the management practices of American and Chinese small firms and identifying in what way and to what extent they are different.

RESEARCH DESIGN

The design used for this research was a comparison between management practices between two groups, American and Chinese small firm owner-managers. To provide a basis for comparison, a questionnaire was drawn up using a series of assertions suggested by Hodgetts (1982) regarding planning, organizing, staffing, and controlling "principles" for small business management. A two-page questionnaire, including 25 statements concerning management practices and some questions about demographic and company profile, was sent to a sample of owner-managers in the United States and Hong Kong. Five hundred small firms were taken randomly from a larger mailing list purchased from the Small Business Administration of the United States. Also, 500 Chinese small firms in Hong Kong (with fewer than 500 employees) were selected randomly from the *Directory of Hong Kong Industries 1994*. The respondents were asked to circle a response indicating whether they strongly agreed, agreed, had no opinion, disagreed, or strongly disagreed concerning the statements. Ninety-four and 37 usable questionnaires were returned, respectively. This gave response rates of 18.8 percent and 7.4 percent, respectively, for the US and Hong Kong samples. As the Small Business Administration of the United States prohibited double usage of any addresses on the purchased mailing list, no follow-up has been conducted. Though the low response rate would to a certain extent influence the validity of this study, this pilot research is the first attempt to advance small business research in a Chinese sociocultural context and to consider the specific cultural influences on Chinese small firms advocated by Kindle (1982) and Waldie (1981) in comparison with their American counterparts.

RESEARCH FINDINGS

The comparison of means between the American sample and Chinese sample, as shown in Table 10.1, reveals that they are different at the 5 percent level of significance in the following management practices: formal employee appraisal (t-value = 3.82, p-value = 0.000); longer-term planning (t-value = 3.26, p-value = 0.002); training program (t-value = 3.17, p-value = 0.002); direct personal contact (t-value = −4.09, p-value = 0.000); downward communication (t-value = 4.87, p-value = 0.000); personal friendship (t-value = 4.36, p-value = 0.000); recruitment based on friendship (t-value = 4.06, p-value = 0.000); written rules (t-value = 3.82, p-value = 0.000); employees follow instruction (t-value = 3.73, p-value = 0.001); and day-to-day management (t-value = 2.37, p-value = 0.022). Chinese owner-managers in Hong Kong are neutral to the importance of formal performance appraisal. However, American owner-managers tend to accept that it is essential. Specifically, Chinese owner-managers have a more favorable attitude toward longer-term planning, compared with their American counterparts. American owner-managers tend to disagree with the notion that training programs are too expensive, whereas Chinese small firms are neutral to that notion. Comparatively, American owner-managers believe much more than the Chinese owner-managers that direct personal contact with employees will generate better results. Interestingly, Chinese owner managers agree with downward communication, while American owner-managers do not. American owner-managers are neutral to developing personal friendship with employees, but Chinese owner-managers show a favorable attitude. Both American and Chinese owner-managers show positive attitudes to hiring people on the basis of friendship; notably, however, American owner-managers have stronger unfavorable attitudes than their Chinese counterparts. Compared with American owner-managers, Chinese owner-managers tend to disagree less with the notion that employees only need to follow instruction. Regarding the use of long-term goals and objectives, American owner-managers tend to disagree more with the notion of concentrating more on day-to-day survival rather than long-term goals and objectives, compared with their Chinese counterparts.

The research results appear to suggest that the American and Chinese owner-managers are different in planning (longer-term planning and day-to-day management), human resource management (recruitment, training, written employee rules, and performance appraisal), and communication (direct personal contact, personal friendship, downward communication, and following instructions).

Table 10.1
Sample Mean Values of Respective Statements

Statements	U.S. Mean	HK Mean	p-value
Job should be clearly spelled out.	1.9	2.2	0.143
* Formal employee performance appraisals are not essential.	3.7	2.8	0.000
* Longer-term planning not important in small business.	4.1	3.4	0.002
* Training programs are too expensive.	3.6	2.9	0.002
Owner/manager should delegate decision making.	3.4	3.4	0.970
* Direct personal contact with employees generates better results.	1.6	2.2	0.000
Operating budgets are not important.	4.1	4.0	0.504
Committees are generally a waste of time.	2.7	3.2	0.060
* Downward communication (superior to subordinate) is much more important than upward communication.	3.9	2.8	0.000
Flexible working hours cannot work in small businesses.	3.4	3.2	0.371
Small businesses need not be concerned with social responsibilities.	3.9	3.6	0.078
Pay the person rather than the job.	3.1	3.0	0.575
Have some excess of inventory rather than risk running short.	3.0	3.0	0.846
If an argument occurs between two employees, the owner-manager should let it blow over.	4.0	3.7	0.155
* Owner-manager not to develop personal friendships with employees.	3.0	3.9	0.000
Written job descriptions are not important.	3.7	3.3	0.131
Decisions should not be made by anyone except the owner-manager.	3.9	3.6	0.073
Responsibility should be delegated, but authority should remain with the owner-manager.	2.7	2.6	0.706
* Hiring people on the basis of friendship.	4.5	3.8	0.000
* Written employee rules are not important.	4.1	3.6	0.030
* Employees only need to follow instructions.	4.4	3.5	0.001
"On-the-job" training is the most effective type of training.	2.3	2.1	0.262
* Concentrate on day-to-day survival rather than long-term goals and objectives.	4.1	3.6	0.022
Owner-managers hold general staff meetings with employees to discuss the work of the organization.	3.8	3.5	0.265
If an employee makes a mistake, discipline him/her right then and there.	3.2	2.9	0.067

Notes: 1 denotes strongly agree; 5 denotes strongly disagree.
*denotes statistically significant at the 5 percent significance level.

DISCUSSION

The reasons for such differences are unclear, but a possible explanation may be found in the influence of cultural values (Siu and Kirby, 1995). The 40 Chinese cultural values proposed by the Chinese Cultural Connection (1987) are widely accepted to explain the behavior of the Chinese. However, Kirby and Fan (1995) examine these 40 Chinese cultural values and find that they are not comprehensive enough to describe Chinese owner-managers and explain Chinese entrepreneurship. Thus, Kirby and Fan propose 59 Chinese entrepreneurial attributes under seven categories—national trait, interpersonal relations, social (family) orientation, work attitude, business philosophy, personal traits, and attitude toward environment—to explain the entrepreneurial behavior of Chinese owner-managers. Details are shown in Table 10.2. This chapter adopts Kirby and Fan's framework to explain the differences. A detailed diagrammatic representation of specific management tenets related to Chinese small business by integrating the general management practices (Hodgetts, 1982), entrepreneurial Chinese cultural values (Kirby and Fan, 1995), and the findings of the current study are shown in Figure 10.1.

Business Philosophy

Chinese owner-managers adopt a longer-term horizon in business planning. The business principles, for example, attaching importance to long-lasting relationships, not gains, long-term orientation, and the doctrine of harmony between people and nature, make Chinese owner-managers think longer-term. Thus, they are often willing to plow earnings into reinvestment and accept lower profits to maintain continuous production and competitiveness for the purpose of long-term profit or survival. These are characteristics of the long-term orientation of Chinese small firms.

Goals and Objectives

Though Chinese owner-managers adopt a long-term orientation in business planning, these research results interestingly reveal that they tend to concentrate more on day-to-day survival rather than long-term goals and objectives. It seems that fatalism (Redding, 1982), or *Yuarn* (Yau, 1988) in the Chinese culture, which is the deep sense of submission to all that happens as inevitable, makes Chinese owner-managers deny the need to calculate and plan for the future. However, *Yuarn* also leads to self-reliance, as suggested by Yau (1988). Chinese owner-managers try to seek interrelations with others or things in order to find out whether they have *Yuarn* or not. Thus, Chinese small firms are highly sensitive to changing tendencies and environments, and this sensitivity is deeply reflected in their day-to-day survival matters.

Table 10.2
Entrepreneurial Chinese Cultural Values

National Trait

1 Patriotism.
2 A sense of cultural superiority.
3 Respect for tradition.
4 Bearing hardships.
5 Knowledge (education).
6 Governing by leaders instead of by law.
7 Equality/egalitarianism.

Interpersonal Relations

8 Trustworthiness.
9 *Jen-ai* /kindness (forgiveness, compassion).
10 *Li*/propriety.
11 Tolerance of others.
12 Harmony with others.
13 Courtesy.
14 Humbleness (modesty).
15 A close, intimate friend.
16 Observation of rites and social rituals.
17 Reciprocation of greetings, favors, and gifts.
18 Repayment of both the good or the evil that another person has caused you.
19 Face (protecting, giving, gaining, and losing).

Social (Family) Orientation

20 Filial piety.
21 Chastity in women.
22 Loyalty to superiors.
23 Deference to age.
24 Deference to authority.
25 Hierarchical relationships by status and observing this order.
26 Conformity/group orientation.
27 A sense of belonging.
28 Reaching consensus or compromise.
29 Avoiding confrontation.
30 Benevolent authority.

Work Attitude

31 Industry (working hard).
32 Commitment.
33 Thrift (saving).
34 Persistence (perseverance).
35 Patience.
36 Prudence (carefulness).
37 Adaptability.

Business Philosophy

38 Noncompetition.
39 Not guided by profit.
40 Moderation, following the middle way.
41 *Guanxi* (personal connection or networking).
42 Attaching importance to long-lasting relationship, not gains.
43 Wealth.
44 Resistance to corruption.
45 Being conservative.
46 Long-term orientation.

Personal Traits

47 *Te* (virtue, moral standard).
48 Sense of righteousness/integrity.
49 Sincerity.
50 Having a sense of shame.
51 Wisdom/resourcefulness.
52 Self-cultivation.
53 Personal steadiness and stability.
54 Keeping oneself disinterested and pure.
55 Having few desires.
56 Obligation to one's family and nation.

Attitude Toward Environment

57 Fatalism (believing in one's own fate).
58 Contentedness with one's position in life.
59 Harmony between man and nature.

Source: Kirby and Fan (1995).

Figure 10.1
Chinese Small Business Management

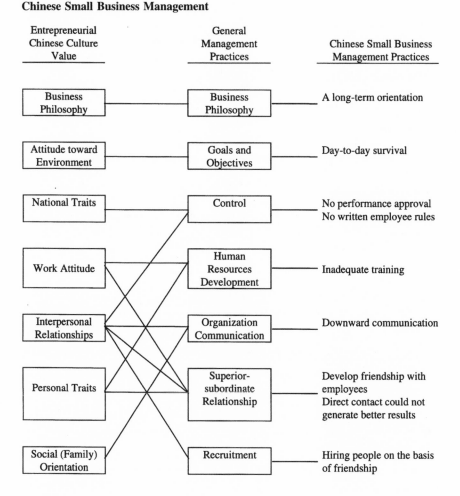

Entrepreneurial Chinese Culture Value	General Management Practices	Chinese Small Business Management Practices
Business Philosophy	Business Philosophy	A long-term orientation
Attitude toward Environment	Goals and Objectives	Day-to-day survival
National Traits	Control	No performance approval No written employee rules
Work Attitude	Human Resources Development	Inadequate training
Interpersonal Relationships	Organization Communication	Downward communication
Personal Traits	Superior-subordinate Relationship	Develop friendship with employees Direct contact could not generate better results
Social (Family) Orientation	Recruitment	Hiring people on the basis of friendship

Control

Chinese owner-managers believe that neither formal employee performance appraisals nor written employee rules are essential or important. Under the influence of "face," management control takes a different form and is more personal than objective, more informal than formal. The poorly performing employee will be informed by the owner-manager that he or she is unsatisfactory in a very subtle way, for instance, by denial of "face" or by withdrawal of supportiveness and friendliness (Redding and Ng, 1982). Thus, objective, systematic, and formal appraisals and written employee rules are not common in Chinese small firms in Hong Kong.

Human Resource Development

The self-cultivation personal trait makes Chinese owner-managers believe that employees should develop the business skills on their own. Also the principle of thrift (saving) work attitude also influences the willingness of Chinese owner-managers to put money into supportive functions, such as training. So, compared with the American owner-managers, Chinese owner-managers perceive training programs as being too expensive.

Organization Communication

Chinese owner-managers believe that employees only need to follow instructions and that downward communication is more important than upward communication. The principles of hierarchical relationships by status, observing order and humbleness, are the driving forces of these phenomena. They make the Chinese believe in modesty and self-effacement. The respect for authority doctrine influences the Chinese to trust without questioning. Redding and Richardson (1986) also confirm that Chinese subordinates are very submissive and play a consultative role in decision making. Given the high power distance in Chinese organization, as suggested by Hofstede (1980), it is understandable that the subordinate will ask few questions and only follow instructions.

Superior-Subordinate Relationship

Chinese owner-managers agree to develop personal friendships with employees but do not believe that direct contact could generate better results. This is understandable, as suggested by Kirby and Fan (1995); work attitudes like industry (working hard), commitment, thrift (saving), persistence (perseverance), patience, and prudence (carefulness) are important attributes to Chinese entrepreneurial success. Thus, direct contact with employees does not enjoy the supreme priority in management. However, the group orientation, the principle of intimate friendship, and the doctrine of harmony with others influence Chinese owner-managers to have close contact and association with employees and also develop a friendship with them.

Recruitment

Chinese owner-managers strongly believe in hiring people on the basis of friendship. It seems that the reciprocation of greetings and favors has provided a strong impetus for Hong Kong small firms to use social networks to operate. Trustworthiness and friendship are essential ingredients in the Chinese social network. Chinese owner-managers become known to a person by means of their relationships with others. Thus, the group orientation makes Chinese owner-managers feel less reluctant to hire employees on the basis of friendship.

FUTURE RESEARCH DIRECTION

Chinese cultural values influence the management practices of small firms in Hong Kong both positively and negatively. On the positive side, Hong Kong small firms, for example, possess a long-term orientation and put emphasis on building a friendly and supportive atmosphere in the organization. On the other hand, the cultural values also generate negative impacts. Training is not perceived as important, nor are objective control systems prevalent in Chinese small firms.

Though there is common agreement that the broad principles of management are applicable to small firms, the findings of this study suggest that these principles, specifically generated from the Western countries, may not be fully suitable for some specific sociocultural contexts, such as Chinese small firms in Hong Kong. Nevertheless, management tenets, ideas, and practices are being more widely used in small firms and are likely to be more intensively used in the future. However, the field of Chinese small firm management is still in its infancy (Siu and Kirby, 1995). Two important factors should guide academics and practitioners as they attempt to extend their knowledge of, and apply broad management principles to, Chinese small firms. First, care should be taken before making generalizations about management in Western situations based on evidence drawn from a particular situation and in assuming that management tools and techniques are equally applicable across all cultures. The specific business environments of Hong Kong (for example, its free economy, molecular organizational structure, and original manufacturing system) demand that caution should be exercised when generalizations are made. Second, research on Chinese small firm management is still embryonic, with major areas largely untapped. Cannon (1991) comments that the role and behavior of the entrepreneur in the development of small firms, for example, the mechanism by which the decisions are made and the skills and aptitudes that underpin it, have received little attention. It is widely held that the key to successful small firm management is the owner-manager. It is vital that the researcher should understand the cultural value orientation of Chinese owner-managers—why they behave as they do and how they make their decisions and choice, under the cultural influences.

From the research findings presented here, two directions for future research emerge. First, it would seem that the traditional Western management tenets may not be fully applicable to non-Western countries. Sociocultural influences should be considered when attempting to understand management practices of small firms in Eastern countries with developing and transitional economies. Second, perhaps traditional Western survey research methods, such as mail surveys, may not be very useful when trying to determine how and why Chinese small firms perform as they do. Qualitative research methods such as in-depth personal interviews or case studies may be one of the possible alternatives for advancing the knowledge of small business management.

IMPLICATIONS FOR SMALL FIRMS IN CHINA

The research results, though concentrated on Chinese small firms in Hong Kong, a very Chinese city with British characteristics, can be extended, to some extent, to other small firms in China. Siu (1995) reveals that owner-managers of Chinese private enterprises, mostly small firms, do not have very clear corporate goals. Networking (*guanxi*) is used not only frequently as a marketing tool but also in production and finance. Owners of private enterprises rely heavily upon ''contracting-out'' production jobs and obtaining financial support from various sources, including kinship and relatives. Chinese managers use compensation and reward rather than development and training in human resource management practices. All these conform to the research results of the present study. Specifically, management scholars (Boist and Child, 1996) propose that Chinese state-owned enterprises will move toward a capitalist regime. The transition of the China economy demands a search for new economic models. It is generally agreed that Chinese state-owned enterprises, inevitably, have to be reformed. Possible solutions, as suggested, are privatization and corporatization (Brown and Porter, 1996; Warner, 1996). Adopting these suggestions will inevitably scale down the operation size and lay off employees. Thus, how fast the reforms are likely to go depends on the degree of scaling down the large state-owned enterprises and the ability of small firms, specifically private and rural enterprises, to absorb the large-scale unemployed, underemployed, or layoffs (Davies, 1997). Nevertheless, issues related to how and to what extent small firms in China should be managed are not discussed in detail. Interestingly, however, management researchers (Chu, 1996; Redding, 1991) reveal that though social and legal factors influence heavily the business success of Chinese small firms, the strength of network ties is the fundamental source of effectiveness in Chinese business. Smart and Smart (1991) also find that Hong Kong small firms make use of personal relations and emphasize ties of kinship and other relations of commonality to attain success in China, where the legal system of economic regulation is underdeveloped, unstable, and subject to political relationships. Thus, the management model of Hong Kong (kinship-based, small family network) small firms may provide positive impetus to China's economic reforms.

CONCLUSION

China's economic reforms have produced many changes. Among the milestones has been the reemergence of private production and free market in the rural sector in Sichuan in 1979. Since then, the wholly private commercial enterprises grew alongside the devolution of authority, in the form of contract responsibility system, director responsibility system, and bankruptcy in the state sector. For the future, the development appears to be clear. First, the Chinese government will withdraw the commitment to state-owned enterprises by cutting financial support to loss-making enterprises, reducing the offer of social and welfare benefits to workers, leaving the state firms to concentrate their scarce resources on business operations. Urban housing, being heavily subsidized and allocated to the state-owned enterprise workers by the government in the past, will be privatized and turned over to the market economy. Chinese managers need entrepreneurial flavor to run the business in a market economy. Schumacher (1975) suggests that large organizations have to achieve smallness within the organization in order to facilitate entrepreneurship. It is expected that Chinese large, state-owned enterprises will scale down their operations to different small firms. Second, the economic contribution of the small business sector has come to the fore in China. It is generally accepted in the literature that small firms play a prominent role in economic development in relation to both growth of income and employment. According to the APEC Survey on Small and Medium Enterprises (1998), small and medium-sized enterprises in China constitute 99.95 percent of the industrial establishments, employ 84.27 percent of the labor force, and contribute 69.49 percent of the total sales of goods. Small firms will keep on playing an important role in China's industrialization. Thus, small firms, in both the private and state sectors, will provide the silver lining and hope for the future economic development of China and also may be a model for China's economy in the forthcoming millennium.

ACKNOWLEDGMENT

The author would like to thank Dr. Robert G. Martin for his kindness to permit the author to use the American data set for comparison purposes.

REFERENCES

Acs, Z. J., and Audretsch, D. B. (eds.). (1990). *The Economics of Small Firms: A European Challenge*. Amsterdam: Kluwer Academic Publishers.

APEC Survey on Small and Medium Enterprises. (1998). Member Report of the People's Republic of China. www.cier.edu.tw/sme/survey/s-prc.htm.

Bannock, G. (1981). *The Economics of Small Firms: Return from the Wilderness*. Oxford: Basil Blackwell.

Birch, D. L. (1979). *The Job Generation Process—Program on Neighbourhood and Regional Change*. Cambridge, MA: Massachusetts Institute of Technology.

Boist, M., and Child, J. (1996). The Institutional Nature of China's Emerging Economic Order. In D. H. Brown and R. Porter (eds.), *Management Issues in China: Volume I*. London: Routledge, pp. 35–58.

Bond, M. H. (1991). *Beyond the Chinese Face: Insight from Psychology*. Hong Kong: Oxford University Press.

Bond, M. H., and Hwang, K. K. (1986). The Social Psychology of Chinese People. In M. H. Bond (ed.), *The Psychology of Chinese People*. Hong Kong: Oxford University Press, pp. 231–266.

Brown, D. H., and Porter, R. (eds.). (1996). *Management Issues in China: Volume I*. London: Routledge.

Brown, E.H.P. (1971). The Hong Kong Economy: Achievement and Prospects. In K. Hopkins (ed.), *Hong Kong: The Industrial Colony*. Oxford: Oxford University Press, pp. 1–20.

Bruch, M., and Hiemenz, U. (1984). *Small- and Medium-Scale Industries in the ASEAN Countries: Agents or Victims of Economic Development?* Boulder, CO: Westview Press.

Cannon, T. (1991). Marketing for Small Businesses. In M. J. Baker (ed.), *The Marketing Book*, 2d. ed. Oxford: Butterworth-Heinemann, pp. 467–484.

The Chinese Culture Connection. (1987). Chinese Values and the Search for Culture-Free Dimensions of Culture. *Journal of Cross-Cultural Psychology* 18(2), pp. 143–164.

Chu, P. (1996). Social Network Models of Overseas Chinese Entrepreneurship: The Experience in Hong Kong and Canada. *Canadian Journal of Administrative Sciences* 13(4), pp. 358–365.

Davies, B. (1997). Painful but Inevitable Restructuring. *AsiaMoney* 8(2), pp. 40–42.

Dwyer, D. J. (1971). Problems of the Small Industrial Unit. In D. J. Dwyer (ed.), *Asian Urbanization: A Hong Kong Casebook*. Hong Kong: University of Hong Kong Press, pp. 123–136.

Dwyer, D. J., and Lai, C. Y. (1967). *The Small Industrial Units in Hong Kong*. Hull: University of Hull Press.

Dwyer, D. J., and Sit, V.F.S. (1986). Small-Scale Industries and Problems of Urban and Regional Planning: A Hong Kong Case. *Third World Planning Review* 8(2), pp. 99–119.

Friedman, M., and Friedman, R. (1980). *Free to Choose*. London: Penguin.

Hodgetts, R. M. (1982). *Effective Small Business Management*. New York: Academic Press.

Hofstede, G. (1980). *Culture Consequences*. London: Sage.

Hong Kong Directory of Industries 1994. Hong Kong: Chamber of Industry and Commerce.

Hull, C. J., and Hjern, B. (1987). *Helping Small Firms Grow: An Implementation Approach*. London: Croom Helm.

Kindle, T. I. (1982). A Partial Theory of Chinese Consumer Behaviour: Marketing Strategy Implications. *Hong Kong Journal of Business Management* 1, pp. 97–109.

King, A.Y.C. (1992). *Chinese Society and Culture* (in Chinese). Hong Kong: Oxford University Press.

King, A.Y.C., and Man, P.J.L. (1979). Small Factory in Economic Development: The Case of Hong Kong. In T. B. Lin, R.P.L. Lee, and U. D. Simonis (eds.), *Hong Kong: Economic, Social and Political Studies in Development*. Armonk, NY: M. E. Sharpe, pp. 31–64.

Kirby, D. A., and Fan, Y. (1995). Chinese Cultural Values and Entrepreneurship: A Preliminary Consideration. *Journal of Enterprising Culture* 3(3), pp. 245–260.

Liu, P. W., and Wong, Y. C. (1992). *Small- and Medium-Sized Firms and Economic Development of Hong Kong* (in Chinese). Hong Kong: Hong Kong Chinese Importers and Exporters Association.

1990 Survey of Industrial Production. (1990). Hong Kong: Census and Statistics Department.

Owen, N. (1971). Economy Policy in Hong Kong. In K. Hopkins (ed.), *Hong Kong: The Industrial Colony*. Hong Kong: Oxford University Press, pp. 141–206.

Redding, S. G. (1982). Cultural Effects on the Marketing Process in Southeast Asia. *Journal of the Market Research Society* 24(2), pp. 98–122.

Redding, S. G. (1990). *The Spirit of Capitalism*. New York: de Gruyter.

Redding, S. G. (1991). Weak Organizations and Strong Linkages: Managerial Ideology and Chinese Family Business Network. In G. G. Hamilton (ed.), *Business Networks and Economic Development in East and Southeast Asia*. Hong Kong: Centre for Asian Business, University of Hong Kong, pp. 30–47.

Redding, S. G., and Ng, M. (1982). The Role of "Face" in the Organizational Perception of Chinese Managers. *Organization Studies* 3(3), pp. 201–219.

Redding, S. G., and Richardson, S. (1986). Participative Management and Its Varying Relevance in Hong Kong and Singapore. *Asia Pacific Journal of Management* 3, pp. 76–98.

Redding, S. G., and Wong, G.Y.Y. (1986). The Psychology of Chinese Organizational Behaviour. In M. M. Bond (ed.), *The Psychology of Chinese People*. New York: Oxford University Press, pp. 267–295.

Schumacher, E. F. (1975). *Small Is Beautiful*. New York: Harper and Row.

Sit, V.F.S., and Wong, S. L. (1989). *Small and Medium Industries in an Export-Oriented Economy: The Case of Hong Kong*. Hong Kong: Centre of Asian Studies, University of Hong Kong.

Sit, V.F.S., Wong, S. L., and Kiang, T. S. (1979). *Small Scale Industries in Laissez-faire Economy: A Hong Kong Case Study*. Hong Kong: Centre of Asian Studies, University of Hong Kong.

Siu, W. (1995). Entrepreneurial Typology: The Case of Owner Managers in China. *International Small Business Journal* 14(1), pp. 53–64.

Siu, W., and Kirby, D. A. (1995). Marketing in Chinese Business: Tentative Theory. *Journal of Enterprising Culture* 3(3), pp. 309–342.

Siu, W., and Martin, R. G. (1992). Successful Entrepreneurship in Hong Kong. *Long Range Planning* 25(6), pp. 87–93.

Smart, J., and Smart, A. (1991). Personal Relations and Divergent Economies: A Case Study of Hong Kong Investment in South China. *International Journal of Urban and Regional Research* 15(2), pp. 216–233.

Topley, M. (1967). Some Basic Conceptions and Their Traditional Relationship to Society. In M. Topley (ed.), *Some Traditional Chinese Ideas and Conceptions in Hong Kong Social Life Today*. Hong Kong: Hong Kong Branch of the Royal Asiatic Society, pp. 7–21.

Waldie, K. F. (June 1981). Management—Western Ways and Eastern Needs—A Cultural Comparison. *Hong Kong Manager*, p. 19.

Wang, S. H. (1977). Family Structure and Economic Development. *Bulletin of the Institute of Ethnology, Academia Sinica (Taipei)* 44, pp. 1–11.

Warner, M. (1996). Managing China's Enterprise Reforms: A New Agenda for the 1990s. *Journal of General Management* 21(3), pp. 1–18.

Yau, O.H.M. (1988). Chinese Cultural Values: Their Dimensions and Marketing Implications. *European Journal of Marketing* 22(5), pp. 44–57.

Chapter 11

Raising the Dragon: Adaptive Entrepreneurship and Chinese Economic Development

Cheah Hock Beng

[I]t can be argued that China has a bright future ahead of it. With entrepreneurial vigour of the Chinese sort, every problem in the Chinese economy can plausibly be redefined as an opportunity. Every bust, inefficient, polluting state enterprise is a potential efficiency gain if it could only be managed by different hands. Every sign of the wasteful allocation of capital in the state-run financial system is evidence of how well things would proceed if only capital was allocated more efficiently. If it has grown this fast while being run badly, think how well China could do if it were run better.

(*The Economist*, 24 October 1998, pp. 13–14)

THE RISE OF THE DRAGON: ASPECTS OF CHINA'S ECONOMIC RESURGENCE

The rise of the four "little dragons" (Hong Kong, Singapore, Taiwan, and South Korea) in the 1960s and 1970s[1] preceded the rise of China (perhaps the mother of all dragons) in the 1980s and 1990s.[2] Since 1978 China's economy has experienced substantial growth, increasing international competitiveness, and a significant "catching-up" process.

Within a space of two decades (1978–1997), China's economy has experienced significant and remarkable changes, associated with a rise in real gross national product (GNP) per capita. One significant change was a shift in China's economic structure. The contribution of agriculture to gross domestic product (GDP) declined from 33.2 percent in 1976 to 19.7 percent in 1997, while the contribution of manufacturing rose from 30.1 percent to 39.5 percent over the same period. This has helped to raise China's ability to export, and increased export earnings facilitated growth in imports. The growth of China's exports was aided by a significant rise in the competitiveness of Chinese products. China has significant world competitiveness in the export of unskilled labor-intensive products, and, since 1975, its competitiveness in this field has risen further. In contrast, in agricultural- and mineral-intensive products, China's export competitiveness has declined below the world average.

These changes have contributed to substantial economic growth and transformation over a period of two decades. These developments demonstrate that there have been significant potential and opportunities for "catching up" by China with more developed countries,[3] opportunities that had been grasped earlier by Japan, Hong Kong, Singapore, Taiwan, and South Korea and, subsequently, by Malaysia, Thailand, Indonesia, and other countries. The changes in the development process can be traced to the entrepreneurial strategies undertaken by the state, by domestic entrepreneurs, and by foreign investors. The role that entrepreneurship (in different forms) has played in this transformation is examined later.

Specifically, it is argued that China's recent economic development has been promoted not by revolutionary innovations undertaken by creative entrepreneurs in China but rather by the rationalization of state-owned enterprises (SOEs); the growth of nonstate enterprises engaged principally in technologically mature and labor-intensive economic activities; product imitation, subcontracting, and other incremental and evolutionary innovations, undertaken mainly by local entrepreneurs in private enterprises; and spatial arbitrage and production and market diversification strategies undertaken by foreign investors and joint ventures. These are diverse forms of what may be termed *adaptive entrepreneurship*.[4] China's experience also suggests that such forms of entrepreneurship can offer significant benefits to developing countries (see Cheah and Yu, 1996; Cheah, 1998b).

However, the benefits of this form of development have been dwindling as the internal and external constraints intensify, and as the success of such development, in China and elsewhere, undermines both the domestic and the international foundations. The recent economic crisis that engulfed various Asian countries since 1997 and that is likely to spread to other regions in the world represents a significant transformation of the domestic and global economic contexts. Intensified competition for export markets from other Asian countries whose currencies have depreciated significantly will compound surplus productive capacity in a range of industries and intensify deflationary pressures. Consequently, the rise of the dragon occurs in a much more fearful world, including growing concerns about the rising dragon itself.

ENTREPRENEURS AND ECONOMIC DEVELOPMENT IN CHINA: THE AGENTS OF CHANGE

The changes just described can be related to developments and activities among the domestic (state and nonstate) and foreign enterprises in China

Figure 11.1
Industrial Production by Ownership of Enterprise (percent)

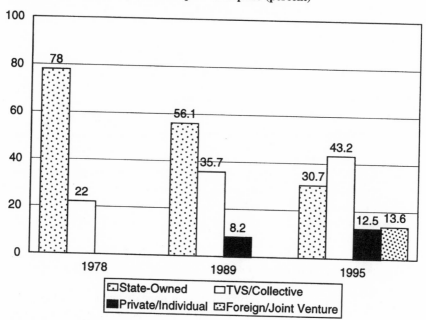

Source: Derived from Harvie (1997): 6.

and the different forms of entrepreneurship associated with them (see Figure 11.1).

Domestic Enterprises

State-Owned Enterprises (SOEs): Rationalization and Elimination of Economic Dinosaurs

Goodhart and Xu (1996: 13–18) have noted that Chinese state enterprises are organized not on a centrally planned, unitary structure that existed in the former Soviet Union but on a more decentralized, "multilayer, multiregional" basis. This makes economy-wide disruption less likely when external shocks occur and also makes it easier to introduce local innovations. In their view,

The Cultural Revolution . . . did have one entirely unintentional effect that was indirectly beneficial to China's long term growth. . . . by further weakening the powers of the central bureaucracy. . . . Power and control . . . was diffused and dispersed much more widely, regionally and locally. This enabled initiatives to be taken at lower (political) levels to establish institutions, both in agriculture and industry (TVEs), which were too small and too local to get (much) state protection. . . . rivalry between regions, provinces, etc., and between SOEs and TVEs injected considerable competition into the system. . . . competition, increased scope for individual initiative, notably in agriculture, and for an increasing share of the economy, in particular the TVE sector. (Goodhart and Xu, 1996: 37)

However, the operational inefficiencies and the substantial debts of the SOEs are a significant drain on state revenues through the requirement for state subsidies and loans from state banks (Harvie, 1997: 4–14). Despite their inefficiencies, the government continues to provide financial and other support to the SOEs because of the large number of workers that they employ and the social safety net (in terms of housing, educational, and medical services) that they provide to their workforce. Retrenchment of a significant number of employees in the SOEs to improve productivity and profitability, in the absence of alternative employment opportunities and of more comprehensive welfare services provided by the state, would lead many retrenched employees to become unemployed and would contribute to even greater social, economic, and political tensions in the country (Goodhart and Xu, 1996: 38). However, continued financial support to the SOEs is seriously undermining the viability of the state banks that provide the credit, much of which the SOEs would be unable to repay.

Reforms introduced in 1984–1986 sought to increase autonomy and accountability of the SOEs for price setting, output sales, and input purchases; to levy taxes on their profits; and to set performance targets for output, profit remittances, and taxes to the government. These measures were strengthened by the enactment of the Bankruptcy Law in 1986 and the Enterprise Law in 1988, and some inefficient and unprofitable SOEs were restructured or shut down. Some changes were also introduced to the employment system and the social benefits system in the SOEs, and from 1991 several large SOEs became joint-stock companies. Nevertheless, various state restrictions on SOE operations (e.g., price controls and quotas for sale of output to the government) continued, together with preferential access for SOEs to cheap raw materials, finance, and tax concessions (see Mai and Perkins, 1997).

After 1993 further reforms of the SOEs were promoted. These, such as the Company Law of 1994, sought to alter the governance structure (increasing management authority and reducing state controls, e.g., through corporatization), introduce a new accounting system, divest some SOEs of their ancillary functions and activities, and reduce staff levels. However, while the rationalization of SOEs (involving the restructuring, privatization, or bankruptcy of these enterprises) may be perceived to result in a dramatic change (and, in some cases, a remarkable improvement) in their operations, the evidence suggests that the change did not generally involve creative innovation, and many SOEs continue to perform poorly. Rationalization through cost-cutting, shedding employees, and adoption of "new" work practices that already operate elsewhere often requires only imitation and adaptation, not necessarily creative innovation. Despite the rhetoric, the move toward a "socialist market economy" appears to be a shift toward just another variant of a mixed capitalist economy.

Furthermore, in practice, various constraints have impeded the introduction of more creative and more revolutionary innovations in relation to the SOEs. Thus, in 1996 the government upheld the principle of maintaining public ownership as the cornerstone of the socialist market economy and maintaining public ownership over major SOEs in strategic sectors, such as petrochemicals. Besides the strategic factor and the danger of greater tension arising from more workers becoming unemployed and losing access to housing, health, and educational services from further rationalization of the SOEs, it has also been noted that "many of the money-losing government-owned firms are controlled by influential CCP [Chinese Communist Party] members. These individuals oppose further economic reforms on more than ideological grounds. Eliminating or downsizing these economic dinosaurs would directly impact the pocketbooks of CCP leaders" (Weidenbaum and Hughes, 1996: 221). In combination, these factors have limited the extent and the rate of reform of the SOEs (Weidenbaum and Hughes, 1996: 220–222; East Asia Analytical Unit, 1997: 331–352).[5] Perhaps the reform of the SOEs can proceed more rapidly and radically if nonstate enterprises were able to take over more of the burden of providing jobs, adequate incomes, and access to social services for the persons still employed in the state sector.

Nonstate Enterprises: Imitation, Subcontracting, Wheeling and Dealing, and Other Adaptive Strategies

While SOEs are concentrated in heavy industry, enterprises in the nonstate sector are engaged mainly in light industry. The nonstate sector includes a broad range of enterprises from urban collectives, to town and village enterprises (TVEs), private and individual enterprises, and foreign-funded enterprises, the latter comprising joint ventures and wholly foreign-owned enterprises. Several studies indicate that this sector has been more dynamic, has grown faster, and has surpassed the state sector in terms of output, employment, and exports (East Asia Analytical Unit, 1997: 355–373; Goodhart and Xu, 1996: 5–6).

Despite this, the nonstate enterprises had poorer access to bank finance, improved technology, skilled employees and managers, and adequate transport and distribution facilities and faced more government impediments. In this situation, nonstate enterprises have had to operate more flexibly and efficiently. Through strategies of imitation, subcontracting, wheeling and dealing, and other adaptive strategies, enterprises in this sector have coped with and overcome their difficulties.[6]

Many enterprises in this sector have capitalized on the lower cost of Chinese labor to gain competitive advantage in low, value-added manufacturing assembly and production, reliant on relatively simple skills and mature technology. They have contributed to China's growing competitiveness in unskilled, labor-intensive activities in recent years. To succeed, this development did not involve creative entrepreneurship, only relatively minor, incremental, and evolutionary adaptations. The relative ease of this development was also a significant factor in the speed and extent of the growth of this sector, once government permitted its emergence.

Foreign-funded enterprises now constitute a significant and growing constituency in this sector. They have facilitated and promoted the influx of simple manufacturing activities, and subcontracting, capitalizing on the large pool of lower-cost labor and other advantages. In this respect, these enterprises are transferring and replicating activities and strategies previously employed in other rapidly growing countries in the region.

Foreign Investors: Market Development, Subcontracting, Spatial Arbitrage, Diversification, Family Networks, and Other Strategies

In recent years, China has been the largest developing-country recipient of foreign direct investment. In the early 1980s, this was mainly in the form of joint development ventures directed toward offshore petroleum exploration. This has been declining and has been surpassed by investments in manufacturing, especially by extensive real estate development, focused on hotels and tourism-related projects (Broadman and Sun, 1997: 1).

Foreign direct investment into China began to take off in 1992, rising from US$11.2 billion in that year to US$43 billion in 1997. However, the location of the investments has been heavily concentrated on the coastal areas (see Broadman and Sun, 1997: 1). The sources of investment have also been rather concentrated, with the bulk of the investment coming from Asia, in particular, Hong Kong.[7] Among the foreign investors, the most significant contrast is between Western (American and European) investors and Overseas Chinese investors.

Western Investors

Foreign investors are generally required to operate as joint ventures (in the form of a limited liability company) in partnership with domestic firms, under arrangements where the domestic partner has greater control over the venture. The foreign partner contributes the finance and know-how, and the local partner contributes the site and the factory and deals with official agencies. The parties share operational management and profits. The joint-venture contracts usually last for 10–30 years. All assets accrue to the domestic partner at the conclusion, with provisions for some compensation to the foreign partner and for renewal of the contract (Weidenbaum and Hughes, 1996: 103–123).

While Western investors and Overseas Chinese investors were both attracted by China's huge market potential and other possibilities, the former tend to perceive negatively the uncertain and unstable aspects of China's environment. Consequently, they have not been attracted to China in the same proportions as the Overseas Chinese and have not profited as much from their investments as the latter.[8]

Apart from language and cultural differences, more fundamental reasons have been traced to the difficulties stemming from uncertainties and instability in China's environment that make it hazardous for most Western enterprises (Weidenbaum and Hughes, 1996:15, see also Elliott, 1998).

The situation can also be compounded further when officials too become directly involved in the situation (see Weidenbaum and Hughes, 1996:151; see also *Business Week*, 1998a).

These and several other circumstances make it seem impossible for Western investors to operate "normally" in China.[9] Consequently, they often seek to have clearer and better regulations, to "normalize" the situation. In many cases, the Chinese government is unable or unwilling to accede.[10]

Nevertheless, some Western investors have been successful in their attempts. One reason for this is their ability to establish a joint venture with Overseas Chinese to invest in China and to gain significant assistance from such a partnership (Weidenbaum and Hughes, 1996:174–179). Examples of American firms that have adopted this strategy to sell low-technology, but marketing-intensive, products include Coca-Cola, Kentucky Fried Chicken, Procter & Gamble, and Wal-Mart.

Another reason that enables some Western investors to succeed in China is their ability to gain special leverage with the Chinese government through possession of desirable high-technology. They include Boeing and McDonnell-Douglas in the aerospace industry and Motorola and General Electric in telecommunications and electronics (Weidenbaum and Hughes, 1996: 162–165). Such investors are the most likely to gain official approval to operate as wholly foreign-owned enterprises. However, in some cases, intercompany and international rivalry is tending to weaken the bargaining power of these investors.

Overseas Chinese Investors

The most important foreign investors in China have been Overseas Chinese entrepreneurs (see Haley, Tan, and Haley, 1998; Weidenbaum and Hughes, 1996; Goodhart and Xu, 1996: 36). These entrepreneurs generally began as small Chinese family businesses (CFBs) in Hong Kong, Taiwan, Singapore, and other countries in Southeast Asia[11] and developed into significant Chinese family business networks (CFBNs) in the Asian region, and, more recently, these CFBNs have begun to extend their activities globally.[12]

The origins and mode of operation of these enterprises illustrate the concept of adaptive entrepreneurship very well. Most CFBs began as small traders, itinerant vendors, artisans, or subcontractors; and many of the entrepreneurs had previously been employed as migrant laborers, small farmers, or employees of other private enterprises (see Wang, 1991; Rolls, 1992, and 1996).[13] Their initial business ventures commenced on a small scale, on an individual basis or a partnership, and often had to rely on support from family members or other persons linked by clan, locality of origin, dialect, or guild affiliation.

"Most Overseas Chinese businesses remain relatively small; [however,] over time, the total size of all a family's business may add up to a large conglomerate'' (Haley, Tan, and Haley, 1998: 117). Indeed, over time, the successful Overseas Chinese entrepreneurs have diversified into a wide range of products, services, industries, and locations. For instance, these entrepreneurs ventured from trading into restaurants and hotels, real estate management and property development, banking and insurance, transportation, agribusiness (rubber, sugar, palm oil, and pineapple plantations), manufacturing (food products, textiles and clothing, and electronics), and a host of other activities within as well as between countries (see Haley, Tan, and Haley, 1998: 58–59). Consequently, ''The net result of these cross-border investment flows by the overseas Chinese community has been the rapid emergence of a Chinese-based economy that is the epicenter for industry, commerce, and finance in Southeast Asia'' (Weidenbaum and Hughes, 1996: 16). In the process, the CFBNs have built up aggregate assets estimated at more than US\$500 billion (Weidenbaum and Hughes, 1996: 25).[14]

Remarkably, the management and decision-making methods of CFBs remain somewhat traditional, unorthodox, and even esoteric in certain respects (compared to modern Western business management methods).[15] For instance, various observers have suggested that the leadership in CFBs:

- Centralize authority with close and active (hands-on) control by the owner and/or the family.
- Maintain paternalistic relationships in a hierarchical organization.
- Undertake flexible and speedy action, based on ad hoc planning and reactive responses.
- Exhibit intense privacy and secrecy over information sources and activities.
- Make decisions intuitively, based on subjective gut feelings, experience, qualitative data, and informal sources of information.[16]
- Are able to see the big picture and to distinguish intuitively winners from losers.
- Perceive situations holistically and manage (craft) emerging opportunities and strategies.
- Rely on connections (*guanxi*), trust, loyalty, and patronage.
- Seek fortuitous circumstances, believe in *feng shui* (geomantics), and cultivate luck.
- Operate effectively and successfully in an ''informational void.''

One reason offered for their success is that membership in the extensive intra-Chinese trading network enables the CFBs to ''economise on the 'high transaction costs' associated with doing business in China and elsewhere in Southeast Asia'' (Weidenbaum and Hughes, 1996:52). While some aspects of the CFB's method of operation described earlier could also be applicable to creative entrepreneurs (who seek to promote revolutionary and frame-breaking innovations), it is argued here that several of the features of that method are particularly apt for undertaking adaptive entrepreneurship (i.e., incremental and evolutionary innovations) in uncertain and unstable environments (see Cheah, 1993; Cheah and Yu, 1996).

Viewed analytically, in such environments, CFBs, acting as adaptive entrepreneurs, seek to discover profitable discrepancies, gaps, and mismatches of knowledge and information that others have not yet perceived and exploited and to capitalize on the opportunity for gain or advantage that the discovery provides. In that process, the CFBs generate more knowledge about the situation, reduce the gap between themselves and the market leaders through a process of catching up, and reduce the general level of uncertainty over time (for themselves and often for others, too). Through activities such as arbitrage, speculation, risk taking, incremental and evolutionary innovation, and production of generic or no-brand goods or even through gross or outright imitation, the CFBs seek to respond quickly and flexibly to perceived market signals and opportunities ahead of others. Such activities distinguish them as adaptive entrepreneurs. Over time, the CFBs create wealth for themselves and others, promote development, and generate a tendency toward equilibrium.

From this perspective, it is not surprising that the CFBs, adaptive entrepreneurs par excellence, have invested substantially in China. While the historical, ethnic, and cultural affinities of the CFBs have been helpful and contributory factors (see Haley, Tan, and Haley, 1998: 28–69), the capabilities and experiences of the CFBs as adaptive entrepreneurs, familiar with operating in uncertain and unstable situations, characterized by significant "informational void," are of particular relevance and value in China as it seeks to manage the transition from a planned toward a more market-oriented economy.[17]

Viewed empirically, research has indicated (see Cheah and Yu, 1996, among others) that the CFBs and their associated networks in Hong Kong and elsewhere have invested in China to maintain or to extend the viability of their small-scale economic activities. Such activities have been very flexible, and they enable firms to survive on relatively small profit margins by being able to respond quickly to changes in market conditions. With limited overheads, machinery, and personnel, the opportunity cost of shifting to other sectors and to new activities is relatively low for such firms. The opening up of the special economic zones and other accessible production locations in China has extended the opportunity and the scope for such firms to operate.

Furthermore, investment in China also increases the scope for production and market arbitrage by overseas CFBs. They can arbitrage production activities, especially for labor-intensive and low-value-added economic activities by tapping on the lower-wage and more abundant supply of relatively unskilled employees available in the special economic zones. This has also been motivated by labor shortages and increased wage and other production costs in their original production locations in Hong Kong, Singapore, Taiwan, and other Asian locations. By these means, the overseas CFBs can maintain or even lower their production costs. Subsequently, the overseas CFBs can arbitrage between markets by selling their products to other (foreign) locations where they obtain higher prices for the goods. This occurs when these firms manufacture products in China for export to more developed country markets. The combination of production and market arbitrages can give rise to very significant profits for the investors.

Investment in China also enables the larger or more established overseas CFBs to extend their opportunities for subcontracting production to other (smaller) enterprises. Overseas CFBs utilize subcontracting when they do not have the necessary production capabilities and also when orders exceed their available production capacities. In some instances, overseas CFBs may operate solely as coordinating agencies, while production is completely subcontracted to enterprises in China and other locations. This practice also increases the flexibility and profitability of the contracting firm, as the subcontractors often bear the brunt of fluctuations in market conditions.

Investment in China also enables overseas CFBs to diversify the nature (product/service/industry) and the location(s) of their operations further. This enables them to have "more eggs in more baskets," thus extending even further the range and the mix of their conglomerates and their networks. By this means, they may acquire increased insurance and the possibility of greater stability in the midst of increasingly competitive and uncertain situations.

In all of the preceding respects, the overseas CFBs have engaged principally in different forms of adaptive entrepreneurship and have not engaged significantly in acts of creative entrepreneurship. Indeed, they have emulated some aspects of business strategies undertaken earlier by Western multinational corporations (MNCs). In the process, the overseas CFBs have become significant MNCs in their own right. This is another aspect of catching up in the economic development process.

The Entrepreneurial State: Evolutionary Innovation Toward a Mixed Economy in China

The notion of the entrepreneurial state is significant, first, when it is likely that the central (as well as other, lower-level) authorities in China will continue to retain partial or full control and ownership of a substantial number of state-owned enterprises for national strategic and other reasons, even after they have been appropriately reformed. The reformation process will itself be unavoidably lengthy.

Second, based on a broader concept of entrepreneurship linked to the quality of innovation and leadership, the efforts of the Chinese leaders and policymakers may also be assessed in terms of the manner and effectiveness with which they manage the process of economic (and other) changes in the society. In this way, just as adaptive entrepreneurs in the business field can adopt strategies ranging from imitation to various forms of incremental and evolutionary innovation, so too at the governmental and institutional level may the key actors be assessed on the quality of their efforts, ranging across a spectrum from "creative" to "adaptive" to "nonentrepreneurial." At this level, the nature, extent, and effectiveness of governmental entrepreneurship (innovativeness) can and do significantly influence critical conditions for corporate entrepreneurs, for better or for worse.

In this regard, the benefits of state entrepreneurship in the development process in China may be measured and assessed by the results reported earlier. While the efforts of the Chinese authorities to shift toward a more market-oriented economy, beginning with the reforms initiated by Deng Xiaoping in 1978, may be regarded as revolutionary and radical in some respects, it is significant that, so far, the reforms have been introduced in a relatively measured and phased fashion over time (extending over 20 years to the present). The authorities have not sought (or desired) to engage in a leap from a planned economy to an unfettered market economy.[18]

The reform process began in the agricultural sector during 1978–1980, when farmers were given greater autonomy in their production and marketing decisions. While a portion of their produce was acquired by the state, the farmers were permitted to sell the remainder, initially at government-prescribed prices and subsequently on the open market. The outcome was a significant surge in agricultural output, diversity, and productivity, improved living standards, and more affordable prices for agricultural produce.

In 1979, emulating the strategy adopted earlier in other rapidly growing Asian countries, the central authorities first opened four special economic zones (SEZs) adjacent to Hong Kong and Taiwan to attract foreign investment and promote export-oriented economic activity and foreign trade. In 1984 the relatively liberal economic policies in the SEZs were extended to Shanghai and thirteen other large coastal cities. In 1988 Hainan Island was made an SEZ, and the Pudong New Area economic development zone in Shanghai was established in 1990. In 1992 the economic reforms were extended to selected cities in the inland provinces and to the borders in the north, the west, and the south (Weidenbaum and Hughes, 1996: 79–88). Enterprises operating in these locations were freed from various restrictions that continue to apply in other parts of the country.

In this manner, the central authorities have adopted a cautious, sequential approach that sought to reform the economy, restructure agriculture and industry, and improve enterprise management and efficiency, while retaining control of strategic industries and SOEs, moderating the rise in unemployment and inflation, controlling political dissent, and maintaining the overall authority of the Chinese Communist Party. This complex juggling act is undoubtedly very demanding and difficult but, conceptually and in practical terms, it constitutes a shift toward a mixed economy. Such a move is not conceptually new, and for several decades various developing and developed economies have struggled to determine the appropriate balance and to find the most effective means and strategies to achieve it (see Polanyi, 1944; Myrdal, 1960; Shonfield, 1965, 1984; Young and Lowe, 1974; Strange, 1986; Levinson, 1988; Naya, 1990; World Bank, 1996, 1997). From this perspective, the efforts of the Chinese central authorities (see Mina and Perkins, 1997; East Asia Analytical Unit, 1997) may be viewed as an act of adaptive (not creative) entrepreneurship, despite the fact

that the consequences could have dramatic significance for a very large number
of the world's population living in (and also beyond) China.

Indeed, some comfort may be gained from this because, in this adaptive process, government officials, professionals, managers of business enterprises, and
academics and scholars in various parts of the world can offer advice, experiences, research, and even practical support to facilitate more effective changes.
While it may often be difficult to obtain consensus among the relevant consult-
ants and advisers on such a complex change, nevertheless, rational discussion
may be possible, and some reasonably sound suggestions and solutions may be
formulated (see Stiglitz, 1998).[19]

In this regard, some useful lessons may be gained from the experiences of
other transitional socialist economies (see Harvie, 1997: 38–53). The Chinese
authorities could also reflect on the experiences of the Singapore development
model and its particular forms of private sector and public sector interaction and
social engineering, guided by a paternalistic political leadership (see Cheah,
1997), as well as the Japanese and Korean development models. The experiences
of the Grameen Bank in Bangladesh may also have particular relevance for
providing effective access to financial resources to the poor in China (see Ravallion and Wodon, 1997; Khandker, 1996; Yunus, 1984). Thus, there is a range
of degrees, aspects, and dimensions on which national leaders and policymakers
too can be entrepreneurial (i.e., innovative).

WHITHER THE DRAGON? PROSPECTS FOR CHINA'S ECONOMIC DEVELOPMENT

Despite the significant achievements so far, the future prospects for China's
development are uncertain for a variety of internal as well as external reasons.
Domestically, the problems of undertaking effective economic restructuring in
a transitional economy will intensify. While there will continue to be significant
benefits from external trade and from the inflow of foreign investments, it is
likely that these will shrink significantly, that the balance will shift adversely,
and that the external difficulties will serve to compound (rather than to amelio-
rate) the domestic difficulties.

The domestic constraints include problems of excess and underutilized productive capacity (see Smith, 1998) and high levels of inventory, declining fiscal
revenues flowing to the central government, and growing indebtedness and financial burden of the SOEs. These are compounding the problem of the insol-
vent banking system. Furthermore, rising unemployment and growing inequality
threaten to foster social dissension (Weidenbaum and Hughes, 1996: 105–109).
Finally, the rising costs of corruption must be added.[20]

Internationally, two sets of constraints are becoming more pronounced. First,
there is the global economic crisis. The surplus productive capacity, voluminous
inventories, and deflationary pressures in China are also duplicated abroad.
There are substantial excess capacity, deflation, falling demand and declining

investments around the world (see Shameen, 1998). Trade frictions between the United States, Europe, and Japan carry the possibility of turning into trade wars, as America becomes the market of last resort for global exports. In this regard President Clinton's recent warning to the Japanese on their trade surplus with America carries ominous overtones, in view of China's growing trade surplus with the United States (see Skelton, 1998; Gray, 1998a; Forney, 1998). The recent currency depreciations of other Asian countries have also helped to reverse, to some extent, their previous decline in competitiveness with China. For these reasons competition will intensify further.

Second, there is a looming technology crisis stemming from the Y2K computer malfunction. This problem, associated with a date specification flaw in computer hardware and software, will cause severe disruptions in many organizations and countries (see Subcommittee on Government Management, Information and Technology, 1998; Cobb, 1998; Cassell et al., 1998). Among other consequences, it threatens serious domestic and international disruptions to trade and financial flows. The remedy for this problem is expensive and time-consuming. Consequently, it is likely that most organizations and economies will fail to resolve the difficulties effectively and in time. Indeed, serious difficulties in domestic and international transactions are likely to occur even prior to the beginning of the year 2000. Unfortunately, many Asian countries, including China, have not responded proactively to the situation and thus are poorly prepared for its severe impact (see Public Management Service, 1998: 19–20; Cassell et al., 1998; ESCAP, 1997; UNDP, 1998; Hiscock, 1998; *Bangkok Post*, 1998; Associated Press, 1999).[21]

Consequently, the times immediately ahead are likely to be more difficult for dragon economies, as well as for most other economies. In the near future, we are likely to see, in a forceful fashion, the collapse of many established companies and the (further) disintegration of some previously viable economies. In the months ahead, when the global economic crisis is compounded by the year 2000 computer malfunction and by failures of national and global leadership, the world will be confronted by a "triple whammy." It will once again become a jungle out there.

In these circumstances, it would be necessary to look ahead at least a decade or more, after the crisis has demolished the present tottering financial and industrial structures, within countries as well as in the world at large. Then it would be necessary to rebuild from the debris of the collapse new industries and institutions that are more efficient and more appropriate for the twenty-first century. It is principally in that context, not just the present one, that the role of entrepreneurship must be considered and that the rise of the Chinese dragon may be contemplated. At that point the necessity and the scope for creative entrepreneurship may be found.[22]

In this regard, creative efforts must focus on the need for a more economically, socially, and ecologically sustainable development process in China (and other countries). This will include the need for a revolutionary transformation in production and consumption processes (see Davies, 1987; Cheah 1998a), as well as a need for "new combinations" of market and nonmarket mechanisms (see Godfrey, 1997; Cheah, 1997), because existing market mechanisms can be as unreliable and as problematic as the nonmarket mechanisms that China has relied upon so far (see Strange, 1986; Levinson, 1988; Gray, 1998b; *Business Week*, 1998b). This can be achieved only by departing from the sterile debate between the purists of free enterprise, on the one hand, and those championing state planning, on the other. It is necessary to be able to recognize the flaws and limitations inherent in both, discover new, innovative ways to promote their respective strengths, and to integrate the merits of both market and nonmarket mechanisms (see World Bank, 1998: 111–129; Shonfield, 1984).[23] By these means, the raising of the dragon can be associated with the achievement of "sustainable abundance" for all of China's population. If this goal can be attained in China, it will have great significance for the rest of the world.

NOTES

This chapter was written prior to the end of 1999.

1. See Vogel, (1991); Watanabe (1992); Sarel (1996); Cheah (1998b).

2. See Goodhart and Xu (1996); Mina and Perkins (1997); Hu and Khan (1997).

3. For a qualified assessment of China's economic performance, see Hsueh and Woo (1996).

4. *Creative* ("Schumpeterian") *entrepreneurship* is associated with radical innovations that create or increase uncertainty throughout an existing system. Creative entrepreneurs seek to profit from the "new combinations" that disrupt an equilibrium situation and produce a movement toward disequilibrium. This involves the change of the existing system. Thus, creative entrepreneurial activities and processes are associated with, and are responsible for, periods of revolution. These activities and processes serve to produce and/or widen the gap between leaders and followers in an industry. In contrast, *adaptive* ("Austrian") *entrepreneurship* is associated with the discovery of profitable discrepancies, gaps, and mismatches of existing knowledge and information, which others have not yet perceived and exploited. The adaptive entrepreneur capitalizes upon the opportunity for gain or advantage that the discovery presents. Adaptive entrepreneurial activities help to increase public knowledge about the situation, reduce the general level of uncertainty over time, and lead to adaptive changes within an existing system. In this way, adaptive entrepreneurship promotes a tendency toward equilibrium and is associated with periods of evolution. These periods provide significant opportunities for followers to catch up with industry leaders. In this way, adaptive entrepreneurs help to define the full potential and approximate limits of a creative innovation. Over time, the dynamic interactions between entrepreneurs responsible for creative responses and entrepreneurs who undertake adaptive responses constitute the entrepreneurial process (see Cheah, 1993).

5. Nevertheless, World Bank data indicate that between 1990 and 1996, proceeds amounting to US$10.4 billion were derived from the privatization of the SOEs.

6. For a revealing, personal account of entrepreneurial wheeling and dealing, see Ye (1996: 106–117).

7. For instance, in 1994 out of the total of US$33.8 billion of foreign direct invest-

ment, nine countries contributed a total of US$31.5 billion. Of this, US$28.1 billion came from six Asian countries. This included US$20.2 billion from Hong Kong/Macao (Tait, 1998: 121;). From 1979 to 1993, Hong Kong provided 68 percent of all foreign investment in China, while Taiwan, the United States and Japan provided 8 percent, 7 percent and 4 percent, respectively (Weidenbaum and Hughes, 1996: 101). However, Broadman and Sun (1997: 17) suggest that as much as 25 percent of the foreign direct investment could have originated from China, due to "round-tripping" to benefit from the incentives provided to foreign investments.

8. Weidenbaum and Hughes (1996: 147–150) identified instances where Overseas Chinese family business networks have gained preferred treatment and the means by which this was achieved.

9. See also Weidenbaum and Hughes (1996: 124–147). Indeed, they have remarked, "Many Western companies, including the largest and traditionally most successful firms, are finding out that they do not possess the requisite capabilities for success in China, at least not yet." (18).

10. Weidenbaum and Hughes (1996: 150) asserted, "To do business in China today, one must—one way or another—have the government as a partner."

11. Significantly, "the family enterprise tends to be the basic economic unit in Southeast Asia" (Weidenbaum and Hughes, 1996: 53). Indeed, "In large measure, the bamboo network consists of cross-holdings of privately owned family-run, trade-oriented firms, rather than the huge publicly owned manufacturing corporations that are typical in the United States, Japan, and Western Europe" (Weidenbaum and Hughes, 1996: 27). This situation has undoubtedly contributed to "crony capitalism" in the region; although it is not the only form of crony capitalism (i.e., business activities based on informal preferential relationships), and crony capitalism in diverse forms is also found widely outside Asia.

12. According to Weidenbaum and Hughes (1996: 5) "It is becoming increasingly clear that the ancient Chinese trading tradition can adjust very well to the high-tech world economy that is currently dominated by the United States, Japan, and Germany, and that this Chinese approach to economic development can generate unprecedented wealth."

13. See the origins of the business empires of the Wuthelam Group, the Charoen Pokphand Group, and others (Haley, Tan, and Haley, 1998: 93–94, 124–125). See also Whitley, (1992: 53–63).

14. Opportunities for public participation in the activities and growth of those CFBs listed on stock exchanges are constrained. Weidenbaum and Hughes (1996: 103–104) have noted that CFBs "maintain considerable discretion over which business opportunities are offered to the public and which stay within the family's private holdings."

15. However, it can be argued that the difference is one of degree and not of kind. Furthermore, CFB practices are also evolving to incorporate more modern management practices as the children of the founders of CFBs return from undergraduate and graduate studies in the West, and as the CFBs begin selectively to employ educated professionals to manage their enterprises (see Weidenbaum and Hughes, 1996: 55; Haley, Tan, and Haley, 1998: 93–94, 96, 155).

16. "Numbers often come last. They are used to confirm the decision rather than to arrive at the decision" (Haley, Tan and Haley, 1998: 100).

17. Despite the capabilities of the CFBs and their attraction to China, the following is worth noting:"Even the most aggressive overseas Chinese investors concede that busi-

ness on the mainland is a risky proposition (as it has also been elsewhere in Southeast Asia). China is still an authoritarian nation, ruled by leaders with a great deal of arbitrary power'' (Weidenbaum and Hughes, 1996: 16).

18. Nor is such a move desirable or necessary. The Chinese leadership's policies and efforts have been perceived to be less radical than those initiated by former leaders of the USSR led by President Gorbachev, when he championed both ''glasnost'' and ''perestroika'' concurrently. Some observers (not least China's present leaders) have perceived the risks of disruption, failure and loss of control (power) of such a strategy to be too high and rationalized on that basis the wisdom of their more cautious strategy so far. Nevertheless, the controversy over a ''big bang'' strategy versus a regulated fizz will never be completely resolved (see Weidenbaum and Hughes, 1996: 89–90).

19. For instance, Stiglitz emphasized the need to enhance tax revenue and create an effective social safety net in the form of unemployment insurance and offered advice on reform of the financial system.

20. In China and elsewhere, corruption, wheeling and dealing, and the negative aspects of ''crony capitalism'' constitute a part of the dark side of entrepreneurship (see Weidenbaum and Hughes, 1996, p. 12).

21. China has been classified in the group of countries least prepared to deal with this problem. Reuters (1997) reported that in China only 8 percent of a survey's respondents had begun remedial action. However, Indian entrepreneurs appear to have taken up the business opportunities that have emerged from this problem (BBC, 1997).

22. Creative and adaptive entrepreneurs in China, within enterprises as well as in government, can help to develop in practice the new combinations of market and non-market mechanisms that integrate their respective strengths. In particular, there is a need for new and better mechanisms and institutions to promote the positive aspects of entrepreneurship, especially among the poor. The Grameen Bank in Bangladesh and the Economic Development Board in Singapore provide some examples worthy of consideration.

23. One specific implication is that the reform of inefficient SOEs should not mean a rush into unfettered private enterprise, for there is an important need for strong social institutions to maintain social capital, help the poor, and moderate inequity in the development process.

REFERENCES

Associated Press. (11 January 1999). China National Petroleum Official Predicts ''Disasters'' from Y2K Bug. http://y2ktoday.com/modules/news/newsdetail.asp?id=663& feature=&type=

Bangkok Post. (4 February 1998). 70% of Businesses in Asia Will Fail, Says Y2K expert.

BBC. (9 December 1997). Looking East to Answer Millennium Conundrum. http://news.bbc.co.uk/hi/english/special_report/1997/bbc_world_computer_week/news-id_37000/37862.stm

Broadman, H., and Sun, Xiaolun. (1997). The Distribution of Foreign Direct Investment in China. World Bank Policy Research Working Paper no. 1720, Washington, DC.

Business Week. (10 August 1998a). China's Army under Fire, pp. 14–17.

Business Week. (26 October 1998b). The Perils of Red Capitalism, pp. 22–26.

Cassell, J., et al. (28 October 1998). Year 2000 Risk Assessment and Planning for Individuals. Gartner Group Strategic Analysis Report.

Cheah, Hock Beng. (1993). Dual Modes of Entrepreneurship: Revolution and Evolution in the Entrepreneurial Process. *Creativity and Innovation Management* 2(4), pp. 243–251.

Cheah, Hock Beng. (1997). Can Governments Engineer the Transition from Cheap Labour to Skill-Based Competitiveness? The Case of Singapore. In M. Godfrey (ed.), *Skill Development for International Competitiveness*. Cheltenham: Edward Elgar, pp. 92–138.

Cheah, Hock Beng. (12–13 June 1998a). Beyond the Crisis: Entrepreneurship Challenges towards the Millennium. Paper presented at the University of Illinois at Chicago and American Marketing Association Research Symposium on Marketing and Entrepreneurship, Hong Kong.

Cheah, Hock Beng. (1998b). "Catching Up": Adaptive Entrepreneurship and Economic Development in Asia. In Y. Takahashi, M. Murata, and K. M. Rahman (eds.), *Management Strategies of Multinational Corporations in Asian Markets*. Tokyo: Chuo University Press, pp. 243–263.

Cheah, Hock Beng, and Yu, T. (1996). Adaptive Response: Entrepreneurship and Competitiveness in the Economic Development of Hong Kong. *Journal of Enterprising Culture* 4(3), pp. 241–266.

Cobb, Adam. (29 June 1998). Thinking about the Unthinkable: Australian Vulnerabilities to High-Tech Risks. *Research Paper* 18 Foreign Affairs, Defence and Trade Group, Parliamentary Library, Canberra, Parliament of Australia. http://www.aph.gov.au/library/pubs/rp/1997–98/98rp18.htm

Davies, S. (1987). *Future Perfect*. Reading, MA: Addison-Wesley.

East Asia Analytical Unit. (1997). *China Embraces the Market*. Canberra: Department of Foreign Affairs and Trade.

The Economist. (24 October 1998). Will China Be Next? pp. 13–14.

Elliott, D. (14 December 1998). Cleaning up Corruption. *Newsweek*, pp. 13–16.

ESCAP (December 1997). Year 2000. *Government Computerization Newsletter*, Bangkok, United Nations. http://www.unescap.org/stat/gc/gcnl/gcnl10.htm

Findlay, C., Phillips, P., and Tyers, R. (1985). China's Merchandise Trade: Composition and Export Growth in the 1980s. *ASEAN-Australia Economic Papers* no. 19. Canberra: ASEAN-Australia Joint Research Project.

Forney, L. (16 December 1998). China, U.S. to Address Trade Deficit. *Asian Wall Street Journal*, p. 10.

Godfrey, M. (1997). Introduction. In M. Godfrey (ed.), *Skill Development for International Competitiveness*. Cheltenham: Edward Elgar, pp. xv–xxix.

Goodhart, C., and Xu, C. (1996). The Rise of China as an Economic Power. Centre of Economic Performance, Discussion Paper no. 299. London: London School of Economics and Political Science.

Gray, J. (27 October 1998a). Protectionist Pressure Grows as US Feels Pinch. *Australian Financial Review*, pp. 7–8.

Gray, J. (4 December 1998b). World Bank Attacks Management of Crisis. *Australian Financial Review*, p. 25.

Haley, G., Tan, C. T., and Haley, U. (1998). *New Asian Emperors*. Oxford: Butterworth-Heinemann.

Harvie, Charles. (1997). Reforming China's State Owned Enterprises: What Can Be

Learned from the Experiences of Other Economies in Transition? Working paper WP97-1, Department of Economics, University of Wollongong.

Hiscock, Geoff. (24 April 1998). 2000 Bugs Lurk in Cracks All over Asia. *The Australian*.

Hsueh, T. T., and Woo, T. O. (1996). Chinese Economic Performance and Foreign Trade. In J. Kuark (ed.), *Comparative Asian Economies*, Greenwich, CT: JAI Press, pp. 305–363.

Hu, Zuliu, and Khan, M. S. (1997). Why Is China Growing So Fast? International Monetary Fund economic issues Paper no. 8, Washington, DC: IMF.

Khandker, S. (1996). Grameen Bank: Impact, Costs and Program Sustainability. *Asian Development Review* 14(1), pp. 97–130.

Levinson, M. (1988). *Beyond Free Markets*. Lexington, MA: Lexington Books.

Mai, Y. H., and Perkins, F. (1997). China's State Enterprises: Nine Case Studies. East Asia Analytical Unit briefing paper no. 7. Canberra: Department of Foreign Affairs and Trade.

Mina, G., and Perkins, F. (1997). China's Transitional Economy: Between Plan and Market. East Asia Analytical Unit briefing paper no. 5. Canberra: Department of Foreign Affairs and Trade.

Myrdal, G. (1960). *Beyond the Welfare State*. London: Methuen.

Naya, S. (1990). *Private Sector Development and Enterprise Reforms in Growing Asian Economies*. San Francisco: ICS Press.

Polanyi, K. (1944). *The Great Transformation*. New York: Rinehart.

Public Management Service. (1998). *The Year 2000 Problem: Impacts and Actions*. Paris: OECD. http://www.oecd.org/puma/

Ravallion, M., and Wodon, Q. (1997). Banking on the Poor: Branch Placement and Non-Farm Rural Development in Bangladesh. Washington, DC: World Bank.

Reuters. (10 December 1997). Asia May Lack Cash for Y2K Bug. http://www.news.com/News/Item/0,4,17211,00.html

Rolls, Eric. (1992). *Sojourners*. St. Lucia: University of Queensland Press.

Rolls, Eric. (1996). *Citizens*. St. Lucia: University of Queensland Press.

Sarel, M. (1996). Growth in East Asia: What We Can and Cannot Infer. International Monetary Fund economic issues paper no. 1. Washington, DC: IMF.

Shameen, A. (20 November 1998). After the boom. *Asiaweek*, pp. 61–65.

Shonfield, A. (1965). *Modern Capitalism*. Oxford: Oxford University Press.

Shonfield, A. (1984). *In Defence of the Mixed Economy*. Oxford: Oxford University Press.

Skelton, R. (21 November 1998). Warning of Trade Battle. *Sydney Morning Herald*, p. 3.

Smith, C. (16 December 1998). GM Seeks Ways to Boost Viability of New China Plant. *Asian Wall Street Journal*, pp. 1, 5.

Stiglitz, J. (20 July 1998). Second-Generation Strategies for Reform of China. Address given at Beijing University.

Strange, Susan. (1986). *Casino Capitalism*. Oxford: Basil Blackwell.

Subcommittee on Government Management, Information and Technology. (8 October 1998). *The Year 2000 Problem*. A Report by the Committee on Government Reform and Oversight to the U.S. House of Representatives, Washington, DC. http://www.house.gov/reform/gmit/y2k/y2k_report/

Tait, M. (ed.) (1998). *Asia Pacific Profiles 1998*. Canberra: Asia Pacific Economics Group.

UNDP. (1998). The Year 2000 Problem (Y2K) and Developing Countries. *INFO21*. New York: UNDP. http://www.undp.org/info21/new/n-y-dc.html

Vogel, Ezra F. (1991). *The Four Little Dragons: The Speed of Industrialisation in East Asia*. Cambridge, MA: Harvard University Press.

Wang, G. (1991). *China and the Overseas Chinese*. Singapore: Times Academic Press.

Watanabe, T. (1992). *Asia: Its Growth and Agony*. Honolulu: East-West.

Weidenbaum, M., and Hughes, S. (1996). *The Bamboo Network*. New York: Free Press.

Whitley, R. (1992). *Business Systems in East Asia*. London: Sage.

World Bank. (1996). *World Development Report 1996: From Plan to Market*. Washington, DC: World Bank.

World Bank. (1997). *World Development Report 1997: The State in a Changing World*. Washington, DC: World Bank.

World Bank. (1998). *East Asia: The Road to Recovery*. Washington, DC: World Bank.

Ye, Sang. (1996). *The Year the Dragon Came*. St. Lucia: University of Queensland Press.

Young, S., and Lowe, A. (1974). *Intervention in the Mixed Economy*. London: Croom Helm.

Yunus, M. (1984). The Grameen Bank in Bangladesh. *Group-Based Savings and Credit for the Rural Poor*. Geneva: ILO.

Chapter 12

Developing Virtuous Corporations with Chinese Characteristics for the Twenty-First Century

Ip Po-Keung

INTRODUCTION

What kind of corporation will be most adaptive and appropriate for China's present stage of economic development? In addition to the institutional and organizational features (''hardware'') of such a corporation, what are the moral and cultural characteristics (''software'') of it? What are the core values in its corporate culture that represent the spirituality of the corporation? Can this culture provide the needed agility, adaptability, and competitiveness for Chinese companies in the global economy?

This chapter proposes a concept of virtuous corporation using a notion of virtues drawn from Confucian resources. A set of Confucian virtues is identified: *Jen, I, Li*, wisdom, trustworthiness, honesty, integrity, responsibility, and hard work, among others. Core values, including Confucian values like harmony, *Jen* as caring, and trust, together with virtues, perform the constitutive and regulative functions in building the morality and spirituality of the corporation. The role of virtues in the development of the virtuous corporation is examined. Ways of institutionalizing virtue development by building the spirituality of the corporation are discussed.

The virtue theory proposed here is not of a reductive or replacement nature. The theory does not intend to claim that all morality can be reduced or is reducible to virtues or virtue morality. Nor does it intend to claim that virtues can replace all other forms of morality, including moral principles, or that virtue ethics can replace other ethics based on principles of rights and justice. What is proposed here can be seen as complementary to existing ethics. For a full moral development of the corporation, virtues play an important but by no

Figure 12.1
Moral Architecture of Corporation

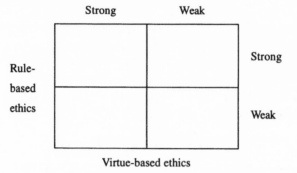

Virtue-based ethics

means exclusive role. Virtues are not sufficient for building a moral corporation.

Moral Architecture of the Virtuous Corporation

Ethics can be broadly be classified into two types: rule-based ethics and virtue-based ethics. Rule-based ethics use rules and principles to justify morality. Virtue-based ethics define morality in terms of virtues. No rules or principles are needed to ascertain the morality of the act or person concerned. Utilitarianism or contractarianism belongs to the first kind. Confucianism or other virtues theories belong to the latter. The nature of ethics that underlies and helps define a corporate culture shapes the moral architecture of the corporation. Similarly, a corporation can be rule-based or virtue-based in its ethics. However, this dichotomy oversimplifies reality. There are cases where both rule-based and virtue-based ethics are combined. Thus, we should allow some form of hybrid that integrates the two into the corporate moral fiber. Figure 12.1 depicts some possible mix of rule-based and virtue-based features.

The corporation that I propose as the virtuous corporation suited for the Chinese context belongs to the type with a mix of strongly virtue-based and weakly rule-based moral architecture. This architecture is broadly congruent with the dominant moral and cultural tradition as represented in Confucianism in China.

THE CHINESE CORPORATION FOR THE TWENTY-FIRST CENTURY

What will the corporation in the twenty-first century look like? In an earlier paper on virtual corporation (Ip, 1998b), I compared the differences between the traditional corporation/organization with the virtual corporation/organization. Even though modern corporations are far from being fully virtual, increasingly, more positive features of virtual corporations have been adopted by more and more corporations to prepare themselves for the next millennium. Table 12.1 depicts the differences between traditional and twenty-first-century corporations. To what extent the future Chinese corporation will have those features of the modern corporations as presented in Table 12.1 is not the focus of discussion here. Our concern is, What are the characteristics that a Chinese corporation needs to have in order for it to develop and flourish not only in the market socialism of the Chinese transitional economy but also in the twenty-first-century global economy?

I propose that such a corporation should possess the following general characteristics:

- It should be able to adapt and respond to both the Chinese developmental context and the global economy.
- It should be able to perform as effectively and efficiently as any other corporations of excellence with comparable competitiveness.
- It should be able to continuously innovate in its products and services.
- It should be able to create wealth and profit but also contribute to the common good of society.
- It should be able to make a significant contribution to the modernization of China.
- Its corporate culture should be a creative transformation of the cultural legacy of which it is a part.
- It should take critical assimilation of its core cultural values into its corporation cultures.
- It should be able to embrace as inclusively as possible all value systems within its culture.
- It should not be inward-looking but outward-looking to be able to forge dialogues and mutual understanding and learning with other corporations both within its culture and in other cultures.
- It should not be parochial in its values outlook but be ready to be open and accommodating with divergent views and values of the world.
- It should take morals and values as its core in its operations and visions.
- It should be able to transcend its narrowly defined economic goals and engage itself in its continuous moral-spiritual development.
- It should be able to learn continuously from itself and from others.
- It should be able to foster trust and cooperation both within the corporation and with its competitors.
- It should take due care and consideration of the impact of its plans and actions on all stakeholders and take due responsibilities for it.
- Its aims and goals should be compatible with the aims and goals of society, its nation, and humankind.
- It should have high awareness of its social responsibilities both as a corporate citizen and as a global citizen and discharge its responsibilities as required.

Table 12.1
Comparing Traditional and Modern Organizations

Dimensions	Traditional Organization	Modern Organization
organization structure	hierarchical	flatten
	bureaucracy	networks
	layers of middle management	no middle management
information flow	centralized	decentralized
	concentrated at the top	dispersed throughout
	unidirectional	bidirectional
decision making	many levels	fewer levels
	centralized	decentralized
	top-down	group
workforce	stationary	mobile
	local	global
	functional/department-based	project-based, team-based
	more in numbers	few in numbers
	single task	multi-task
	rigid	flexible
product/services	longer cycle	shorter cycle
	noncustomized	customized
	traditional	virtual
workplace	limited by location and time	flexible, mobile
asset	conventional	virtual
corporate culture	mistrust and check	trust and respect
	control and command	participatory

- It should respect and observe the universally accepted minimal ethical standards of corporate conduct.
- It should respect and observe the basic values universally accepted by the moral community.

These are indeed very broad and general conditions. They are surely not exhaustive. A corporation that meets all these conditions will be a highly idealized corporation. Corporations in reality, due to their different histories and unique circumstances, may realize these conditions in various degrees or realize the conditions at different stages of their development. There are diverse forms of corporations in terms of ownership and management responsibility in China today: state-owned enterprises, collectively owned rural county enterprises, jointly owned companies, privately owned enterprises, and foreign-owned corporations, to name the major ones. Under publicly owned companies, there exists a variety of forms: solely state-funded companies, collective economy, joint-stock system, joint-stock partnership system, entrusted management, and property management responsibility system (Li, 1998:13–14). With the exception of the foreign-owned companies, corporations should meet the conditions listed earlier. Foreign-owned corporations, though they need not meet *all* the conditions, should conform to a majority of them as they are applicable to them.

For the present purposes, we confine the discussion to the institutionalizing of basic values and the virtues in corporations in connection with the development of the appropriate corporate culture for the Chinese corporation. In what follows, I refer to the corporation that builds virtues as the integrative part of its corporate culture. Furthermore, a corporation that commits itself to virtues and is persistent in its practice of virtues is a virtuous corporation. I contend that in addition to meeting other conditions or features adumbrated earlier, a successful Chinese corporation should be a virtuous corporation.

Values in Corporate Culture

Corporate culture helps to enhance a corporation's adaptability in today's highly competitive environment. Corporate cultures can be strong or weak. Strong-culture corporations have a rich and complex system of values that are shared by the employees. The cultural complex of a corporation comprises values, key actors, rites and rituals, communication networks, and so on. Key actors are those people who personify the culture's values and as such provide tangible role models for others to follow. The rites and rituals are the mundane daily routines of the corporation, prescribing employees' desirable behaviors. The communication network is the "carrier" of the corporate values and heroic mythology, storytellers, "spies," "priests," and other actors. It forms a hidden communicative and social hierarchy that serves as a way to get things done or get access to information about the organization, its people, and their relationships (Deal and Kennedy, 1984; Davis, 1984; Hampden-Turner, 1990).

Values embedded in the organization form the heart and soul of corporate culture. Defining "success" in concrete and understandable terms for employees, values form the basis of a sense of shared mission for all employees and guide their daily conduct. Values differ in scope. Some are wide and general; others are focused and narrow. Strong values command people's attention; weak values are often ignored. Shared values are reflected in the mission and principal ethical standards of the corporation. If employees know what standards they are expected to uphold, then they are much more likely to make decisions that will conform to them. They are more likely to have a stronger sense of ownership of their responsibilities, which enhance job performance and work commitment.

Successful corporations put great emphasis on values. They display some important commonalities. They stand for something that they perceive as worthy of pursuit. They have a clear and explicit vision about how they aim to run their businesses. The management in the company takes great pains in shaping and fine-tuning these values to adapt and respond to the economic and business environment of the company. These values are then communicated throughout the company so that they are known and shared by all. The values of a corporation also help to form the basis of its cognitive, evaluative, decision-making, distributive, and communicative processes. Shared values are reflected in the corporate image to the outside world. Shared values affect corporate performance (Deal and Kennedy, 1984: 31–34).

In sum, the corporate culture of a corporation functions as a formidable normative and motivational framework for employees' conduct and performance. It helps to lay down for employees the basic values, beliefs, norms for decisions, and activities in both the strategic and operational endeavors of the company. What would a corporation's culture be like if it adopted the core values of Confucianism? I define a corporation as Confucian if its corporate culture (major values and practices) is Confucian. In what follows, I identify the core Confucian values and virtues that form the heart of corporate culture of a Chinese virtuous corporation.

Core Values of the Chinese Virtuous Corporation

What are the core values of Chinese virtuous corporations? I take the values of *harmony, Jen* as caring, and *trust* as the three core Confucian values to be implanted in the corporate value complex. In addition, the modern value of *respect for persons*, which has universal acceptability, should also be included. To briefly articulate these core values:

Harmony

Harmony should be the primary goal for human–nature, human–human, and human–self relationships, a cherished cultural tradition in China. Harmony should be the principal value underlying goals, shared mission of the members of the corporation, and shared purposes of the teams. It also should be the basis of human ethical relationships within the corporation and beyond. There should be harmony of other values and beliefs. Caution: harmony should not be achieved at the expense of diversity and freedom. Homogeneous harmony is boring and dangerous. It stifles creativity and free spirit. Harmony should be compatible with pluralism. Later in this chapter, there will be more discussion of this value in connection with the dark side of Confucian familial collectivism.

Caring

The moral feeling or sentiment of caring indeed is a natural manifestation of the Confucian mega virtue *Jen*. A corporation should show compassion and care for all its stakeholders, especially those less able to defend themselves (for example, employees, consumers, and nature). It should take due care of the welfare and interests of its employees and consumers, as well as society and nature, in conducting its business. Avoiding causing harm to stakeholders is the minimal care that a corporation should observe.

Trust

As well as a manifestation of the virtue of *Jen*, trust is a value that corporations cannot afford to ignore. Trust enhances cooperation and good performance by greatly reducing transaction costs in the course of business operations. It thus helps to boost productivity. Great corporations all have a strong culture of trust (Ip, 1998a, 1998b).

Respect for Persons

To respect a person is to respect the dignity of the person, to accept his or her person humanity as well as his or her uniqueness. Respecting the person also includes respecting the rights and autonomy as well as the integrity of the person. Corporations should go beyond the rhetoric of respecting the person and put the value into genuine practice by providing an effective enforcement mechanism and establishing rules and regulations for such respect. One of the most effective ways to do this is to institutionalize individuals' rights as employees' rights in the corporation and to establish enforcement mechanisms for their implementation and protection. Along with this "institutionalized" form of respect is an environment that enables employees to have the opportunity to grow and flourish in their professional and personal lives. People are the most important asset of the corporation. Only persons can produce and appreciate values. As a universally accepted value, respect for persons, though not explicitly endorsed in the Confucian moral enterprise, is not incompatible with the basic spirit of Confucianism. Indeed, the concept of *Ren* as the capacity to love others embraces a strong sense of respect for humanity, albeit in an implicit way. After all, to say that one loves humanity without respecting humanity is a contradiction in terms. As discussed later, this value requires particular emphasis among all four basic values, in view of the negative ramifications of the familial collectivism of Confucianism.

These values, though core, are not exhaustive. There are other values that the corporation needs to assimilate into its cultural fabric. For example, the Chinese socialist value of serving the people is one excellent candidate. More importantly, this value fabric is the moral space within which virtues are to be developed, enhanced, and promoted. Values and virtues form the edifice of the spirituality or moral backbone of the corporation.

Confucian Virtues: *Jen* and *I* as Megavirtues

Confucian ethics is predominantly *humanistic*, *obligation-based*, and *collectivistic* in nature. Its collectivism is vividly displayed in its emphasis on *collective* values and interests over *individual* values and interests. It is obligation-based because morality of human conduct is primarily articulated in terms of obligations. Since the family as the archetype of the collectivity occupies a core position in Confucian ethics, the version of collectivism that it endorses may aptly be deemed *familial* collectivism. Furthermore, Confucian ethics is not a *rule-based ethics*, like utilitarianism or contract theory, but basically a *virtue ethics* that defines morality primarily in terms of virtues.

Confucian ethics is built on the *Jen-I-Li* moral architecture, which defines and sustains morally and socially acceptable conduct. *Jen* refers to both a *capacity* for and an *act* of utmost benevolence and love.[1] *Jen* is what I refer to as one of the two *megavirtues* of Confucian ethics. The exercise of *Jen* generates a host of benevolent acts and conducts, which are in effect the manifestation of Jen in moral practices. Buttressing *Jen* is another megavirtue, *I*, which means moral rightness or righteousness. It also is deemed the principal moral norm for conduct and decisions. (*I* occupies a very central position in the doctrines expounded by Mencius. I take it to be a central tenet in Confucius ethics.) *Li* represents the many etiquettes, norms, and protocols in both everyday and institutional lives. Though *observing Li* itself is a virtue, *Li itself* is not a virtue, but the rules and norms that sanction conduct and attitudes. The basis for judging whether a certain *Li* is morally acceptable has to rely ultimately on the megavirtues of *I* and *Jen*. Broadly understood, the *Jen-I-Li* normative structure, with its array of moral virtues, provides an elaborate normative system governing morality of an individual's personal and interpersonal life. Indeed, *Jen* and *I* as megavirtues can be pictured as the core sitting at the center of an elaborate, interconnected web of virtues, each of which bears some relationships to each other, and many of which are manifestations of *Jen* and *I*. The whole web serves as a broad and comprehensive moral network to define and direct moral conduct. In addition to these three virtues, the virtues of wisdom and trustworthiness-honesty are equally important in one's character. Indeed, traditional Chinese culture took *Jen*, *I*, *Li*, wisdom, and honesty-trustworthiness as the five principal virtues in society.

Virtues as Attributes of a Virtuous Person

The qualities of a Confucian virtuous person can be seen as *virtues* of the person. In the classical conception, the following attributes as virtues are readily identifiable. The Confucian virtues are manifested in two forms: attributes of a virtuous person (superior man) and the qualities of a man of *Jen* (man of humanity). Putting these attributes of the two persons together, we have the following virtues of a person[2]:

righteous, wise, diligent in his action and duties, acts before he speaks, speaks according to his action, prudent in speech and words, acts according to his words, has filial piety for his parents, displays brotherly respect for his brothers, associates with men of moral principles, loves learning, loves men, broadminded and non-partisan, takes virtues seriously, observes rules of propriety, has good will towards people, accommodating, dignified but not proud, courageous, steadfast, self-reflective, self-motivated, fair-minded, chung shu (observe and exercise the gold rule: do not do to others what you do not want others to do to you), has clear moral sense, loyal, faithful, serious, principled and consistent (nonarbitrary), open minded (not dogmatic), flexible (not obstinate), not egotist, tolerant, reciprocates, compassionate, frugal, hardworking, perseveres.

Confucian virtues are principally social. Human relationships sit at the center of the ethical concern. Social harmony through the exercise of *Jen, I,* and other social virtues is one of the primary goals of ethics. Most of the Confucian virtues are applicable to the business context. Also, virtues can be grouped at three levels: individual, team, and corporate, each having special features and roles of its own (Ip, 1998a).

The Role of Virtues in Virtuous Corporations

The simple answer to the question, "Why are virtues needed?" is the inadequacy of the codes of conduct to provide the needed moral guidance to employees. Despite the serious efforts of many corporations to design and develop their own codes of conduct, codes *alone* are not effective means to enhance the morality of their employees. No matter how detailed the codes of conduct that are formulated, there tend to be areas that the codes fail to cover. There are always areas or situations that are morally ambiguous for which the codes fail to offer effective guidance. Employees in such situations have to use their own often uneducated and thus arbitrary discretion to make a judgment and decision. It is here that people feel anxious and uncertain about how to act or judge.

More importantly, when the codes are in direct conflict with personal interests, there is always a danger that employees will not follow the codes, especially when the temptation is great. Can codes of conduct *alone* be sufficient to provide the needed support and guidance to employees in situations of great temptation?

The answer seems to be no. What is the motivation for people to comply with codes or rules when noncompliance can bring more benefits than compliance? Can moral character help to reduce the danger of violation? In general, what makes people comply with rules and codes? I think the concern and commitment of the people concerned play a crucial role here. If people have genuine concern and real commitment to codes and rules, there is a high likelihood for rule-compliance. Indeed, what are referred to here as concern and commitment belong to the domain we call character and, ipso facto, moral character of the person (Kupperman, 1988). Presumably, the strength of the moral character (virtuous character) of the employee concerned can serve as a good predictor of whether the employee will follow the rules and codes. Without a virtuous employee, there is always the risk that the codes will not be consistently adhered to. Virtues seem to be the "last defense" in this kind of situation.

Can virtues alone be enough to provide employee support and guidance for actions and decisions? The answer seems to be no. Virtues have to be exercised in conjunction with codes and other means, which together form an interconnected action framework and constraint for moral conduct and responses. Virtues form an inseparable part of the whole repertoire of moral resources for proper moral responses.

Factors in Corporate Virtue Development

Following Confucius, we take it that virtues can be learned and taught. However, virtues have to be nurtured, encouraged, and developed in tandem with a host of other institutional, organizational, and motivational factors. To warrant effective changes in, or development of the moral character of the employees, the team to which they belong and the corporation where they earn their living should also be (or be developed to be) virtue-enhancing. A holistic approach to virtue development is needed. Such an approach will embrace factors including corporate mission, core values, policies, codes of conduct, systems and procedures, leadership, moral training and development, and ethics officers, among others. Virtues should be developed in close complementary relationships to the corporate mission and core values. The aims of virtue development should be clearly defined and communicated throughout the corporation. The ultimate aim of virtue development is to develop *autonomous moral persons* who are committed to live a virtuous corporate life.

In addition to the factors suggested earlier, effectively developing virtues in the corporation requires a program that includes the following major elements:

- Leadership
- Effective and open communication
- Enhance moral ownership and autonomy
- Continuous, sustained training and education

- Reward system for virtues
- Regular monitoring of results and improvement

Leadership

A successful program of virtue development must have strong leadership and strong support from the very top. Directors and chief executive officers (CEOs) should demonstrate their commitment to the program. The CEO and his or her representatives in senior management must take personal charge of the program. *Leadership by example* is probably one of the most powerful tools to foster change. Top leadership in the corporation as well as heads of departments and units should serve as good role models for employees. They should demonstrate their commitment by respecting virtues and, more importantly, "walk their talks." The influence from the top should not be underestimated. Employees should be made aware that virtues are positively endorsed in the corporate culture.

Effective and Open Communication

To build an effective and open communication system within the corporation is important. The aims and objectives of such a change should be clearly communicated throughout the whole company. Free discussions and criticisms should be encouraged. Units heads, managers, and CEOs should participate in discussions and dialogues. Management should make sure that everyone is involved, every issue is thoroughly discussed, and problems are identified and hopefully solved. An atmosphere where people can freely communicate moral problems without fear or embarrassment should be fostered. People should be made comfortable in discussing moral issues honestly and openly. They should be helped to understand their importance in corporate and personal lives.

Enhance Moral Ownership and Autonomy

To supplement the top-down moral leadership, a bottom-up involvement of all employees in the education process is equally important. A *participatory* approach is necessary. Employees should be involved in the identification and selection of the set of virtues that the corporation will adopt. Through participation, staff have a better grasp of the meaning of virtues and how they are related to moral practice. Better understanding will enhance their sense of *ownership* of virtues related to their workplace and task functions. Enhanced ownership contributes to employee moral self-mastery and autonomy. Over time, employees, through relentless practice and proper guidance, will finally become their own moral masters. Their maturity in virtue development can enable them to be good coaches and moral mentors to other junior staff.

Continuous Training and Education

It makes little sense to demand that employees take moral issues seriously if they do not have the awareness and the knowledge and skills to handle moral issues. Moral competence has to be taught and educated through various forms of continued education and training. Regular training is necessary to equip employees with the required aptitudes and competence. Effective training ultimately empowers employees in their virtue development and moral competence. *Ethics officers* may be appointed to provide this continued training and counseling.

Reward for Virtues

Though people's major motive to become virtuous persons is not based on material reward, some form of rewards, albeit nonmaterial, may give due recognition to achievement in this area. It helps to sustain the right motivation of people to continue to be virtuous and to motivate those virtue-blind to be more sensitized to virtues and the virtue-deficient to become virtuous. It can also help to strengthen employees' awareness of the importance of virtues as recognized by the corporation.

Regular Monitoring of Results and Improvement

Virtue development, like other moral development, is a long and complicated process. One should not expect measurable results overnight. However, regular monitoring of the results of the programs is necessary to make sure that they are effective and relevant. Continued learning from the results, regular assessment of the system, and continued improvement should be the norm.

What motivates employees to value virtues? What motivates them to exercise virtues when they are needed? For employees, their corporation's culture, CEO, immediate superior, peers, and circumstances all constitute the institutional/organizational context as well as the circumstantial context within which they perform. Employees' virtues are subject to the influences of these forces, too. Employees' *moral character as virtues* cannot be seen as immune from the corporate culture, the workplace, and the character of their superior and peers. Their character is plastic and in the process of shaping and reshaping itself by external forces as well as by their own effort. Through the conscious and sustained effort of enlightened education and training, virtues can be implanted in an employee, further strengthened, consolidated, and endorsed.

THE DARK SIDE OF THE CHINESE CORPORATION AND WAYS TO CURE

I have so far concentrated on the positive side of the Confucianism and focused on the virtue aspects of the Confucian value complex. However, negative elements within the complex of the Confucian value system need to be identified and addressed, especially in connection with the building of the virtuous corporation. The negative elements that may hinder the development of a robust Chinese virtuous corporation are familial collectivism, blind obedience to authority, subservience, authoritarianism, and nepotism, which constitute the downside of Confucianism.

Let us first address the issue of familial collectivism. Familial collectivism[3] has its roots deep in Chinese culture and classical Confucianism. In traditional China, central to the set of behavioral norms framed by the *Jen-I-Li* system was the family-based principle of *filial piety*. People observed filial piety almost with blind faith. As a cardinal principle, it dictated the desirable and proper human relationships within the family and beyond. The emperor of the Confucian state indeed ruled his subjects very much like a father taking care of his children. Heads of states, under the mandate of heaven, ran the country like running a family. Thus, there is a natural extension of filial piety from the family to the state. The extension of this principle to the political sphere generated the principle of *loyalty*. The object of loyalty was the emperor, who in a sense was depicted as the head political figure. *Classics on Filial Piety* explicitly stated this extension: "To serve the emperor with filial piety is tantamount to loyalty." Also, it had an important place in the moral architecture: "Filial piety is fundamental to *Jen*."

As a result of the paramount importance given to filial piety in both family and state, it dominated and defined all other salient human relationships, as society was a relatively underdeveloped social entity in traditional China. On the other hand, filial piety presupposes a hierarchical type of human relationships that are natural within the family context. However, when filial piety as a cardinal principle is practiced as an all-encompassing principle, the hierarchical human relationships that go with it become pervasive in all social relationships. There is nothing wrong for a hierarchical relationship to exist in the family structure, at least to some extent. It is, however, dangerous to have this hierarchical human relationships be *the* principal human relationships within society. The pervasive practice of filial piety sanctioned a *hierarchical* structure of human relationships in society, which is undesirable for the development of the value of equality of persons and with it the equal respect of persons, which are so valued in modern society.

The Hierarchical Relationship Underlying Filial Piety

The social and institutional manifestation of the Confucian familial collectivism is the *family* or the *clan*. Throughout Chinese history, the most prominent basic institution of China has been the family. Within the family, the *hierarchical relationship* dominated all major human relationships. This was a natural consequence of enshrining filial piety as the cardinal human relationship. There was no equality among persons within this social setting. The hierarchically structured family as a basic institution thus dictated the substantive content of permissible conduct in which a person could engage. The upshot of this social arrangement was that there were no equals within this dominant social environment.[4] The notion of *equal persons* and *equal respect for persons* simply did not have a place in this fundamentally important social setting. Permissible conduct or behaviors within such a social setting would take the form of *obligations* and *duties* rather than rights.

On the societal level, there were the *five basic human relationships* as conceived by Confucianism. However, the underlying nature of these relationships was essentially one of *subservience and domination*. Again, equality and equal respect of persons simply had no place in these all-encompassing social orderings. The five relationships—emperor–officials; father–son; brother–brother, husband–wife; and between friends—with the exception of the last one, all exhibited a strong dominator-subordinate relationship. Within the five salient social relationships, three cardinal norms governed and constrained them. They were highly *status-bound* and *status-regarding* norms. The emperor, the father, and the husband occupied these norm-generating and norm-dictating statuses and positions. They invariably demanded a *subservient observance* and respect from the official, the son, and the wife, respectively. There were no reciprocal respects from the former to the latter. Indeed, respect was *nonreciprocal* and one-way. As a result of this norm-setting of human relationships, the relationships were one of domination-cum-subordination. There was no equality among these relationships. Other social relationships and configurations would spin around these unequal and domination-cum-subordinate social arrangements.

Reinforcing this domination-subordination relationship was the unifying norm of filial piety as alluded to earlier. Therefore, within the basic institution of the family, the structure of the human relationship was highly inhibitory of the emergence of the culture of equal respect for persons, which would be essential to the development and recognition of individual rights.[5]

There were mutual reinforcements between ideology and institutions in traditional China. Confucian familial collectivism provided the moral and ideological foundation for the family. The development of the family as an institution in turn helped to sustain the correctness of Confucian familial collectivism, which lay at its very foundation. Beyond the family, the remaining basic institutions like the state, society, and legal system were just as inhibitory of individuality and respect for persons as the family.[6]

CONFUCIAN FAMILIAL COLLECTIVISM IN ACTION: CONFUCIAN CORPORATION

On the basis of the preceding discussion, it is not difficult to envisage how Confucian familial collectivism defines and shapes a corporation in its basic values and practices. I define a corporation as Confucian if its basic values and practices are Confucian. A Weberian, ideal-type Confucian corporation will presumably endorse as its core values collectivism, harmony, obedience to authority, paternalism, familial connections, and particularism, among others. It will probably have a hierarchical organizational structure and authoritarian, top-down style of decision making. The Confucian corporation will also be obligation-based with regard to its demand on employees' loyalty and commitment, as well as interpersonal relationships.

The core values of the Confucian corporation in effect furnish a framework within which it designs, develops, and implements its policies, with regard to both its strategic and operational goals and activities. Such goals, policies, and operations have a profound impact on its employees. The interesting question is to see how these values relate to the values introduced earlier: harmony, caring, trust, and respect for persons. Are the two sets incompatible with each other? If so, how could we resolve the incompatibility?

Given what has been said about the negative impact of Confucian familial collectivism on the values of equality and respect for persons, it is not unnatural to raise concern about the prospect for the individual person within a corporation dictated by familial collectivism. Let us highlight some of the major reasons for this concern. First, there are tensions between the familial collectivism and the respect for the person and the related values. The major ones are harmony, particularism, and paternalism.

Harmony

Harmony itself is a highly cherished goal for organizations. However, in the context of a collectivism-based corporation, without the strong safeguard of equal respect for the person, the individual's interests and needs as well as rights will often be unduly suppressed or compromised for the alleged collective good of the company. Sometimes, without an effective mechanism for checking abuses and a transparent management system, what is referred to as collective good is often in effect the disguised personal good of the proprietor or his or her family members. In normal circumstances, conflicts within the organization tend to disturb and disrupt harmony and should be avoided or minimized. However, conflicts or disharmony can also be seen as effects of a variety of causes, not all of which are bad. Therefore, they should not be automatically seen as detrimental to the well-being of the corporation. Reasoned conflicts in the form of honest and rational disagreement over policies and practices within the corporation can help expose deep-seated prejudices and unveil unquestioned assumptions and can unravel problematic areas that required rethinking and reforms as well as avoid dogmatism and open up new ways of thinking and doing things. They are also instrumental in unleashing from employees the needed drive and creativity that will enhance the corporation's competitive edge. However, without effective protection of the individual's rights, including the right to free speech, a corporation is unlikely to benefit from free and open discussions, as well as honest and unfettered exchange of ideas, which can prevent the corporation from degenerating into conservatism, complacency, stagnation, and a host of other corporate ills. Without firmly instituting the rights and equality of the person, the quest for harmony may not be beneficial to the individual as well as the long-term interests of the company.

Particularism

Particularism is a way of treating people that is based on *who the person is*, not on *what the person can do*. One of the downsides of particularism in the corporate context is that it is based on an *affective principle* and not a rational principle with regard to personnel matters, including hiring, firing, and promotion. Particularism also displays itself in the form of family connectedness in personnel matters. Those with family connections will be given advantage over those who do not have such connections. Indeed, family connectedness often is used as a criterion for appointment, promotion, and worthiness of trust. But this stands in contradiction to the rational principles based on performance, experience, and qualification. As a result, particularism very often sanctions the practice of hiring or promoting the less talented and less able person and at the same time excluding from the corporation talented and well-performing people who are not family members or clan-related. This will almost certainly damage the competitiveness and well-being of the corporation, as good people are an asset that very few good corporations can afford to lose. Particularism can also easily lead to nepotism, which may create injustice and damage staff morale and thus lower the efficiency of the organization.[7]

A more general form of family connectedness is the *guanxi* (relationships), which lies at the heart of the Chinese society. Family connectedness in the strong sense relates mainly to relationships within the family, with blood ties as the basis; however, *guanxi* as family connectedness is also family connectedness in the weak sense, because what is deemed as having a *guanxi* depends on whether the persons involved in the *guanxi* know each other in person. The more intimate the knowledge that persons have about each other, the stronger the *guanxi*. In an elliptical sense, for the Chinese, having a *guanxi* with a person is very much like bringing him or her into some form of family relationship with oneself; that is, bringing the person into the family circle. In a sense, the dependence of *guanxi* can be seen as a reflection of the familial collectivism, which conceives a person and his or her behavior in the context of familial relationships. A person with his or her individual rights, needs, and interests unattached to the social relationships in which he or she belongs is a pretty alien image in Chinese culture. Like relying on family connectedness, reliance of *guanxi* as a criterion to do business and to make decisions, though instrumental or efficacious in the business culture of Chinese communities, may sometimes fly in the face of rationality. Too much reliance on *guanxi* at the expense of other factors in a business dealing may prove to be not in the best interest of the corporation in the long run.

Paternalism

Paternalism goes hand in hand with authority-obedience and authoritarianism. Enlightened paternalism is arguably acceptable because it is for the considered benefits of those being ''paternalized.'' However, paternalism, especially in its authoritarian version, which is often practiced in Confucian corporations, should not be encouraged because it would suppress the autonomy of employees as subordinates. Authority is necessary within an organization if things need to be done. Authority-obedience that is often blindly practiced is bad for an employee's creativity and freedom to think and act. Diversity of opinions and views as well as independent thinking are very difficult in an environment dominated by blind and excessive observance of authority as well as unenlightened paternalism. The absence of diverse opinions and independent minds as a direct result of the lack of rights protection would make the organization boringly uncreative and poor in innovations.

These core values form an interwoven web of normative constraints that dictate the way business ought to be conducted, as well as how people ought to behave and to be treated. In view of the inhibitory effect of Confucian familial collectivism on the individual, it is not difficult to see such values as not conducive to an environment that encourages personal initiatives and creativity. Without individual rights properly instituted, hierarchy is no friend of equality, as familial collectivism is hostile to individual rights, which presuppose some form of equality.

Second, the organizational structure and processes within a Confucian corporation are also incompatible with the environment that enables and empowers employees. The hierarchical organizational structure, with its authoritarian mode of communication and decision-making processes, centralization of information, and the domination-subservience human relationships, resembles the traditional organization type, which is becoming obsolete. Such an outmoded organization structure is ill-equipped for the next century. It is an organization that is a far cry from the modern one, which is well suited for teamwork, employee empowerment, open and free communication, equal respect for employees, mutual trust, creativity, and other organization niceties. This is because employee empowerment, open and free communication, and equal respect for employees are based on values that include respect of the rights and equality of the individual person. The organizational structure and processes as defined by Confucian familial collectivism unfortunately endorse values that contravene them.

Finally, the obligation-based normative structure also contravenes the rights-based nature of the corporate person. Therefore, in terms of value compatibility, structure-process compatibility, and normative structure compatibility, corporate persons will find the familial, collectivistic, Confucian corporation a particularly alienating and harsh environment to conduct their business, if they can survive in it at all.

EMPIRICAL EVIDENCE ABOUT CONFUCIAN CORPORATION

Empirical findings about Chinese business organizations are consistent with those problems just identified. Let us highlight some of the problems with respect to leadership and decision making as well as management control within the corporate context (Redding and Wong, 1986).

Leadership and Decision Making

Silin (1976) reports that leaders hold information and disseminate it at their discretion to subordinates. By controlling the information, the leaders can subject subordinates to a certain dependency insofar as the decision-requires-information situation is concerned. This observation agrees with another comparative study that shows centralization of power of decision making, usually to a dominant owner (Pugh and Redding, 1985). Leadership style is authoritarian or autocratic, especially in information sharing with subordinates (Huang, 1984). These invariably reflect embedded domination-subordination relationships as well as hierarchical human relationships in Chinese business organizations.

Management Control

Management control refers to the processes of articulating organizational goals and objectives, monitoring the results, assessing the results, and making adjustments in goal realization. With regard to management control of the company, two distinct characteristics distinguish Chinese companies from their Western counterparts. First, the determination of corporate goals is usually an internal family matter. Nonfamily members are relieved of the responsibilities of formulation of corporate goals. This has a lot to do with the particularism of the Chinese corporate culture. Second, corporate performance, particularly regarding finance and profitability, is often shrouded in secrecy.

To enhance management control, Chinese companies institute means that include nepotism, obligation networks, nonobjective performance assessment, and paternalism (Mok, 1973). Again, Confucian familial collectivism dominates. Notwithstanding familial collectivism, not every family member is treated with benevolence or equality. The less powerful ones are often ruthlessly treated (Wilson and Pusey, 1982). Superiors tend to be condescending to their subordinates, and public humiliation of subordinates is not uncommon and may even be socially tolerated. (Redding and Wong, 1986: 280).

The second means of achieving organization behavior is by nonobjective assessment. The structure of Chinese organizations often exhibits these features: there is a low level of structuring; roles are less precisely defined; standard procedures are less prevalent; "staff" as opposed to "line" personnel are far less evident (Redding and Wong, 1986: 276). As a result, there is a lack of a structured system of performance measurement, which subsequently leads to a lack of data on which individual performance can be assessed. On the other hand, responsibilities are loosely defined. An employee's contribution to the company is not evaluated on some objective criteria but is judged in terms of his or her loyalty or affective relationships to the superior. The negative effect of paternalism on organization should not be underestimated. The centralization of power leads to tension in vertical relationships at the lower levels. Supervisors in Chinese firms did not feel that they had sufficient authority to meet their responsibilities, as they were often bypassed by their own superiors who went straight to their subordinates without consulting them (Deyo, 1978). As regards the relationships of collective values and individual values, the impact of collectivism on individual psychological makeup in the corporate context is also rather pronounced. As observed by Redding and Wong (1986: 285), Chinese managers and employees are reported as giving a higher rank to social needs than to ego needs, a characteristic that stands in stark contrast to Western managers and employees.

Another recent study on Chinese business organizations in Taiwan also reveals interesting findings about Confucian corporations, which were referred to as ''rule-by-man corporations'' in the study (Huang, 1984).[8]

The study used twelve indicators to measure employees' responses in different organization types, including the Confucian corporation. The indicators included the self-perception of demand of the work; willingness to take initiative at work; willingness to undertake responsibility; delegation of authority to employees; openness; team identity; concern for the welfare of the employees; communication and liaison; interpersonal harmony; fairness in treatment; clarity in rules and regulations; and rationality of the system (Huang, 1984: 42–49). The Confucian rule-by-man companies scored lower marks than those of the foreign-owned and rule-by-law companies in almost all twelve aspects. The explanation for this was that since the Confucian rule-by-man companies lack clarity in institutional guidelines and directives for the employees, and power is so centralized in the hands of one or two persons, they effectively disempower employees by not adequately delegating power to employees and giving them ownership. Such an organizational arrangement could also adversely affect the openness, group sense of belonging, personal initiatives, willingness to undertake responsibilities, communication, and cooperation of employees as well as organization harmony at the workplace.

Redressing the Balance—Strengthening the Respect for Persons

It seems clear from the preceding discussion that there is in Confucianism as familial collectivism a repressive ideological and institutional regime against equality and respect for persons. To the extent that Confucian familial collectivism entails values that contravene the value of equality and respect for persons, it is certainly not the desirable basis for building a corporate culture. To combat these negative effects induced by familial collectivism, the first thing to do is to be vigilant about the darker side of the Confucian corporation, especially those negative portions of the corporate culture that underlie it. Recognizing the valuable virtues in Confucianism should not blind us to those downsides. As proposed in the earlier part of this chapter, the value of respect for persons should be given special attention, among all the four basic values. The value of respect for persons in the corporate context can be made more concrete in terms of the notion of corporate person.

I define a corporate person as a person who is well equipped with the understanding, sentiment, will, and skills to discharge his or her (hereafter, using masculine terms) corporate responsibilities and assert his corporate rights as well as to effectively conduct his business within the corporate or organizational setting. He has a keen awareness of his identity as a corporate person, including awareness of his relationship to the corporation and to his fellow workers. As well as showing his loyalty toward his corporation, he recognizes his rights and duties as a citizen in society. He respects and is committed to the reasoned values in the corporate and social arenas. Central to these values are the values of rights and equality. A corporate person respects the rights of his fellow workers and commits himself to the value of equality of persons. A corporate person in his full maturity would presumably demonstrate the preceding qualities to their fullest extent. In actuality, however, he demonstrates different degrees of maturity regarding these qualities. Respect for persons thus amounts to respect for the corporate person.

Extra effort should be made to enforce the principle of respect for persons by effectively institutionalizing the development and protection of individual rights as an antidote to the predominantly collectivistic culture. To do so should not be seen as paying undue emphasis to individual rights at the expense of collective goods. The important thing is that a proper balance should be maintained between the individual and the collectivity. As a result of a long tradition of collective interests dominating the social, political, and familial lives of individuals in China, it is time to redress the balance between collectivity and the individual. In view of the lack of a tradition championing and respecting individual rights, to give an extra boost to individual rights not only is timely but is beneficial to the corporation ready for the twenty-first century.[9]

CONCLUSION

In building the Chinese corporation for the twenty-first century, there is increasing recognition of the need for developing its spiritual component together with the material infrastructure. Chinese corporations that are able to capture and assimilate the riches of its own cultural heritage while correcting its collectivistic excesses will be those that not only have the efficiency and effectiveness for optimal competitiveness but also have the vision and capacity to take social responsibilities and business ethics seriously. There is no doubt that the fusing of core values and virtues into the culture of the corporation forms a crucial part of that capacity and vision. Though virtue development should not be seen as the be-all and end-all of corporate moral and spiritual development, it surely is a solid means toward enhancing the morality and spirituality of corporate life.

NOTES

1. The subjectivity of *Jen* as a moral capacity is vividly demonstrated by this celebrated saying of Confucius: "Is humanity [*Jen*] far away? As soon as I want it, there it is right by me." It clearly means that the ability to exercise *Jen* is within ourselves. *Jen* is not something imposed from outside. Confucius also highlights the self-mastery aspect of *Jen*: "To practice humanity depends on oneself. Does it depend on others?" Having established our innate ability of *Jen*, Confucius identifies other aspects of it in the *Analects*. Furthermore, apart from being a megavirtue, other virtues are manifestations of *Jen*.

2. The Confucian virtues as manifestations of *Jen* are identified via the attributes of man of *Jen*/Humanity and virtuous person (superior man) (Chan, 1963). Man of humanity and virtuous person refer to the same thing. For details of the sources see my paper (Ip, 1998a).

3. Confucian familial collectivism has either a strong sense or a weak sense. Its weak sense refers to it as an ideology, while the strong sense represents both ideology and institutions. Unless otherwise stated, the strong sense of the word is in general used.

4. Regarding equality, some recent empirical studies observed that "individuals do not perceive themselves as related to each other on some fundamentally equal basis. Instead the individual is at the centre of a series of concentric circles, the closest having the strongest blood ties. What is significant is that rights and obligations differ according to the relative positions in such circles" (Redding and Wong, 1986: 284).

5. That the family in modern Chinese society still exerts a dominant influence on the individual has been shown by recent empirical studies. Shalaff's (1981: 18) study of Hong Kong female factory workers has provided evidence for this observation: "In the centripetal form the family becomes a power base to manipulate other institutions. . . . [It] gathers in its forces by demanding the primary loyalty of its members and mobilizing their labor power, political, and psychological allegiances on behalf of kinsmen. The centripetal norms and values aid families in their competition against other kin groups for scarce resources" (quoted from Redding and Wong, 1986: 284).

6. Refer to "Confucian Familial Collectivism and the Underdevelopment of the Civic Person" for a fuller discussion (Ip, 1996).

7. There are advantages and disadvantages in connection with nepotism. Nepotism can provide cohesion as well as strong motivation to uphold corporate policy by the overlapping personal and corporate goals of key executives. Its liability is that by not allowing outside professional managers in the company, it keeps the organization small. Nepotism also helps breed the formation of cliques, usually built on clan regional affiliations (Leeming, 1977). Conflicts among different cliques are not uncommon phenomena, like tense interpersonal relations based on differences in obligation networks. Due to its particularistic interpersonal connections, "Overseas contacts are usually based on uncles and cousins living overseas. Business contacts are friends, and virtually all business is based on personal contacts" (Leeming, 1977: 51). Another commentator (Deyo, 1983: 216) observes: "Chinese firms emphasize trustworthiness and loyalties to a far

greater extent than in Western firms. Well-known is the tendency to hire kinsmen or closely trusted persons for top-level positions, rather than to search for persons of the best qualifications. Lower and middle-level managers tend to be internally recruited, while lower-level persons are often hired on the basis of recommendations by supervisors or trusted persons.''

8. A majority of the small and medium-sized businesses under study were rule-by-man type, loosely corresponding to our Confucian corporation. Their distinctive features are that there are unclear institutional rules and regulations or the lack of them or lukewarm and partial implementation of them; that the founder or the owner usually dictates how business has to be run; that the power resides in the hands of a few individuals, all of them either family members or close relatives; and that very seldom are outsiders appointed to key positions in the higher echelon of power within the company.

The research conducted in Taiwan used comparative data to establish the relationship between the morale of the workers and different organization types, including the rule-by-man companies. Using data from the survey of 130 workers from 130 different companies belonging to four different types of organization, interesting findings are noted that help to shed light on how corporate culture impacts on an organization and the morale of its workers.

9. Some may argue, however, that there is a degree of underdetermination of ideas within the Confucian moral corpus, for example, the ideas espoused in *Great Learning*, to the effect that it is possible to generate some notion of the corporate person from its basic tenets. That is, it is not implausible to reconstruct a notion of the corporate person within the Confucian moral corpus. One could argue that within the Confucian moral architecture of *Ren-I-Li*, there is no explicit rejection of rights, nor is there a strong endorsement of all forms of inequality, even though the preference over filial piety did entail some forms of social inequality. Seen in this light, it is suggested that Confucianism in its abstract and formal version possibly underdetermines a concept of corporate person that is rights- and equality-based. Proponents of such a view, however, must not overlook the fact that familial collectivism is the inseparable core of Confucianism that contributed critically to the underdevelopment of the corporate person. In other words, even if we subscribe to the view that there is some degree of underdeterminism of the Confucian moral architecture over the concept of corporate person, Confucian familial collectivism is primarily responsible for the inhibition of rights and equality.

REFERENCES

Berger, P. L. (1983). Secularity: West and East. Cultural Identity and Modernization in Asian Countries. KoKugakuin University Centennial Symposium.

Birchall, D., and Laurence, L. (1995). *Creating Tomorrow's Organization: Unlocking the Benefits of Future Work*. London: Pitman.

Chan, W. T. (1963). *Source Book in Chinese Philosophy*. Princeton, NJ: Princeton University Press.

Cheng, C. K. (1944). Familism: The Foundation of Chinese Social Organization. *Social Forces* 23(1), pp. 50–59.

Davis, S. M. (1984). *Managing Corporate Culture*. Cambridge, MA: Ballinger.

Deal, T. E., and Kennedy, A. A. (1984). *Corporate Cultures—The Rites and Rituals of Corporate Life*. Reading, MA: Addison-Wesley.

Deyo, F. C. (1978). Local Foremen in Multinational Enterprise: A Comparative Case Study of Supervisory Role-Tensions in Western and Chinese Factories of Singapore. *Journal of Management Studies* 15, pp. 308–317.

Deyo, F. C. (1983). Chinese Management Practices and Work Commitment in Comparative Perspective. In L.A.P. Gosling and L.Y.C. Lim (eds.), *The Chinese in Southeast Asia: Vol. II. Identity, Culture and Politics*. Singapore: Maruzen Asia, pp. 215–230.

Fairbank, J. K. (ed.). (1957). *Chinese Thought and Institution*. Chicago: University of Chicago Press.

Fei, X. T. (1948). *Rural China* (in Chinese). Shanghai: Guancha She.

Gambetta, D. (ed.). (1988). *Trust: Making and Breaking Cooperative Relations*. New York: Basil Blackwell.

Hampden-Turner, C. (1990). *Corporate Culture: From Vicious to Virtuous Circles*. London: Hutchinson.

Hesselbein, F., Goldsmith, M., and Beckhard, R. (eds.). (1997). *The Organization of the Future*. San Francisco: Jossey-Bass.

Hsieh, H. W. (1967). The Status of the Individual in Chinese Ethics. In C. A. Moore (ed.), *The Chinese Mind*. Honolulu: University of Hawaii Press, pp. 307–322.

Hsu, F.L.K. (1948). *Under the Ancestor's Shadow*. New York: Columbia University Press.

Hsu, F.L.K. (1967). *Under the Ancestor's Shadow: Kinship, Personality, and Social Mobility in Village China*. rev. and expanded. New York: Doubleday.

Hsu, F.L.K. (1981). *Americans and Chinese: Passage to Differences*. 3rd ed. Honolulu: University Press of Hawaii.

Huang, K. K. (1984). Confucian Ethics and Corporate Organizational Forms (in Chinese). In Commercial Times Business Series Group (ed.), *Chinese Management*. Taipei: Times Cultural, pp. 21–55.

Ip, P. K. (1996). Confucian Familial Collectivism and the Underdevelopment of the Civic Person. In L. N. Lo and S. W. Man (eds.), *Research and Endeavours in Moral and Civic Education*. Hong Kong: Hong Kong Institute of Educational Research, Chinese University of Hong Kong, pp. 39–58.

Ip, P. K. (1998a). Developing Virtues in Corporations: Learning from Aristotle and Confucius. In T. Coady (ed.), *Public Morality and Transcultural Interaction*. Melbourne: University of Melbourne Press, pp. 112–131.

Ip, P. K. (March 1998b). The Ethics of Trust in Virtual Corporation. Paper presented in International Conference on Management and Philosophy, Taiwan.

Kupperman, J. (1988). Character and Ethical Theory. In P. A. French, T. E. Uehling, Jr., and H. K. Wettstein (eds.), *Midwest Studies in Philosophy Volume XIII, Ethical Theory: Character and Virtue*. Notre Dame, IN: University of Notre Dame Press, pp. 95–112.

Leeming, F. (1977). *Street Studies in Hong Kong*. Hong Kong: Oxford University Press.

Li, J. (5–11 January 1998). Diversified Forms for Materializing Public Ownership. *Beijing Review*, pp. 13–16.

Misztal, B. A. (1996). *Trust in Modern Societies: The Search for the Bases of Social Order*. Cambridge: Polity Press.

Mok, V. (1973). The Organization and Management of Factories in Kwun Tong. Occasional Paper, Social Research Centre, Chinese University of Hong Kong.

Pence, G. E. (1984). Recent Work in Virtues. *American Philosophical Quarterly* 21(4), pp. 281–297.

Pugh, D. S., and Redding, S. G. (January 1985). A Comparative Study of the Structure and Context of Chinese Businesses in Hong Kong. Paper presented at the Association of Teachers of Management Research Conference, Ashridge, England.

Redding, S. G., and Wong, G.L.L. (1986). The Psychology of Chinese Organizational Behavior. In M. H. Bond (ed.), *The Psychology of the Chinese People*. Hong Kong: Oxford University Press, pp. 267–295.

Shalaff, J. (1981). *Working Daughters of Hong Kong*. Cambridge: Cambridge University Press.

Silin, R. (1976). *Leadership and Values*. Cambridge: Harvard University Press.

Wilson, R. W., and Pusey, A. W. (1982). Achievement Motivation and Small Business Relationship Patterns in Chinese Society. In S. L. Greenblatt, R. W. Wilson, and A. A. Wilson (eds.), *Social Interaction in Chinese Society*. New York: Praeger, pp. 83–95.

Wright, A. F. (1964). *Confucianism and Chinese Civilization*. Stanford, CA: Stanford University Press.

Wright, A. F., and Twitchett, D. (eds.). (1962). *Confucian Personalities*. Stanford, CA: Stanford University Press.

Index

About the Editor and Contributors

ABOUT THE EDITOR

FRANK-JÜRGEN RICHTER has lived, worked, and traveled extensively throughout Asia. Fluent in Mandarin and Japanese as well as his native German, he holds a doctorate from Stuttgart (Germany) University, has studied business administration and mechanical engineering, and done other postgraduate work at Tsukuba University, Tokyo. Dr. Richter has written articles for various professional and scholarly journals, authored two books, and is the editor of a previous book for Quorum, *Business Networks in Asia: Promises, Doubts, and Perspectives* (1999), and a forthcoming book, *The Asian Economic Catharsis* (2000).

ABOUT THE CONTRIBUTORS

CHEAH HOCK BENG is a Senior Lecturer at the School of Economics and Management, University College, University of New South Wales. His teaching and research interests include Human Resource Management, Organizational Development, and Entrepreneurship. In 1989 he was a visiting Research Fellow at the Snider Entrepreneurial Center, Wharton School, University of Pennsylvania, where he examined the Schumpeterian and Austrian conceptions of entrepreneurship and proposed a new perspective of the entrepreneurial process. Since then he has explored more extensively the ramifications of this perspective of entrepreneurship for organizations, management, and economic development.

CHEN BAIZHU is Assistant Professor at the Marshall School of Business, University of Southern California. His research interests center on the study of financial institutions, international economics, and economic development, particularly in relation to China and East Asia.

CHEN JIN, a former visiting researcher at the Wharton School of the University of Pennsylvania, is an Associate Professor at Tianjin University of Commerce. He is a Ph.D. candidate at Tokyo University and an affiliated research fellow at MIT. He has published widely in international management issues and economic journals.

DENG SHENGLIANG is Managing Director of Shell Companies in Northeast Asia and Professor of international business and marketing at the University of Saskatchewan, Canada. Professor Deng has been deeply involved in corporate strategic planning and international marketing areas for more than 20 years, with a wealth of research, teaching, and consulting experiences and a worldwide reputation.

FENG YI is an Assistant Professor at Claremont University. His areas of specialization include international political economy and methodology. He has published extensively, and his papers appeared in such journals as *British Journal of Political Science*, *European Journal of Political Economy*, *Journal of Peace Research*, *Journal of Conflict Resolution*, and *International Interactions*.

IP PO-KEUNG has taught at Lingnan College, Tunghai University, and the Open University of Hong Kong, where he was Dean of the School of Arts and Social Sciences from 1992 to 1998. His publications include works in envirnomental ethics, business ethics, and bioethics. Currently, he is Research Associate of the Institute of Asian Research, University of British Columbia, and is working on a book on Chinese business ethics.

DAVID LI is Assistant Professor of Economics at the University of Michigan, Ann Arbor, and a fellow of the National Center for Economic Research (NCER) at Tsinghua University. Between 1997 and 1998 he was a National Fellow at the Hoover Institution at Stanford University. His research interests are economic theory, corporate finance, economics of transition, and the Chinese economy.

LU TONG is Associate Professor of the Institute of World Economics & Politics, Chinese Academy of Social Sciences, Beijing. She teaches M.B.A. courses in international trade and international business. Her areas of research interest include internationalization of firms, foreign market entry, strategic management, and theory of multinational corporations. She was a visiting scholar at the Department of Economics, Dartmouth College, and at the Department of Marketing, Strathclyde University, U.K. She is a member of the Chinese World Economy Society.

LUO YADONG is Associate Professor of International Management at the College of Business Administration, University of Hawaii. His research interests are in the area of international management, with a focus on global strategy, international cooperative ventures, foreign direct investment, and Chinese management and business. He has published over 70 research articles in professional journals and two recent books, *International Investment Strategies in the People's Republic of China* and *China 2000: Emerging Business Issues*. Before he came to the United States in July 1992, he served as a provincial official in China in charge of international business for six years.

QI HANTANG is Senior Lecturer in international business strategy at the School of Business and Management, University of Greenwich, U.K. In 1994 he came from the Management School of Fudan University, China, to Lancaster University, where he has been researching the strategic development of Chinese township and village enterprises. His research interests are strategic management, international business, and wider China-related management issues.

SIU WAI-SUM is Acting Head and Associate Professor of the Department of Marketing, Hong Kong Baptist University. He obtained a doctoral degree from the University of Durham, U.K., studying the marketing practices of Chinese small firms. He has published over 50 journal articles on Chinese entrepreneurship, small firm marketing, international marketing, and marketing education.

EDWARD TSE is Vice President of Booz-Allen & Hamilton and the managing partner of its Greater China operations. A native of Hong Kong, he consults with multinational companies and Chinese enterprises on strategy, operations, and organization.

WANG XUELI is a lecturer at the School of Economics and Management, Tsinghua University.

XU XIAOJIE is Research Fellow of Petroleum Strategic Studies with China National Petroleum Corporation and Associate Professor with Petroleum Management College, University of Petroleum, China. His research areas are mainly in corporate organizational studies, Asian oil and gas market analysis, and geo-strategic planning. He was a visiting scholar at the University of Saskatchewan, Canada, and the University of Houston. Currently he is also an honorary Research Fellow of the University of Houston and an energy expert invited to work with several international energy institutions, including the International Energy Agency and James Baker Institute, Rice University.

ZHANG LIJUN is a lecturer at the school of Economics and Management, Tsinghua University (Beijing). His research interests include international management, Asian economies, and state enterprise reform.